Battle
of
Britain 1917

Battle
of
Britain 1917

The First Heavy Bomber Raids on England

Jonathan Sutherland and Diane Canwell

Pen & Sword
AVIATION

First published in
Great Britain in 2006
By Pen and Sword Aviation
An imprint of
Pen and Sword Books Ltd
47 Church Street
Barnsley
South Yorkshire
S70 2AS

ISBN 1 84415 345 2

Typeset by Mac Style, Nafferton, E. Yorkshire
Printed and bound by

Pen and Sword Books Ltd incorporates the imprints of Pen and
Sword Aviation, Pen and Sword Maritime, Pen and Sword Military,
Wharncliffe Local History, Pen and Sword Select, Pen and Sword
Military Classics and Leo Cooper.

For a complete list of Pen and Sword titles please contact
Pen and Sword Books Limited
47 Church Street, Barnsley, South Yorkshire, S70 2AS, England
E-mail: enquiries@pen-and-sword.co.uk
Website: www.pen-and-sword.co.uk

CONTENTS

Introduction

The primary aim of this book is to investigate the Gotha and Giant bomber raids on the British Isles from 1917 to 1918. Although in terms of the strategic outcomes of the First World War the German aircraft offensive against Britain can be seen as little more than an irritating diversion to the strategists, it presented a significant series of encounters between limited numbers of men, both in the German squadrons and the British defensive units.

In order to place the the German bomber offensive into context, it is important to look at the relative successes and failures of the German navy and army Zeppelins, which began their own bombing offensive against the British Isles as early as 1915.

The British first had to cope with seemingly impervious German airships flying at extreme altitudes for that age during the day. Their defensive aircraft were few and mostly incapable of reaching the altitudes to engage the raiders. As British aircraft improved and the War Cabinet realized the potentially devastating impact of German airships being able to roam and bomb at will over Britain, the Zeppelins were no longer as safe as they had been in the past.

As the German airships shifted towards night operations they were replaced by an altogether more dangerous and devastating threat to Britain, the long-range Gotha bomber. These aircraft, still flying at relatively high altitudes, posed a huge threat that the British could not easily counter. Although they could not carry the weight of bombs that the airships had been able to, they were far more accurate. British aircraft at the time lacked the performance to reach their altitude in order to intercept them. Even when they tried to engage them, the Gotha's speed and manoeuvrability meant that very few effective interceptions could be made.

All of these encounters over the British Isles took place at a time when the primary objective of the Allies was to defeat the Germans on the Western Front. Whilst comparatively speaking the Gothas did little material damage and inflicted high casualties only on a handful of occasions, the German intent was clear. They saw any British aircraft or anti-aircraft gun transferred or kept away from the Western Front as a victory. Occupying British minds in the defence of their own country rather than launching offensives on the Western Front was seen as a long-term and enduring objective.

The number of German aircraft deployed at any one time was limited to a single squadron of Gotha bombers based in Belgium. Only later would even larger German bombers, the Giants, reinforce this effort. Nonetheless, considerable numbers of British aircraft and personnel were diverted from the primary task of defeating the Germans on the ground in mainland Europe.

The other major consideration at the time, as far as the British were concerned, was the running battle being fought between supporters of a unified air force and those who believed that the Royal Naval Air Service (RNAS) controlled by the Admiralty, and the Royal Flying Corps (RFC), controlled by the British Army, should remain separate entities. This separation was retained for most of the war and only in the closing phases did the RNAS units and the RFC squadrons merge to some extent, despite the fact that the Royal Air Force (RAF) was created as a separate entity to encompass both services.

In the last phases of the war, Britain still faced three major threats from the air. There was still the ever-present Zeppelins and their reputation for mass destruction, added to which were the effective and devastating Gotha bombers. The final threat came from the far larger, and potentially as dangerous, Giant bombers. Mercifully, the Germans never managed to produce more than a handful of Giants and by that stage of the war, the British defence squadrons were adept at dealing with the aerial threat.

As it was, the Zeppelin threat, although seriously dented sometime earlier, was dealt a death blow on the night of 5–6 August 1918 when the latest Zeppelin, the L70, was shot down in flames. The German bomber threat had been dealt a serious blow on the night of 19/20 May 1918 when a large number of Gothas were intercepted, shot down or crashed on land. The operational strength of the German England Squadron, home to the Gotha, had never exceeded many more than thirty-six aircraft, the loss of four over England alone provided proof that the offensive had reached its conclusion and that henceforth the German effort would be on the mainland of Europe.

The scoreboard for the entire offensive, including the earlier airships, makes pretty grim reading. Total British aircraft crew casualties were twenty-eight throughout the period. The Germans, on the other hand had lost 158 army and navy airship crewmen and fifty-seven Gotha crewmen as a direct result of aircraft being destroyed over Britain or forced to ditch or into the sea. In addition, the Germans also lost thirty-seven men due to crash landings and other accidents.

Financially, the situation looks rather different. In addition to the vast numbers of British aircraft (variously priced at £1,406 for a Sopwith Pup and £3,000 for a Bristol Fighter), the British maintained thirty-five operational airfields and around 139 emergency and other landing fields. Added to this were the vast numbers of personnel, the anti-aircraft guns and, of course, the military and civilian casualties and the damage to buildings and the war effort.

The German costs were also phenomenal. The 122 airships alone cost an estimated £12 million. The early versions cost an average of £50,000 each, later models a prohibitive £150,000 each. The cost of supporting them has been estimated at the very least to be £5 million, including the hangars, airfields and other facilities needed to operate the vast weapons. In all, the Germans lost sixty-six in operations outside the British Isles and a further seventeen on bombing missions over Britain. The estimated cost of the Gotha was around £9,000 and the Giant a staggering £19,000.

At the outbreak of the war Britain could muster just 270 aircraft of various types in both the RNAS and the RFC, the total manpower being some 2,073. By the end of the war, this had expanded dramatically. In total the RAF could muster 291,170 officers and men and 22,647 aircraft.

The first Battle of Britain never involved vast numbers of men or aircraft, yet it left an indelible mark on strategic thinking. Just like the German bombing offensive of the First World War, the much-vaunted strength of the *Luftwaffe* in the Second World War would be defeated. Ultimately, the few of 1915–18 would give way to the equally magnificent few of 1940.

CHAPTER ONE

The First German Raids on Britain: The Zeppelin Offensive, 1914–16

On 13 October 1912, several eyewitnesses reported seeing a vast German airship over Sheerness. Then on the night of 22/3 February the captain of the *City of Leeds*, *en route* from Grimsby to Hamburg, reported seeing a large airship heading for the Humber. These were early endurance trials, probably of the German navy's first Zeppelin, the L1. But as far as the British were concerned, the sightings were never substantiated and the Germans flatly denied that they had entered British air space.

The first of Count Ferdinand von Zeppelin's aerial express train projects had been abandoned in 1894. But by 1900, the LZ1 project was well underway. In 1907, the LZ3 showed sufficient promise to prompt the German government to lay down a challenge to von Zeppelin to create an airship capable of twenty-four hours of flight. The LZ5 achieved this specification in 1909 and the German military began its, initially reluctant, involvement with airships.

The military interest was, at this stage, limited, but von Zeppelin pressed on and his LZ10 (1911) carried 1,500 passengers in a year. Meanwhile, the German navy took an even more cautious approach and did not order their first airship, the LZ14 (L1) until April 1912.

Despite the fact that the Hague Conference of 1899 had forbidden nations at war to drop bombs or explosives from the air (indeed, in 1907 they had specifically mentioned undefended targets), the British saw the potential of the airship. In 1908, the Committee of Imperial Defence (CID) began to investigate the potential dangers of both airships and aircraft. By January 1909, it had concluded that despite the limited payloads of airships and aircraft, Britain would be vulnerable to attacks on dockyards, industrial targets and shipping.

Nonetheless, it also concluded that both airships and aircraft were still at an experimental stage and as such would not pose a serious threat to the nation. It did, however, approve £35,000 for the development and construction of a naval rigid airship. It was thought that this project would provide valuable insights into the potential threats from the air. This funding allocation led to the construction of the R1 *Mayfly*. The airship was doomed, however, and broke its back during mooring trials.

During May and June 1910, the General Staff and the Admiralty were represented at the Paris International Conference on Aerial Navigation. Both were in general agreement that despite peacetime pledges to ban the use of airships against civilian targets, the Germans would use the vessels to induce panic. They were of the opinion that the airships would not cause a great deal of damage, but that, nevertheless, anti-airship guns and other devices would need to be developed.

By 1911, both the army and the navy had begun to develop their air fleets; in this they were seriously lagging behind the rest of Europe. The CID was of the firm opinion that effort and expertise should be pooled and this led directly to the formation of the Royal Flying Corps in 1912.

Despite views to the contrary, the army and the navy took divergent paths. To begin with the army favoured French aircraft, but after a time they began its rely on the Government Royal Aircraft Factory at Farnborough. The navy, meanwhile, purchased a variety of machines from a number of different British companies.

The CID was still concerned with the potential threat of airships. They were unsure whether aircraft would be capable of destroying airships, knowing that the airships could operate in far more adverse weather conditions than aircraft. At this stage, in July 1912, they were of the opinion that the only effective counter measures against airships were airships.

In the following month the military wing of the RFC was charged with the task of protecting ports and other strategic targets in the event of war. Meanwhile, the Admiralty began to establish coastal airbases, although it was the War Office's responsibility to ensure that a foreign power did not gain air superiority over Britain. The War Office, however, did not have a comprehensive view of how the various disparate elements would cooperate and provide an overlapping defence of Britain. Indeed, by 1914 it had committed the majority of the existing aircraft squadrons to any expeditionary force that might be required in mainland Europe. A draft proposal for the defence of Britain was finally published in draft form on 27 July 1914. It would require 162 aircraft to be distributed to six squadrons, two based in

Scotland, one in the Humber area, another at Orford Ness and one each at Dover and Gosport.

By this stage any hope of a unified air force had disappeared. The Admiralty controlled the naval wing of the RFC, which on 1 July 1914 became the RNAS. Whitehall had always considered the RFC to be a single branch, but on 1 August 1915 the RNAS officially became a separate entity, both on paper and in fact.

Britain declared war on Germany on 4 August 1914. To protect against any potential attack by Zeppelins there was a motley collection of inadequate aircraft. Indeed, the pilots and their commanding officers were perfectly aware that their aircraft would be inadequate to deal with the Zeppelins; one commanding officer proposed that his pilots ram them. On the day that war was declared the Admiralty positioned three anti-aircraft guns to protect Whitehall and even proposed that four RFC aircraft should operate from Hyde Park. There was still a distinct lack of aircraft available for defence.

It was originally proposed that the Admiralty was in a far better position to deal with any incoming German aircraft or airships, and should therefore take responsibility for the defence of Britain. It was also proposed that the Admiralty immediately begin positioning aircraft around the east coast.

There were several false alarms during August and September 1914, but in truth had any of the defence aircraft or ground spotters seen a German aircraft they would not have been able to have distinguished it from an Allied one. With alarming honesty, on 22 October Winston Churchill informed the War Cabinet that at present he could not guarantee the protection of London. There was also still wrangling between the War Office, the Admiralty and the army. It was proposed that the RNAS deal with air defence whilst any army aircraft should be deployed to assist ground forces in the event of a German invasion of Britain.

Both the RFC and the RNAS were making huge demands on aircraft production capabilities. The navy had ordered 400 aircraft and the RFC even more. If there had been a Zeppelin attack on Britain at this stage it would have been met by aircraft whose principal offensive weapon was a Martini-Henry carbine with incendiary bullets. Under development was a grenade designed by F. Marten Hale, petrol bombs developed by the Admiralty Air Department and other bizarre weapons filled with petrol and TNT.

As it was, the first German attacks did not come from Zeppelins but from naval seaplanes. In December 1914 Germany's first seaplane squadron became operational at Zeebrugge. The first sortie was launched against Dover on 21 December 1914. It was a solitary aircraft, which appeared at 1300 and managed to drop two bombs close to the Admiralty Pier. A second, slightly more successful attack, took place, again against Dover, on 24 December. The aircraft, a Friedrichshafen FF29 is credited with having dropped the first bomb on British soil at 1045. The success was hardly amazing as it only managed to make a crater in the garden of a civilian living near Dover Castle and break a few windows.

A more audacious attack took place on 25 December when a single FF29 was heard over Sheerness at 1220. It came under fire from several anti-aircraft batteries before passing Gravesend, Tilbury and Dartford and managing to drop a few bombs. However, it had already attracted the attention of several RNAS and RFC aircraft out of Dover, Eastchurch, Grain, Joyce Green, Farnborough and Brooklands. Once again the raider escaped unscathed, but the reaction of the British aircraft served as an encouragement to the British authorities.

A far more serious incursion took place on the night of 19/20 January 1915, when the German navy Zeppelins L3 and L4 targeted the Humber area. A proposed attack on the Thames estuary by the L6 was cancelled when it was still short of the British coastline as it was suffering from engine problems. The L3 reached Great Yarmouth at 2020 and it commenced bombing. The L4 was lost and rather than attacking its intended targets it dropped several bombs near Kings Lynn and into Norfolk villages. There were only two defensive sorties that night, both from the RFC at Joyce Green. There had been ample warning and indeed the first report had been given from Lowestoft at 1940.

During February there were few attacks and those that were made were undertaken by FF29s against coastal shipping. No damage was reported and only two defensive sorties in total were launched.

There was a single attack by four German aircraft in March. On the 20th a daylight raid was launched on coastal shipping near Dover by three FF29s and a German flying boat. At 1125 an anti-aircraft battery at Thameshaven proudly announced the first German kill of the war, but in fact they had hit an RFC Gunbus.

The period between April and October 1915 saw nineteen German airship attacks on Britain. Production had been stepped up and both the army and navy were beginning to receive new versions based on the Zeppelin designs.

The first attack was an opportunist one on the night of 14/15 April, involving a single German navy Zeppelin, the L9. It had been proceeding on a reconnaissance mission over the North Sea, carrying bombs, and found itself close to the British coast. At 1945 it crossed the coastline at Blyth and, mistaking Wallsend for Tynemouth, it dropped some incendiaries. A single Bristol TB8, flown by Flight Sub-Lieutenant P. Legh, responded. Legh headed for the likely target, Newcastle, but failed to see the Zeppelin slipping away.

The German navy launched another attack, this time on the Humber area, on the night of 15/16 April. The L5 was spotted off Southwold at 2140 and at around 2340 it dropped some bombs on Lowestoft. The L6, meanwhile, bombed Maldon shortly after 2330. The L7, having reached the British coast somewhere between Hunstanton and Great Yarmouth, did not penetrate into British air space and headed home at 0240 without dropping a bomb. There were just two defensive sorties on this night, both by the RNAS Great Yarmouth, but no contact was made.

A single German Albatros BII made a daylight sortie against northern Kent on April 16. Aircraft from Dover, Eastchurch and Westgate were scrambled, but none of them managed to see the raider, who had only dropped four bombs at around 1220 near Sittingbourne and another into the River Swale before it turned towards Faversham, dropped five more bombs and then exited near Deal at 1250.

There were ineffectual attacks that nonetheless caused some damage on the nights of 29/30 April and 9/10 May. Both were carried out by the LZ38, a German army Zeppelin. The first attack hit Ipswich and Bury St Edmunds, with the raider coming in over Felixstowe at around 2400 and exiting via Aldeburgh at 0200. The second raid was against Southend, and took place at 0250. It made two passes over the town, mainly dropping incendiary bombs. On this occasion one person was killed and two were injured.

The LZ38 struck again on the night of 16/17 May, 26/27 May and 31 May/1 June. Its attacks were becoming somewhat more accurate: the first attack hit Ramsgate, the second Southend and the third, more seriously, London. On this third occasion the LZ38, commanded by Captain E. Linnarz approached the British coast at Margate at 2142. He headed towards London via Shoeburyness and dropped thirty bombs and ninety incendiaries on Stoke Newington, Stepney and Leytonstone, exiting via Foulness. On this occasion seven people were killed and thirty-five injured. The defensive response came exclusively from the RNAS, which mounted fifteen sorties that night.

There was a false dawn for the British in May and June 1915. On the night of 16/17 May the German army's LZ79 was badly damaged over Belgium and even more successfully the LZ37 was destroyed on the night of 6/7 June. Both of the German airships had been attacked by 20lb bombs. In reality, however, the development of the British home defences was lagging behind and the British were relatively powerless to respond.

June saw the turn of the German navy, commencing with attacks by the L10 and the SL3 on the night of 4/5 June. Nine RNAS and RFC sorties were launched. The L10, intent on attacking Harwich, actually bombed Gravesend. The SL3 tried to head for Hull but due to strong headwinds it turned back after dropping a few bombs into the countryside.

The navy struck again the following night (6/7 June) with the L9, accompanied by the army's LZ37, LZ38 and LZ39. This raid was to cause the heaviest casualties so far. An early sighting was made, probably off Great Yarmouth, at 1730. As it transpired none of the German army airships reached Britain and all of them turned around because of navigational problems. The L9, however, crossed the British coast at Cromer at 2000 and was over Bridlington at 2310. At around 0050, now over Hull, it dropped ten bombs and fifty incendiaries, killing twenty-four and injuring forty. There were just three defensive sorties from the RNAS out of Great Yarmouth and Killingholme. Even though the LZ37 had not crossed into British airspace, it was intercepted over Ostend by Sub-Lieutenant R. A. J. Warneford, who was awarded the VC for the first kill inflicted on a Zeppelin. He attacked it over Ghent at 0225 and managed to drop six × 20lb bombs on it. The airship exploded, but bizarrely one of the LZ37s crew managed to survive despite falling $1\frac{1}{2}$ miles to the ground in the forward gondola. The gondola struck a roof and the survivor, Alfred Muhler, was tipped out of it and landed on a bed. Unfortunately, Warneford died ten days later in a flying accident.

On the night of 15/16 June the German navy Zeppelins L10 and L11 were deployed to attack the Tyneside area. The L11, as it transpired, did not take part in the raid as it encountered engine problems, but the L10 approached the British coast at 2045, when it was still daylight. It lingered off the coast until sunset, when it entered British air space to the north of Blyth at 2345. It headed south and dropped 3,500lb of bombs on Wallsend, Jarrow and South Shields. The only British response was aircraft scrambled from the RNAS at Killingholme, Whitley Bay and Great Yarmouth. No contact was made and the L10 slipped away unmolested.

During July there was just one German raid on Britain, carried out by two German aircraft, an Albatros floatplane and a Gotha WD2 floatplane. There were nine defensive sorties against this attack on Harwich. They were spotted at 1120, flying high, by the Inner Gabbard light vessel. The two raiders dropped bombs near to Harwich but failed to do any damage or inflict any casualties. The RNAS scrambled aircraft from Chelmsford, Eastchurch, Felixstowe and Westgate and just a single aircraft left Joyce Green, the RFC's only contribution.

On the night of 9/10 August the German navy Zeppelins, L9, L10, L11, L12 and L13 intended to attack London, but not a single bomb fell there. The L9 was spotted off Flamborough Head at 2015 and it headed to the south of Hornsey at 2315 then moved on to attack Goole, which it mistakenly believed was Hull. The L10 had crossed at Aldeburgh at 2140 and headed for Shoeburyness. Some of its bombs, instead of dropping onto targets near the Thames, hit Eastchurch aerodrome, but the majority fell harmlessly into the Thames estuary. The L11 appeared at Lowestoft at 2218, believing that it was approaching Harwich. All of its bombs were dropped into the sea. The L12, believing it was at Great Yarmouth, actually appeared at Westgate at 2248 and dropped bombs on Dover at 0030. Meanwhile the L13 turned back due to engine problems. The L12 came under the most brisk attacks, bracketed by searchlights and under fire from anti-aircraft guns. Flight Sub-Lieutenant C. E. Brisley, in an Avro 504B, attempted to engage but the L12 disappeared into cloud. As it transpired it had been hit, almost certainly by the anti-aircraft guns from Dover, and it was forced to land off Zeebrugge. During the Germans' salvage missions RNAS aircraft out of Dunkirk and Dover tried to destroy it, but it was successfully towed into Ostend.

The L9, L10, L11 and L13 were back on the night of 12/13 August. This time they were determined to press an attack on London. The L9 and L13 all had to turn back prematurely, however, and the L11 skirted Harwich, Thanet and Deal before also disappearing home. The L10 appeared off Lowestoft at 2125, but instead of attacking London it targeted Harwich. All in all seven people were killed and twenty-three were injured as a result of the attack and the RNAS flew just four sorties out of Great Yarmouth.

There was one further attack in August, on the night of 17/18, when once again the German navy attempted to launch an attack on London. This time the L10, L11, L13 and L14 were earmarked for the raid. The L13 was forced to turn back because of engine difficulties and the closest the L14 got to London was the Norfolk coastline, also as a result of engine problems. The L11 was sighted over Herne Bay at 2130 and only managed to drop bombs on Ashford before exiting at 2345. The L10 was altogether far more successful: it entered Britain via Bawdsey at 2055 and between 2230 and 2245 it dropped several bombs on Walthamstow, Leyton and Wanstead. Only two British pilots saw it. Flight Sub-Lieutenant C. D. Morrison of RNAS Chelmsford and his fellow pilot, Flight Sub-Lieutenant H. H. Square, both flying Caudron G3s, attempted to give chase, but it escaped.

September saw several attacks by both army and navy Zeppelins, the first being launched by the army on the night of 7/8 September.

The target was London and detailed for the attack were the LZ74, LZ77 and SL2. The LZ74 came over Bradwell at 2255 and dropped its bombs on Cheshunt at around 2400. It managed to drop one bomb on Fenchurch Street before racing to head home via Harwich. The LZ77 approached Britain via Clacton at 2240 and headed inland, but then moved towards Saxmundham, where it dropped a handful of bombs before heading out towards Lowestoft, leaving British air space at 0220. Meanwhile the SL2 had approached via Foulness at 2250 and at around 2400 had bombed Southwark and Woolwich. In all eighteen people were killed and twenty-eight were injured. Just three defensive sorties were flown that night, all by RNAS BE2Cs out of Felixstowe and Great Yarmouth.

It was the turn of the navy on 8/9 September, with the L9, L13 and L14 involved in the attack. The L14 was spotted off Cromer at 2010 and mistaking East Dereham for Norwich, it dropped its bombs before heading back home at 2200. The L13 came in over Wells at 1935. It first headed towards King's Lynn and then on to London. It dropped some bombs on Golders Green at 2240, but its main attack spread from Euston to Liverpool Street, causing significant amounts of damage. It then turned and exited Britain via Great Yarmouth at 0200. The L9 attacked Skinningrove, having approached to the north of Whitby at 2115. It commenced bombing at 2135 and headed home at 2145. There were seven defensive sorties, all by the RNAS, out of Redcar and Great Yarmouth. A sortie was also flown by Flight Lieutenant V. Nicholl in a Sopwith Schneider from on board a converted Lowestoft trawler, *The Kingfisher*.

A single German army Zeppelin, the LZ77, aimed to attack London on the night of 11/12 September. It crossed the coast just to the north of the River Crouch at 2315 and hoped to head towards London. In the event, however, it bombed the area around North Weald and then left Britain via Great Yarmouth at 0025. There were only three defensive sorties that night, by RNAS Chelmsford and a BE2C of the RFC from Rittle.

There was another ineffectual German army attack by the LZ74 against London on the night of 12/13 September. The airship crossed the coast at Walton-on-the-Naze at approximately 2245. It headed towards Halstead, hoping it was moving in the right direction for London, but it became hopelessly lost and dropped its bombs over East Anglia, exiting via Southwold at 0018. A single BE2C, piloted by Flight Sub-Lieutenant F. T. Digby of RAF Eastchurch was scrambled at 2255, but he had no chance of catching the Zeppelin and returned to base at 2347.

During the daylight hours of 13 September there was a hit-and-run coastal attack against Margate by a German floatplane that was spotted at 1740. It crossed Cliftonville, dropping ten bombs, killing two people and injuring six. Two RNAS BE2Cs out of Westgate were scrambled but the raider was too fast and slipped away. Later that day three German navy Zeppelins, the L11, L13 and L14 were launched against London. The L13 and L14 turned back owing to bad weather, but the L11 continued. It was damaged by anti-aircraft fire over Harwich, causing it to jettison its bombs and hasten for home, having inflicted £2 worth of damage.

There were no other attacks in September, but the German navy launched an ambitious raid against London on the night of 13/14 October. Involved were the L11, L13, L14, L15 and L16. All except the L11 were spotted in the Bacton area between 1815 and 1845. The L13 attacked Hampton waterworks and then bombed Guildford before jettisoning the last of his bombs over Woolwich shortly before 2400. The L14 managed to drop four bombs on the Shorncliffe army camp, killing fifteen soldiers, before it went on to drop bombs on Tunbridge Wells and Croydon, exiting via Aldeburgh at 0145. The L15 penetrated as far as central London by 2145. It dropped a stick of thirty bombs between the Strand and Limehouse before turning and exiting via Aldeburgh at 2355. The L16, again aiming for London, mistakenly identified the River Lea as the River Thames and hit Hertford rather than east London. It exited to the north of Bacton shortly after 2400 hours. Meanwhile at 2030 the L11 had appeared close to Bacton and almost immediately came under fire from a mobile anti-aircraft battery. The crew clearly panicked and dropped their bomb load around Coltishall, heading off home via Great Yarmouth at 2115. There were only six defensive sorties, all flown by the RFC out of Joyce Green, Hainault Farm and Suttons Farm. Collectively the Zeppelins had killed seventy-one, injured 128 and caused over £80,000 worth of damage.

This was the last raid of the year and it was already becoming clear that to a large extent these sorties were being carried out with relative impunity.

The New Year opened with a series of largely ineffective float- and seaplane attacks on Dover and Folkestone, causing few casualties and little damage. The first major attack took place on Liverpool on the night of 31 January/1 February 1916. The German navy Zeppelins L11, L13, L14, L15, L16, L17, L19, L20 and L21 took part, and inflicted seventy deaths, 113 injuries and nearly £54,000 worth of damage. Instead of hitting Liverpool, however, they in fact hit Derby, Burton-on-Trent, Tipton, Wednesbury, Loughborough, Scunthorpe, Ilkeston and Walsall. They crossed the British coast between 1640 and 1910 across an area covering from Happisburgh to the Wash. The War Office immediately thought that they would be making for London, and various aircraft were scrambled, but were unable to find any sign of the raiders. In fact the closest one got to the capital was 60 miles away. No fewer than twenty-two sorties were flown from a variety of RNAS and RFC air bases and squadrons.

February began with just two attacks by German seaplanes, the first against Broadstairs and Ramsgate and the second against Lowestoft, Walmer and shipping in the English Channel. The Zeppelins were uncharacteristically silent during February and did not return to action until the night of 5/6 March.

The beginning of March saw a morale-boosting victory for the British. A German FF29 had attacked Margate between 1810 and 1822, dropping seven bombs. It was hit by fire from British patrol boats as it scampered back across the North Sea to base. The pilot was taken prisoner, but the observer drowned.

Most of the Zeppelins were now undergoing mechanical over-hauls and having more reliable engines fitted. Three German navy craft, however, the L11, L13 and L14 ventured out on the night of 5/6 March in support of a German surface fleet operation. Initially they were due to attack targets around the Tyne and Tees area, but there were strong north-westerly winds that night and as a result they opted for targets further south, amidst heavy snowstorms. The L14 was spotted to the north of Flamborough Head at 2230. It dropped some bombs on Beverley then, having found the Humber River, dropped more on Hull at around 2400. The L11 had also found Hull by 0100, and it commenced dropping bombs on the city. The L13 had found the Humber River and was spotted at 2115. It headed towards Newark and dropped bombs there at 0110. The extremely poor weather conditions confused the crew and amazingly they found themselves over the River Thames around 150 miles further south than they believed they were. They hunted for targets, but eventually headed off home at 0220.

Hull took the brunt of the attack. Eighteen people were killed, fifty-two were injured and around £25,000 worth of damage was inflicted on the city. There was just one defensive sortie that night, primarily due to the heavy snow, which was launched by Flight Sub-Lieutenant C. C. Wyllie in a BE2C from RNAS Eastchurch. He failed to find any of the raiders.

On 19 March, four FF33Bs, a single Hansa-Brandenburg NW and a Gotha Ursinus were launched against various targets in Dover, Deal and Ramsgate in another hit-and-run attack. Three German floatplanes were seen approaching Dover at 1350; they dropped twenty-four bombs on Dover and nine on Deal. At 1410 another fifteen bombs were dropped on Ramsgate and Margate. The RNAS scrambled aircraft from

Dover, Eastchurch, Grain and Westgate and the RFC also scrambled aircraft out of their base at Dover.

Flight Commander R. J. Bone, the commanding officer at RNAS Detling, had flown to Westgate in order to have a picnic that afternoon. As soon as the alert came in that raiders were in the area, he took off at 1410 and almost immediately spotted one of the German aircraft. He gradually gained on it as it flew towards the Belgian coast. After about forty minutes he climbed to around 9,000ft and could see the German seaplane below and ahead of him. He made a diving attack, firing at it at close range and receiving return fire. Bone banked and made a second attack, this time wounding the observer. He then closed to 20ft and fired a burst into the enemy aircraft and saw its engine misfire and begin to smoke. Bone was forced to turn around, as he was running out of fuel, and another aircraft was sent out to bomb the wrecked plane, but it found nothing. The Germans had towed it into Zeebrugge.

On the last day of March the Germans planned to launch a combined army and navy Zeppelin raid against London and East Anglia. All of the army Zeppelins (LZ88, LZ90 and LZ92) had to turn back, however, because of bad weather, and the navy's L9 and L11 had to return because of engine problems. This left the L13, L14, L15, L16 and L22 to carry out the attacks. The first one to be spotted appeared off Dunwich at 1945; it was the L15, which then headed towards London before coming under fire at 2140 from anti-aircraft guns in Purfleet, Erith and Plumstead. It dropped its bombs on Rainham but was hit by the Purfleet battery at 2145. Two of the gas cells were ruptured and the crew began jettisoning everything that was not screwed down. They hoped to be able to reach Belgium, but were forced to ditch 15 miles to the north of Margate shortly after 2300. One crewmember was drowned and a British destroyer picked up the others.

The L13, which had come in over Dunwich at approximately 2000, began to gain height and dropped twelve bombs on a munitions factory in Stowmarket. They missed and the airship came under fire from anti-aircraft guns. Two cells were ruptured. The crew jettisoned the rest of their bombs and managed to escape via Southwold at 2220.

The L14 crossed the British coast at Sea Palling at 2105 and headed directly towards London, dropping bombs at Sudbury, Braintree and Brentwood *en route*. It then headed for Thameshaven, where it dropped fourteen bombs at 0130, believing that it had attacked Tower Bridge. It exited British air space at Aldeburgh at 0250.

The L16 crossed the British coast to the north of Great Yarmouth at 2210. It believed it was bombing Hornsey, but in fact it hit Bury St Edmunds. On its way back out of Britain via Lowestoft it dropped a single bomb and crossed the coast at 0115.

The final Zeppelin, the L22, was suffering from engine difficulties but was making reasonable progress towards Grimsby. It dropped bombs at Humberston and Cleethorpes, one of them hitting a chapel that was being used as a billet by the British Army. The explosion killed twenty-nine and injured fifty-three soldiers.

Some twenty-four defensive sorties were launched that night, commencing at 2105. The first plan of action was to put up a defensive ring around central London. Second Lieutenant Claude A. Ridley lifted off from Joyce Green at 2130 and just six minutes later saw the L13 illuminated by searchlights. He attacked at extreme range but the airship slipped away. Second Lieutenant Alfred de Bathe Brandon did contribute to the demise of the L15, however. He arrived on the scene just after the Purfleet anti-aircraft gun had hit it. He dropped three explosive darts onto the hull and continued to chase it, accompanied by Second Lieutenant H. S. Powell out of Suttons Farm. Both pilots were awarded the ME for their contribution.

The German navy Zeppelins L11 and L17 aimed to strike London on the night of 1/2 April 1916, but because of the weather conditions, they opted to attack targets to the north instead. The L17 approached first but there was still some daylight so it lurked offshore. Around an hour later, now to the south-east of Hornsey, it encountered serious engine trouble, jettisoned its bombs at sea and returned home. The L11 was spotted over Seaham Harbour at 2305, it first attacked Sunderland then Middlesbrough, exiting at Saltburn at 0030. The majority of the twenty-two killed and 130 injured were in Sunderland. The RNAS at Redcar, Scarborough and Whitley Bay and No. 36 Squadron, Cramlington, and No. 47 Squadron, Beverley, launched seven defensive sorties.

On the night of 2/3 April the German army and navy launched an uncoordinated attack. The navy's L14, L16 and L22 targeted the Forth area whilst the army and LZ90 went for London. The navy airships were supposed to be accompanied by the L13 but it had to turn back because of engine problems. The army attack was singularly unsuccessful. The LZ90 was seen over Chelmsford at 2330, and came under fire from anti-aircraft guns based at Waltham Abbey. It immediately jettisoned 90 bombs and exited via Clacton at 0100. The LZ88 was no more successful, having crossed at Orford Ness at 2300 and then headed towards Ipswich. Believing it was over Harwich, it dropped its bombs near the mouth of the River Deben and then headed for home at 0120.

The naval Zeppelins' primary target was the Royal Navy base at Rosyth and the Forth railway bridge. The L14 could not find either of the targets and instead, between 2330 and 0015, dropped its bombs on

Edinburgh and Leith, exiting via Dunbar at 0100. The L22 began dropping its bombs at 2115 in the vicinity of Berwick-upon-Tweed, believing it was attacking munitions targets near Newcastle. At around 2350 it released the last of its bombs on Edinburgh. The L16 crossed the British coast just to the north of Blyth. It dropped most of its bombs in open country, but some hit the Cramlington airfield. It was gone within ninety minutes. The RNAS and RFC launched fourteen sorties, but it is unlikely that any of the defensive aircraft spotted any of the raiders.

The L11, accompanied by the L17, launched a highly ineffective raid on the night of 3/4 April. They had intended to make an attack on London, but strong headwinds dissuaded them from carrying out their mission. Indeed the L17 turned about when it was still 10 miles short of the Norfolk coastline. The L11 pressed on, crossing the coast near Cromer at 0130. All it managed to achieve, however, was to drop a few bombs into the countryside before it exited to the north of Great Yarmouth at 0300. There was poor visibility that night and as a consequence only four defensive sorties were launched; two from RNAS Great Yarmouth, another from Covehithe and the remaining one a BE2C piloted by Captain Arthur Ashford Benjamin Thomson (known as Ack-Ack Beer Thomson). He had left Doncaster at 2300 and searched in vain for the two Zeppelins. By 0125 he was desperately short of fuel. He came in low, searching for a landing place, and ended up hitting a tree on a 600ft hill near Market Rasen. Remarkably he escaped with few injuries.

The L11 and L16 were launched once again on 5/6 April. The L13, which was supposed to have accompanied them, had to turn back with engine problems. The L11 crossed the coast at Hornsey at 2105 and shortly afterwards began drawing anti-aircraft fire on its approach to Hull. Clearly the anti-aircraft fire was getting too hot for it and it turned about, hoping to reach Hull on a different course. Once it had got back over the sea it suffered an engine failure and headed towards Hartlepool. It suffered a second engine failure at 0125 near Skinningrove, where it dropped a few more bombs before heading off.

The L16 was seen to the north of Hartlepool at 2330, where it attacked colliery targets to the west of Bishop Auckland at around 2400. It then exited via Seaham Harbour at 0115.

There was very low cloud cover during the night and just five defensive sorties were launched. One aircraft was launched from Scarborough despite the fog. No. 36 Squadron Cramlington scrambled two BE2Cs but sadly both crashed on landing and one pilot was killed. Two more aircraft were scrambled from No. 47 Squadron, Beverley, again BE2Cs. They hunted for the L11 but failed to find her.

On 23 and 24 April there were two aircraft attacks on Dover, but neither managed to inflict any damage or casualties. A far sterner test came on the night of 24/25 April when the navy launched another attack on London, this time carried out by the L11, L13, L16, L17, L21 and L23. In total, however, they only managed to kill one person, injure another and cause just under £6,500 worth of damage.

The L16 was the first airship to be spotted, off Cromer at 2215. The L13 followed at 2220 and the L21 was spotted 5 miles to the south of Lowestoft at 2310. Shortly afterwards at 2350 the L23 crossed to the north of Great Yarmouth and the L11 at 0030 over Bacton. The last arrival that night was the L17, which was spotted to the north of Skegness at 0140, but it did not stay very long and turned back across the coast in about twenty-five minutes. Owing to the headwinds it immediately became apparent that an attack on London would not be possible. The Zeppelins therefore fanned out, hunting for targets in East Anglia. The L21 was seen over Stowmarket at 0015 and the L16 over Newmarket at 0030. Very few bombs were dropped and most of the airships exited between Sheringham and Happisburgh between 2330 and 0145. The only damage caused during the raid was against Lowestoft, probably by the L21 at around 0400. It had turned about along the coast before heading back home. The RNAS and the RFC launched some twenty-two sorties. Three Bristol Scouts out of RNAS Great Yarmouth spotted one of the airships and pursued it until it was lost in the clouds.

Quite by accident Flight Commander V. Nicholl and Flight Lieutenant F. G. D. Hards, hunting for the airships, encountered the L9 some 40 miles east of Lowestoft at around 0438. It was carrying out a reconnaissance mission and was flying at an altitude of only 2,600ft. Both men were in BE2Cs, armed with bombs and darts, and they chased the L9 for 25 miles. Hards believed that some of his darts had hit the airship, but he was mistaken and the L9 slipped away to safety.

The German army launched the LZ87, LZ88, LZ93 and LZ97 on the night of 25/26 April, targeting London again. The LZ26, which had been in service since 1914, did not leave base at the same time as the others and was forced to abandon its part in the mission as it encountered French fighters over the North Sea. The LZ97 crossed the British coast at Blackwater River at 2200 and proceeded to attack what it believed to be the centre of London from 2245; in fact its bombs fell on Ongar and Barkingside. It turned about and exited to the north of Clacton at 0035.

The LZ87 had no better luck, having dropped some bombs on Deal Harbour at 2155 and manoeuvred to avoid anti-aircraft fire from Walmer. It decided that discretion was the better part of valour and turned for home. The LZ88 got no closer to London. It entered Britain somewhere near Whitstable at 0030 and headed towards Canterbury. It then dropped some bombs in the countryside and exited via Westgate at 0135. The final Zeppelin, the LZ93, dropped several bombs close to Harwich in a quarter-hour stretch from 2230 and then headed home.

The RNAS from Eastchurch, Rochford and Westgate launched some sixteen defensive sorties. The RFC launched aircraft from Dover and No. 39 Squadron's bases at Hounslow, Suttons Farm and Hainault. It was the LZ97 that came in for the closest attention. Second Lieutenant William L. Robinson encountered the Zeppelin as it was closing on Barkingside. He fired a machine-gun burst, but then his gun jammed. It continued jamming and he only managed to get off twenty rounds before he lost sight of the airship.

On the night of 26/27 April a single German army Zeppelin, the LZ93, attempted to attack London. However, it began suffering from engine difficulties whilst it was still off the coast. It headed towards Deal, where it dropped three bombs, then crossed the River Thanet and exited shortly afterwards. The RNAS at Westgate and three flights of the RFC launched eight sorties, but no contact was made.

A more serious attack took place on the night of 2/3 May with the German navy Zeppelins L11, L13, L14, L16, L17, L20, L21 and L23 targeting the Royal Navy facilities at Rosyth and the Forth railway bridge. A single German army Zeppelin, the LZ98 was also launched against Manchester. Again poor weather caused difficulties. Earlier the navy Zeppelins, with the exception of the L14 and L20, headed for targets in the Midlands rather than those in Scotland. The L11 was seen over Holy Island at 2220. It dropped two bombs on Amble and then disappeared. The L23 was seen over Robin Hood's Bay at 2115 before it turned north and attacked the ironworks at Skinningrove before dropping more bombs on Easington, leaving Britain at 2225.

The L23 dropped a single incendiary on Danby High Moor, which caused a substantial blaze. The L16 mistook it for a burning military target and released all of its bombs onto the moor. A handful were also dropped elsewhere before it exited Britain, leaving via Saltburn at 2325. The L17 was similarly fooled by the blaze. It dropped some bombs near Skinningrove but the majority of its payload landed on the moor. The L13, having arrived off the British coast to the south of Whitby at 2230, believed that Danby Moor was Hartlepool and dropped several bombs in the vicinity before exiting via Scarborough at 0050. The final airship in this group, the L21, came in to the north of Scarborough at 2140. It attacked York and then headed back out to sea via Bridlington at around 2400.

Of the two that continued to Scotland, the L14 came in across the Scottish coastline to the south of St Abbs Head at 2025. It completely missed the Forth and dropped its bombs in open country near Arbroath, exiting around Fife Ness at 0100. The L20 was seen to the south of Montrose at 2155. It believed that it was over Loch Ness at around midnight but unable to find any targets it randomly dropped a few bombs and exited via Peterhead at 0240. It was utterly lost and eventually crash landed near Stavanger in Norway.

The remaining Zeppelin abroad that night was the German army's LZ98, which was close to Spurn Head at around 1900. Adverse weather conditions forced it to abandon its approach towards Manchester, however, and it headed home after around an hour.

The RNAS and RFC managed to launch at least fourteen sorties, possibly more. Bad weather impeded their ability to operate and their chances of spotting one of the targets.

Between 3 May and the night of 9/10 July 1916 incursions into British airspace were carried out by a variety of German aircraft. There were four raids, half by day and half by night. The sum total of their endeavours was one death and six injuries. Substantial numbers of defensive sorties were launched but there were no aircraft casualties on either side.

The German navy resumed its airborne offensive on the night of 28/29 July. It launched the L11, L13, L16, L17, L24 and L31. Ten Zeppelins had originally been earmarked for the attack but four had been forced to turn around. Those that managed to approach Britain encountered heavy fog. The majority entered Britain between Spurn Head and Great Yarmouth from around 2400 to around 0235. Altogether they dropped around seventy bombs. There were no casualties and just £257 worth of damage was done. The L13 was the only airship that penetrated far inland; apparently it was seen over Newark. Owing to the appallingly bad weather only one defensive sortie was launched. Captain R. C. L. Holme of No. 33 Squadron, RFC Bramham Moor, lifted off at 0200, but when he had just got over the airfield, he realized that visibility was appalling and turned back, managing to land safely.

The German navy tried once again on the night of 31 July/1 August 1916, with the L11, L13, L14, L16, L17, L22, L23 and L31. Between them they only managed to inflict £139 worth of damage, however, and there were no casualties. The eight airships approached Britain between 2240 and 0200 over a wide area stretching from Covehithe to Skegness. The furthest they penetrated was the Isle of Thanet (L31), Newark (L16), March (L14) and Haverhill (L22). Again there was dense fog, which caused difficulties for the Germans and inhibited the response of the home defence squadrons. Five defensive sorties were launched; The crews of RFC No. 51 Squadron, Mattishall, came closest to injury when a single bomb landed close to the airfield. It was almost certainly dropped by the L17. One aircraft was immediately scrambled and was aloft for fourteen minutes before it stalled and crashed, killing the pilot.

Undeterred by the failure of this attack, the German navy launched its Zeppelins once again on 2/3 August. The majority approached via the coast of East Anglia between 2345 and 0100 (Orford Ness in the south and Wells in the north). The L21 was reported as having reached Thetford, the L17 was seen over Eye and the L13 got as far as Wymondham. The L11 caused the only real damage of the night when it bombed Harwich. The L31 was seen off the Kent coast and simply dropped its bombs in the sea off Dover. Thirty-two sorties were launched against the Zeppelin attack.

Another navy attack was launched on the night of 8/9 August, comprising the L11, L13, L14, L16, L21, L22, L24, L30 and L31. The main force was seen between 0015 and 0200 between Flamborough Head and Tynemouth. Of this group only the L24 managed to bomb a strategic target, this time Hull, which suffered the majority of the casualties inflicted that night. The L14 came in over Berwick-upon-Tweed at 0025 and left rather abruptly at 0200 at Alnwick. The L16 was reported as being seen over Hunstanton at various points between 0030 and 0100. Just two defensive sorties were launched, both by the RNAS, one out of Redcar and the other out of Whitley Bay. The only aircraft to engage the Zeppelins was a BE2C flown by Bruno P. H. de Roeper, who pursued either the L21 or the L22, following it until it was around 20 miles off Flamborough Head.

A single German aircraft attacked Dover at 1227 on 12 August. It approached at extremely high altitude and dropped just four bombs, one of which fell on the RNAS airfield at Guston Road. Owing to the extremely poor visibility that day only one British aircraft of the ten scrambled from Dover, Manston and Westgate actually saw the raider. This was a BE12 flown by Second Lieutenant C. A. Hore of RFC No. 50 Squadron, Dover. He managed to follow the aircraft for around half an hour, during which time he was attempting to climb to the same altitude. He eventually lost it, however, in a thick bank of cloud.

There was one brief attack on the night of 23/24 August by the German army Zeppelin LZ97, which appeared over Bawdsey at 2355. After jettisoning its bombs into the countryside it departed at Orford Ness at 0015, causing no casualties or damage. No defensive sorties were launched.

The last attack in August 1916 took place on the following night, the 24th/25th. The German navy sent the L16, L21, L31 and L32. By the standards of most of the previous raids they inflicted considerable material damage, in excess of £130,000. Nine people were killed and forty were injured. The target was once again London, and the raid was intended as a hammer blow. Originally twelve Zeppelins had been earmarked for the mission, but for a variety of reasons eight had turned back. The L16 was singly unsuccessful that night. It approached Ipswich and began bombing to the north-east of the city at 0015. The L21 was seen over Frinton at 0143, passing at an extremely high altitude. It was aiming to attack Harwich and began dropping bombs at 0200, but most of them fell far too short of their targets. The L32 had approached Folkestone at 0210 and skirted along the coast towards Deal, but for some inexplicable reason dropped all of its bombs into the sea before making off.

The most successful airship that night was the L31, which approached Margate at 2330. Two hours later it was over London, which was where most of the damage and all the casualties were inflicted. It was the first time the capital had come under attack since October 1915. The RNAS and the RFC launched sixteen defensive sorties, none of which managed to hit any of the raiders. Flight Sub-Lieutenant E. T. Bradley, flying out of Eastchurch in a BE2C, saw the L31 near Southend. Also in the area at that time was Flight Commander C. Draper in a Sopwith $1^1/_2$ Strutter, who saw the same airship. Both lost sight of it, however, as it headed out to sea. Both Bradley and Draper also saw the L32, as did Squadron Commander R. L. G. Marix, on the Kent coast.

The airship had a close shave when it was caught in the Dover searchlights. Captain John W. Woodhouse of No. 50 Squadron, Dover, in a BE2C, was returning from a mission having dropped an agent behind enemy lines. He closed with the L32 and emptied one and a half drums of ammunition into it. The airship took evasive action and whilst Woodhouse was reloading he lost sight of it. It was also spotted briefly but plainly by Major M. G. Christie, also in a BE2C, of No. 50 Squadron, Dover as it disappeared into the clouds.

This period of Zeppelin domination had ended with little real damage to either military or civilian targets and a significantly lower level of casualties than had been anticipated. Despite the fact that the Zeppelins had been able to roam almost at will across Britain, poor weather conditions and even poorer navigation conspired to prevent them from launching a prolonged or devastating assault on London. Whilst the British response had been chaotic, it had not been entirely without success. British crews could claim Zeppelin kills and caused some fear among the Zeppelin crew.

CHAPTER TWO

The End of the Zeppelins: September 1916–May 1917

On the night of 2/3 September 1916 the German army launched their first and only coordinated Zeppelin attack on London. It was an utter disaster, largely because of atrocious weather conditions and poor navigation.

The German navy Zeppelins L11, L13, L14, L16, L17, L21, L22, L23, L24, L30 and L32 were involved. The navy's Schütte-Lanz's SL8 and the army SL11 were deployed. The army also sent their Zeppelins, LZ90, LZ97 and LZ98.

The L14 made landfall close to Wells-next-the-Sea at around 2150. Owing to a number of problems, including weather and navigational and technical difficulties, six navy airships (L11, L13, L22, L23, L24 and SL8) abandoned the attack on London and tried for other targets.

Searchlights at Lowestoft spotted an airship at around 2300. Flight Lieutenant E. Cadbury and Flight Sub-Lieutenant S. Cemball, in B2Cs out of Great Yarmouth and Covehithe respectively closed in, but the airship disappeared. It was most probably the L30, which went on to bomb Bungay. Alternatively, it could have been the L11, as later in the war, when one of the crewmembers was captured, he reported that the L11 had been attacked by at least two aircraft, which could have been those flown by Cadbury and Cemball.

Flight Sub-Lieutenant E. L. Pulling, in a BE2C from Bacton, had initially taken off just after midnight on 3 September in response to reports of German airships. He returned to base at 0043 and took off once more just fifteen minutes later. After about fifty minutes he saw bombs exploding close to the aerodrome at Bacton. This was the work of the L24, which was trying to bomb Great Yarmouth. Despite the visual clues Pulling could not find the airship. After returning to base and taking off once more at 0257 he failed again to locate L24.

Meanwhile, No. 33 Squadron at Beverley had scrambled to meet the threat of the L22. It had passed within 10 miles of the airfield and was bombing Humberston. To the south, London had been alerted at around 2240, when the SL11 appeared off Foulness. A further alert was raised at 2305 when the LZ90 was spotted off Frinton. The LZ90 slipped away to the east and attacked Haverhill, whilst the SL11 took a circuitous route to approach London. By 2300 aircraft of No. 39 Squadron were patrolling between North Weald and Joyce Green.

Lieutenant W. L. Robinson (B Flight, No 39 Squadron, Suttons Farm), in a BE2C, caught sight of a Zeppelin illuminated by searchlights close to the end of his patrol period. It was discovered to be the LZ98, which had crossed New Romney at around 2400 and had begun bombing Gravesend at 0115. Robinson closed in on it, but because of cloud and the fact that it was gaining height he lost sight of it. He headed back to base at North Weald and at 0150 decided to detour to investigate a red glow in the distance. Around fifteen minutes later he encountered the SL11, which had been bombing the northern outskirts of London. He was considerably higher than it and attacked with the advantage of around 800ft of altitude. He emptied a full drum into the belly of the airship then reloaded and attacked the side. There was still no noticeable effect so he descended until he was 500ft below the airship and emptied yet another drum into the underside. This time there was a red glow and the airship burst into flames.

Second Lieutenant J. I. Mackay (A Flight No. 39 Squadron), also in a BE2C, had left North Weald at 0108. At that time his was the only aircraft from his flight aloft. He was somewhere over Joyce Green when he saw the SL11 about 12 miles to the northeast. It took him twenty-five minutes to reach it and by the time he did so it was aflame. Shortly afterwards he saw another German airship off to the north-east and chased it, but with no success. It was later believed to be the L32, which was heading back to base after a bombing attack on Ware.

Second Lieutenant B. H. Hunt of C Flight, No. 39 Squadron, Hainault, was also aloft at this time, having left base at 0122. He was close to the SL11 when it began to fall. In the light he saw the L16, which was around $1/_2$ mile away, having just bombed a village close to Hatfield. He lost sight of it but later spotted the L32. He could not find her, however.

Robinson was awarded the VC for his destruction of the SL11, but there was other work to do that night. No. 50 Squadron tried and failed to find the LZ98 when it arrived off the Kent coastline. Flight Commander A. R. Arnold had left RNAS Grain in a Farman F56, also hunting for it, but instead he saw the demise of the SL11. He then lost his bearings and tried to head for Broomfield Court, close to

Chelmsford, but in the mist he landed in a ploughed field and turned the aircraft over. He escaped with an injured ankle and a few abrasions.

After the poorly coordinated attack there was no further German action over Britain until 22 September, when an unknown aircraft attacked during daylight hours. It was spotted off the coast at Deal at 1500 hours and five minutes later it dropped seven bombs on Dover. Major N. G. Christie and Captain Williams of No. 50 Squadron, Dover, flying a Vickers FB19 and a BE12 respectively, lifted off at 1510 and tried to close with it. No. 50 Squadron had no warning of the attack until the bombs actually fell. The German aircraft was probably a navy Albatros.

The German navy Zeppelins made another appearance on the night of 23/24 September 1916. In all likelihood the total force included the L13, L14, L16, L17, L21, L22, L23, L24, L30, L31, L32 and L33. The newer airships crossed Belgium and approached London from the south, whilst the others headed for the Midlands. The L21 crossed the British coast at Aldeburgh at 2140. Aircraft from Great Yarmouth were scrambled to find it, and indeed Flight Lieutenant C. J. Galpin attacked an airship about 30 miles east of Lowestoft, but he lost it whilst he reloaded at around 2055. In all probability the L30 crossed the British coast at Cromer. Flight Sub-Lieutenant E. L. Pulling, in a BE2C from RNAS Bacton, tried to find her but failed.

The slower-moving airships approached the British coast over Lincolnshire at some point between 2200 and 2300 hours. The L17 planned to attack Nottingham, but most of its bombs fell into open countryside. The L13 had bombed around Sleaford and an unnamed pilot from RNAS Cranwell had engaged her, but low cloud was favouring the airships.

Meanwhile, the L21 bombed Stowmarket and other airships were approaching London. The L33 crossed at Foulness at 2240 and began dropping bombs over Bow at 0012. It was hit by anti-aircraft guns, from either the Wanstead or the Beckton battery and was badly damaged. As it lost height, it was attacked by a number of aircraft. It was now almost defenceless, as the commander had ordered heavy items to be jettisoned, including machine-guns. It finally grounded just to the north of the Blackwater River estuary at Little Wigborough. The crew set fire to the airship and then surrendered to a local policeman.

At around 2245 the L31 and L32 crossed the British coast at Dungeness. The L31 approached London and began dropping bombs at 0030 then headed for Great Yarmouth, leaving the British coast at 0215. The L32 had slipped behind due to engine problems and by the time it reached south-east London at around 0100 the anti-aircraft batteries and searchlights had been alerted and it came under fire.

Having dropped the majority of its bombs on South Ockenden it began to head north. Three of No. 39 Squadron's pilots were hunting for it. Indeed Second Lieutenant F. Sowrey, in a BE2C of B Flight out of Suttons Farm, having taken off at 2330, saw it at about 0045 still 10 miles south of the River Thames. He emptied a drum of machine-gun bullets into its underside, then attacked for a second time, firing at the gun positions in its gondola. He turned for a third attack, firing into the hull. The L32 lurched and burst into flames. It plummeted to the ground, crashing near Billericay at 0120. Second Lieutenant J. I. Mackay of A Flight, No. 39 Squadron, out of North Weald, in a BE2C also managed to fire a few shots into the L32, but Sowrey could claim the kill.

On the night of 25/26 September the German navy Zeppelins L14, L16, L21, L22, L30 and L31 were all part of a raid on both London and industrial targets in the Midlands. The L23 was supposed to join in the attack, but it turned back as a result of technical problems. At 2005 the L14 and L16 crossed the British coast near Hornsey. At 2300 the L14 dropped bombs on York and then headed for Leeds, but turned for home after it had dropped some bombs on Wetherby. At 2145 the L21 crossed the British coast at Sutton-on-Sea. After skirting Sheffield at 2300, it dropped bombs on Bolton at 0045 and then headed back for the coast, leaving via Whitby at 0305. A similar track was taken by the L22 around fifty minutes later, but it made bombing runs against Sheffield. Meanwhile, the L31 crossed at Dungeness at 2135. It approached Portsmouth at 2350 then headed for St Leonards and left at 0230 from Dover.

There were just fifteen defensive sorties by the RNAS and the RFC that night. The RNAS scrambled aircraft from Calshot, Cranwell, Manston, Great Yarmouth, Bacton and Holt. The RFC had primarily responded by scrambling aircraft of No. 33 Squadron, out of Coal Ashton and Bramham Moor, while No. 50 Squadron scrambled out of Dover and Bekesbourne. Although some of the aircraft saw the enemy airships they were unable to engage.

On 1/2 October the German navy launched another night attack involving the L14, L16, L17, L21, L24, L31 and L34, the L13, L22, L23 and L30 all turned back prematurely. There was heavy cloud that night across central England, and not exactly perfect weather over the North Sea either. The L31 approached the coast at Lowestoft at 2000 and headed towards London. Most of the rest of the airships came in between Cromer and Theddlethorpe between 2120 and 0145. The L17 managed to penetrate to within 15 miles of Norwich, the L16 was reported as having attacked targets near Horncastle, the L14 was seen near Digby, the L24 was seen over Hitchin and the L21 over Oakham.

The L34 managed to get as far as Corby, but it dropped most of its bombs into the countryside.

Meanwhile, the L31 was making steady progress towards London. Searchlights at Kelvedon Hatch illuminated it at 2145 and it was spotted again close to Buntingford at 2230. By 2340 it was near Cheshunt and caught in the beam of several searchlights. It was at this point that Second Lieutenant W. J. Tempest, flying a BE2C of A Flight, No. 39 Squadron, North Weald, came onto the scene. He was at approximately 14,500ft and about 15 miles away from the airship. He could see it in the distance amidst a barrage of anti-aircraft shells. He attempted to close with it but his petrol pressure pump failed and he had to hand pump the petrol. He had been spotted by the L31, but it was also attracting the attention of other pilots in the area. Second Lieutenant J. I. Mackay and Second Lieutenant P. McGuiness, also of A Flight, were accompanied by Lieutenant L. G. S. Payne of C Flight. When the crew of the L31 saw all these aircraft they began to jettison their bombs and head west. Tempest, meanwhile, had got within firing range. He fired two bursts and then swung round to finish the drum. Before he had a chance to fire off all of the bullets, however, the L31 erupted into flames. It crashed near Potters Bar at 1154. Despite still suffering from pressure pump problems, Tempest managed to land back at North Weald at 1210.

On 22 October, at 1337 hours, one German aircraft attacked Sheerness. In all likelihood it was a Luft Verkehrs Gesellschaft (LVG) CIV seaplane. It managed to drop several bombs, but only four of them fell on the land. The RNAS started scrambling aircraft out of Dover and Manston from 1348 but no contact was made. Approximately an hour later a second aircraft approached North Foreland. It was fired on by two naval vessels and turned back. In all likelihood this aircraft was the one claimed by Lieutenant D. M. B. Galbraith of RNAS Dunkirk. He was piloting a Nieuport and saw a German seaplane coming in from a westerly direction at around 8,000ft. He dived to attack it and emptied two drums of ammunition, seeing it crash into the sea off Blankenberghe at 1530.

The following day saw another hit-and-run attack, this time against Margate by a single aircraft. In all likelihood it was again a seaplane. It approached Margate at an altitude of around 12,000ft and at 1005 dropped three bombs on Cliftonville. Several RNAS aircraft were scrambled from Dover, Eastchurch, Manston and Westgate but only one, a Bristol Scout D, flown by Flight Lieutenant J. A. Carr from Manston, spotted it, but by the time he had visual contact it was too far away and he had no hope of catching it.

On the night of 27/28 November 1916 the Midlands and Tyneside were the targets of the German navy Zeppelins L13, L14, L16, L21, L22, L24, L34, L35 and L36. It was to be a disastrous night for the Germans, who lost two of their Zeppelins, the L21 and L34.

The group targeting Tyneside comprising the L24, L34, L35 and L36, approached the British coast at around 2215. The other group, aiming for the Midlands, came in from 2110 between Spurn Head and Filey. The only real damage caused by this second group was inflicted by the L21, which killed four people in Hartlepool.

A BE2C of A flight, No. 36 Squadron, Seaton Carew, piloted by Second Lieutenant I. V. Pyott, was flying over Hartlepool at 2330, at an altitude of 9,800ft when he saw the L34 clearly illuminated in the Castle Eden searchlight. He dived and attacked, and then banked around to fire bursts into its hull. A small flame erupted and then in seconds the entire airship was ablaze. It fell into the sea just off the mouth of the River Tees. Its destruction frightened the crew of the L35 and they immediately turned for home.

Meanwhile, the L22 had been severely damaged by anti-aircraft fire, probably from around York, and was heading home. The L21 passed between Leeds and Sheffield and commenced bombing, but was suffering from engine problems. It flew to the south of Nottingham, straight into several British squadrons' patrol zones. At 0250 it was reported that it was heading for home, but there were several aircraft searching for her. Captain G. H. Birley of B Flight, No. 38 Squadron, Buckminster, spotted it, caught in his own airfield searchlight. It was flying at about 7,500ft and Birley was about 2,000ft higher. He dived to attack but lost sight of it. He continued to search until he saw it again at an altitude of around 11,000ft, apparently making very little headway because of its engine problems. Birley came in to attack from an altitude of 9,000ft and emptied a drum at it.

Meanwhile Second Lieutenant D. S. Allan, of A Flight, No. 38 Squadron, Leadenham, in a BE2E spotted it at 0300. It was flying at a height of 13,000–14,000ft. Allan tried to engage it but lost sight of it. At around 0400 it was spotted once more, this time by Lieutenant W. R. Gayner of C Flight, No. 51 Squadron, Marham. It was now close to East Dereham, but just as he was coming into range in his FE2B the engine stopped and he was forced to crash land at Tibbenham. By 0605 the L21 had reached Great Yarmouth and could be seen clearly in the dawn light, flying at 8,500ft. It was spotted some 9 miles east of Lowestoft by Flight Lieutenant Egbert Cadbury, who had flown out of RNAS Burgh Castle shortly after 0600 hours. Anti-aircraft guns around Great Yarmouth were firing at it, which alerted Flight Sub-Lieutenant E. L. Pulling, in a BE2C from RNAS Bacton, and Flight Sub-Lieutenant

G. W. R. Fane, also in a BE2C from Burgh Castle. Cadbury made an attack from below and emptied four drums into it. Its crew fired back just as Fane came to within 100ft of its starboard side, but his Lewis gun jammed. Pulling now made his attack, but his gun also jammed after just a handful of shots. He pulled away and as he did so the L21 burst into flames. Cadbury's attack with tracer, incendiary and explosive ammunition had probably done the trick. As Pulling had been the last man to fire at the airship, however, he was given the most credit and was awarded the DSO. Cadbury and Fane were awarded the DSC.

On 28 November 1916 an LVG CIV made a daring raid into the heart of central London. Commencing at 1150, the pilot, Deck Officer Paul Brandt, dropped six bombs in a line from the Brompton Road to Victoria Station. He and his fellow crewmen also managed to take several photographs. The target was the Admiralty building and the attack came perilously close, in fact just 13,000ft away. The aircraft had taken off from an airfield near Ostend and had arrived to the north of North Foreland at around 1035. It had approached London via Croydon and Mitchum and in all likelihood had been mistaken for a British aircraft, hence the long delay before anyone was scrambled from various RFC squadrons, commencing shortly after 1300.

Having carried out its audacious attack, the aircraft headed home, crossing the British coast close to Hastings. It was forced to crash land close to Boulogne at 1415 after the aircraft suffered from engine failure, however, and both crew members were captured.

Despite the fact that they had been the target, the Admiralty did not receive notification of the incursion until 1234 and consequently the Royal Flying Corps was not told to scramble until 1245. It took another fifteen minutes for the aircraft to get aloft, by which time the raider had already reached the British coastline and in all likelihood would never have been intercepted.

This was the last attack of 1916, a year which had seen a massive reinforcement of the home defence systems. There were no less than eleven home defence squadrons, the majority of which had three flights. Around 140 night landing grounds had also been established. Each squadron had been assigned a searchlight company. The anti-aircraft defences around London had been reinforced, with around sixty-five specifically deployed to defend the capital out of the total of 200 available. The RNAS also had an additional thirty aircraft to support the home defence.

Up until this point there had been 160 German airship incursions over the course of forty-two raids. They had managed to drop over 162 tons of bombs, in addition to the 2.5 tons that had been dropped by thirty-nine German aircraft. Although the damage and casualties had been minimal, the Germans had succeeded in one of their major tasks, that was to deflect resources away from the Western Front and force the British to use up equipment and manpower in the defence of the British Isles. Indeed some 17,000 men were directly involved in home defence.

Unfortunately, many of the home defence squadrons had to carry out their duties with a motley selection of aircraft. The latest models were automatically assigned to the Western Front, whilst the home defence squadrons had a mixture of prototypes and other unwanted aircraft. Some of them, whilst adequate to deal with airships, had no chance of catching the German seaplanes. Gradually, however, through 1917, they would begin receiving newer and better quality aircraft.

There were also other demands that needed to be fulfilled. The planned expansion of anti-aircraft gun manufacture was halted when there was a call for British merchant ships to be equipped with guns to protect them against U-boats. There was also a need to find at least thirty-six experienced pilots and provide nine replacement pilots a month to man new FE2B night-bomber squadrons. In the end experienced pilots from the home defence squadrons were stripped out and transferred. Similarly, some of the BE2Es of the home defence squadrons were transferred to the Western Front. It was firmly believed by many that the worst of the German airship raids had been dealt with and that their menace was nowhere near as grave as it once had been, so defence cuts were an acceptable risk.

The first attack of the New Year took place on 14 February 1917. A Sablatnig SF5 came in to attack coastal shipping at around 0800. It approached from an altitude of around 10,000ft, dropped around fifteen bombs and was immediately came under fire from anti-aircraft guns at Deal. There were no casualties and the raider escaped intact.

Two days later a similar attack was made by the same type of aircraft against coastal shipping. It was first spotted at 0750 to the east of Ramsgate flying at an altitude of 11,000ft. RNAS aircraft from Manston and Westgate were scrambled but the SF5 came in so fast and struck so quickly that none of them could intercept it. No casualties or damage were inflicted by the attack.

During the night of 16/17 February the German army Zeppelin LZ107 was spotted off Walmer at 0145. Although an RNAS aircraft was scrambled from Manston and five from No. 50 Squadron, RFC, none of them managed to close with the airship and it did not drop any bombs on British soil. It was probably simply returning from a bombing raid on Calais.

There were further German floatplane attacks on 1 and 16 March. The first came in from Zeebrugge and attacked Broadstairs at 0945. Six people were injured and a minimal amount of damage was caused. The RNAS and RFC mounted several sorties, but the raider escaped unscathed. The second attack was against Westgate and coastal shipping, with the raider being spotted at around 0520. Around twenty bombs were dropped but only minor damage was caused. Sorties from Dover, Manston and Westgate by Nos. 37 and 50 Squadrons were launched, but to no avail.

A potentially more serious attack took place on the night of 16/17 March, when five German navy Zeppelins, the L35, L39, L40, L41 and L42 targeted London. The L42 turned back very early but managed to drop a few bombs, causing no damage. Between 2220 and 2240 the L35 and the L39 crossed the British coast near Thanet. The L35 headed first for Ashford and left the British coast via Dover at 0025. Meanwhile the L39 left via Pevensey at 2350. The L39 did not make it home, as it was shot down by French artillery. The L40 came in over Herne Bay at 0100 and left close to New Romney at 0215. The L41 was only spotted over Dungeness at some point between 0140 and 0205. Collectively the airships did very little damage and nobody was killed or injured. Aircraft from RNAS Eastchurch and Manston were scrambled, as were a number of aircraft from RFC's Nos. 37, 39, 50 and 78 Squadrons.

During the remainder of March there were two ineffectual attacks by German aircraft against Dover on the 17th and against coastal shipping on the 25th. The attacks continued during April, but only two were reported, one against Ramsgate on the night of 5/6 April and another against coastal shipping during daylight hours on 19 April.

A second brave attack by a single German aircraft against London took place on the night of 6/7 May. An Albatros CVII, flying from an airfield near Ostend, approached the northern outskirts of London at 0100. It dropped five bombs between Holloway and Hackney and then sped off, crossing the British coast near Deal. Only four defensive sorties were mounted, owing to the speed of this attack, with two flying out of RNAS Manston and two from A Flight, No. 50 Squadron, Bekesbourne.

Navy Zeppelins returned to make another attack on London during the night of 23/24 May. Involved this time were the L40, L42, L43, L44, L45 and L47. The RNAS and the RFC managed to mount seventy-six defensive sorties. The Germans did minimal damage and only claimed one death. The Zeppelins were first spotted somewhere off the coast of Great Yarmouth at 2145. At around 0018 the L40 crossed the British coast to the south of Lowestoft. The L42 came in shortly afterwards over the Naze, the L45 crossed to the south of Orford Ness at 0100 and the L43 at a similar position at 0215. The L44 was stranded for some time off the coast between Lowestoft and Harwich after it lost power to its engines. The L47 by all accounts did not penetrate British airspace.

The L43 was flying at an altitude of 20,000ft, and from that height its crew mistook Harwich for Sheerness and proceeded to drop bombs on Suffolk villages, believing them to be London. The British responded by scrambling RNAS aircraft from most of their East Anglia bases, supported by RFC aircraft of Nos. 37, 39, 50 and 51 Squadrons. The only British aircraft to spot one of the raiders was a BE12A flown by Lieutenant G. D. F. Keddie of B Flight, No. 37 Squadron, Stow Maries. He saw a Zeppelin off the coast of Harwich and gave chase for around twenty minutes. Then he lost sight of it and his engine started to give problems, so he was forced to land at Covehithe. In all probability it was the L44, which had been suffering from engine problems off the coast. The airship finally reached its own base at 1900 hours. The major problem for both the airships and for the defending aircraft was the poor weather. There was particularly poor visibility and the closest any of the airships had got to London was the L42, which turned around near Braintree at 0145.

CHAPTER THREE

The England Squadron

W hen the German army's offensive in the autumn of 1914 had brought them close to the Channel coast, a former balloon pilot, Major Wilhelm Siegert, proposed the creation of bomber squadrons which could deliver attacks on London. He believed that strategic bombing would bring an abrupt end to the war.

At that stage the only suitable aircraft were small two-seaters, underpowered and incapable of carrying a heavy bomb load. They could only be used effectively against London if the Germans first captured the Pas de Calais. The German High Command was confident that this would happen, and that Siegert's plan would work. They therefore authorized the creation of the *Fliegerkorps der Obersten Heeresleitung*, the 'Air Corps of the High Command'.

As it was, of course, the Pas de Calais was never captured, so the new corps was stationed at Ghistelles, near Ostend in Belgium. For security reasons it was bizarrely codenamed *Ostend Brieftauben Abteilung* – 'Ostend Carrier Pigeon Squadron'. Initially experienced aircrew were allocated to the *Fliegerkorps*, which consisted of two wings with a total of thirty-six aircraft. They were small B-type aeroplanes with no defensive armament, and the crew had to rely on pistols and rifles for close defence.

The German 4th Army was halted by the British at Ypres in November 1914 and any hope of transferring the squadron to the Pas de Calais evaporated. So not only were the aircraft inadequate, but they were also too far away to pose any threat to London. The Germans had not been idle in their attempts to create larger bombers (*Grossekampfflugzeug*), however and various aircraft manufacturers had already begun the design work.

Siegert and his squadron were likewise not idle. They launched bombing attacks on various Allied targets, including Dunkirk. In the spring of 1915 the squadron was divided into four separate units. One was sent to Metz, a second to Galicia and two reconnaissance units,

A66 and A69, were created. It served on the Eastern Front until July 1915 and in January of the following year it was redesignated as *Kampfgeschwader I der Ohl* ('Battle Squadron I'). Almost immediately it was renamed *Kagohl I*.

This squadron comprised six flights, each with six two-seater C-type aircraft. They were soon launched on bombing operations around Verdun.

In September 1916 *Kagohl I* was again reorganized. Three of the flights under Captain Gaede began operations around the Somme, whilst Flights 2, 3 and 5 were posted to the Balkans. At around this time both half-squadrons (*Halbgeschwaders*) were issued with prototype *Grossekampfflugzeug* aircraft, the GII, but they had severe problems with their Mercedes engines and were soon withdrawn from operations. By September 1916 the GIV prototype was ready, having learned many lessons from the GII and the next model, the GIII. Manufacture of these aircraft was now approved and at long last Siegert's plan could be put into action.

As we have seen, navy Zeppelins had been bombing London since the middle of 1915, but after the loss of Hieinrich Mathy and the L31 over Potters Bar in October 1916, few had dared to attack the capital. The prospect of being able to attack London in an entirely different manner caught the imagination of the German armed forces.

General Ernst von Hoeppner became *Kommandierender General der Luftstreitkräfte*, the first commander of the separate German air force. He wrote the following memorandum shortly after he took office:

Since an airship raid on London has become impossible, the Air Service is required to carry out a raid with aeroplanes as soon as possible. The undertaking will be carried out in accordance with two entirely separate schemes:

1. Bombing squadrons equipped with G (large) aeroplanes
2. Giant flights equipped with R (Giant) aeroplanes

The G (large) aeroplane for this task is now ready, and the R (Giant) so far developed that its use will be practicable in the near future. It is therefore possible to consider carrying Scheme 1 into effect.

Scheme 1 will be carried out by Half-Squadron No. 1 using Gotha GIV aeroplanes. The requisite number of thirty aeroplanes will be ready by 1st February 1917.

By despatching eighteen aeroplanes, each carrying a load of 300kg of bombs, 5,400kg could be dropped on London, the same amount as would be carried by three airships, and so far three airships have never reached London simultaneously.

Scheme 1 can only succeed provided every detail is carefully prepared, the crews are practised in long-distance overseas flight and the squadron is made up of especially-good aeroplane crews. Any negligence and undue haste will only entail heavy losses for us, and defeat our ends.

The new bomber squadron would henceforth be named *Englandge-schwader*. The *Obersten Heeresleitung* endorsed von Hoeppner's plan and gave the operation the codename *Türkencreuz* ('Turk's Cross').

It was the earnest hope of the Germans that daytime aircraft attacks on London and other targets would have a profound effect, at least on morale. The *Obersten Heeresleitung* also believed that the bombers would be effective against lines of communication, military encampments and factories producing munitions. A hoped-for subsidiary effect was that British anti-aircraft defences would be withdrawn from France, which would lessen the dangers for German aircraft over mainland Europe. Above all, the Germans recognized that in establishing a relatively small strike force of thirty aircraft, they had the opportunity to cause disproportionate panic and cost to the British, thus diverting them from their main war effort on the Western Front.

From the outset *Englandgeschwader* would target Downing Street, the Bank of England, the Admiralty and media premises around Fleet Street. This would strike at the heart of the British establishment and prove beyond any reasonable doubt that not even the British decision-makers and opinion-formers were safe from attack. Secondary targets were established between Folkestone and Harwich. These would be chosen if the aircraft ran into poor weather or were suffering from engine problems. Also included in this list of secondary targets were other key strategic locations, including Tilbury and Woolwich.

The Gotha GIVs required specially levelled landing strips. It had been proved that the earlier types were prone to mechanical breakdown and worse if they were exposed to bumpy take-offs and landings. As a result, four new airfields were to be constructed, all around the Ghent area. The first was at Mariakerk, the second at Melle-Gontrode and the remaining two at Oostacker and St Denis Westrem. St Denis Westrem and Melle-Gontrode were ready in April 1917. Mariakerk and Oostacker would not be ready until the July. As a result, the squadron was stationed at Ghistelles, which was already the base of the existing *Halbgeschwader No. 1*. It was perilously close to the Western Front and only 10 miles behind the lines, with the result that Allied aircraft constantly over flew it. Whilst waiting for the Gothas, the squadron continued to operate with C-type aircraft, which was a wise precaution as there were innumerable delays in the delivery of the new aircraft.

Captain Ernst Brandenburg had been personally selected by von Hoeppner to command the new squadron, replacing Gaede. It was proposed that it would have six flights, each with six bombers. *Halbgeschwader No. 1* was fully incorporated into *Kagohl III*, with No. 1 flight becoming No. 13 flight, under the command of Lieutenant Vierbeg, No. 4 flight becoming No. 14, under Lieutenant Weese and No. 6 flight becoming No. 15, under Lieutenant Walter. Brandenburg was soon able to create flight No. 16, under Lieutenant von Seydlitz, but his remaining two flights, Nos. 17 and 18, would not be fully operational for some months.

Each bomber had a crew of three. Commanding the aircraft was a navigator and bombardier, not a pilot officer, and in addition to navigation and bomb aiming, he manned the front machine-gun. He occupied the nose of the Gotha, a large space but filled with equipment. In addition to the machine-gun and navigational and bomb-aiming aids, there was also an oxygen cylinder. The bombsight was a 3ft long vertically mounted Goertz telescope, which was used to direct the dropping of internal and external bombs. The smaller bombs were fixed to racks in the fuselage and the heavier ones were fitted underneath the wings and fuselage.

The pilot was either an officer or a senior non-commissioned officer; many of them were former cavalrymen. The third member of the crew was usually another non-commissioned officer, whose role was to defend the rear of the aircraft with a pair of machine-guns. The configuration of the fuselage allowed the rear gunner to be able to fire at enemy aircraft attacking from the rear and from below, which was usually a blind spot.

Brandenburg, who was in his early thirties, had a headquarters staff of seven, including himself. His Adjutant was Gerlicht and five other officers were responsible for intelligence, motor transport, meteorology, photography and technical issues. Brandenburg's own Gotha's rear fuselage was painted red so that he could easily be recognized in flight. Two other Gothas were allocated to the headquarters staff.

In March 1917 the first of the GIVs arrived at Ghistelles. As we have seen, experience with the GII in the Balkans had shown that the Mercedes 220hp engines were unreliable, and there were also other problems. The structure was not strong enough and the ailerons had been fitted only to the top wing, so the pilot had to be constantly aware and could barely relax. Although the GIII was a considerable improvement, having a stronger fuselage and better Mercedes 260hp engines, very few were available by December 1916, as it had only gone into production the previous October. Ailerons were fitted to both the upper and lower planes and this aircraft was very much the prototype for the GIVs that would be used by the squadron.

Brandenburg and his men were delighted to see the improvements in the GIV compared to the two previous models. Overall protection had been improved, the rear gunner could fire above the fuselage and through the ventral gun tunnel, and a dynamo, fixed to the right-hand engine, electrically heated the machine-guns so that the oil in their mechanism would not freeze when the aircraft was flying at high altitude. The aircraft carried several drums of ammunition, each holding 200 rounds of armour-piercing Mauser bullets. Every fourth round was a tracer bullet to aid accuracy.

It was decided that the aircraft would carry a mixture of 50kg and 12.5kg bombs for daylight raids. Up to seven 50kg bombs were fitted onto racks under the nose and immediately underneath the pilot and the commander. It would be the commander's responsibility to operate the bomb-release system. The 12.5kg bombs were stored in a magazine fitted with a sliding door and the pilot was responsible for pulling the lever to release them. The 50kg bombs were around 7in in diameter and 5ft long. Their explosive component consisted of hexanitrodiphenylamine and trinitrotoluene (TNT) in a 60:40 mix, and in theory, they were capable of destroying a three-storey building. In practice, over 30 per cent failed to explode and a further 10 per cent exploded prematurely in the air.

The 12.5kg bomb's were packed with a mixture of TNT and phosphorus. They were primarily considered anti-personnel weapons, rather than being capable of doing serious damage to buildings. The bombs themselves were about 3.5in in diameter and approximately 30in long. They had a very sensitive fuse and the mixture of explosives was especially useful to the bomb aimer, as when they detonated they threw up a white cloud. Around 90 per cent of these bombs hit their targets.

Bomb aiming was relatively rudimentary, although based on sound science. The bomb aimer would work out how long it took for the target to cross a part of the sighting scale. The bomb aimer would look through the eyepiece of the sight and, as the target passed below, start a stopwatch. He would be able to judge the point when the bombs needed to be dropped by calculating the height of the aircraft and comparing it to a chart. He would then set the bomb sight to provide a course for the pilot.

The Germans were acutely aware that if they attacked Britain in daylight then they would be spotted and the alarm raised at the earliest opportunity thereby attracting the attention of fighter aircraft and anti-aircraft batteries. It took a GIV carrying 1,200kg of bombs around an hour to climb to 18,000ft. The other key consideration was that a return trip to London was 350 miles. It was calculated that 600kg of bombs, plus essential equipment, including ammunition and machine-guns, would total 900kg. This meant that the aircraft would need 15 gallons of oil and 175 gallons of petrol. The existing petrol tank was inadequate and therefore an additional 70 gallon gravity tank was added to each aircraft, which would give each GIV two more hours of flying time. It was decided, however, that each aircraft should carry only 300kg of bombs, so as to leave a margin for error.

Even this was not sufficient, however. It was apparent that direct flight paths would, in a short period of time, be made impossible by balloon aprons, concentration of anti-aircraft guns and more closely based British fighters; detours would have to be made. In addition to this, cloud cover was a concern, as were other weather conditions. It was therefore decided during the early stages that each Gotha would carry just 150kg of bombs.

Whilst the original Gothas, which were produced by Gothaer Waggonfabrik, met performance standards, those made by licensees tended to fall significantly below the minimum required. The initial batch was flown to their targets at around 16,000ft, but owing to the deficiencies of some of the licensed models, they were forced to come in at just 12,500ft.

Assuming a 300kg load, a GIV would be fitted with eight 12.5kg bombs and four 50 kg ones. Some, of course, had even lighter loads or none at all, as some were used for photoreconnaissance, whilst others were used as decoys to draw away British fighters. Despite its cumbersome look, and its loaded operational speed of no more than 80mph, it was still, relatively speaking, quite manoeuvrable. The RFC deployed fairly slow-moving fighter aircraft and the Gotha was a match for these, both in speed and, to a lesser extent, in manoeuvrability. Problems did arise when it hit a headwind, as its speed would be reduced to little more than 50mph. Poor weather played its part in no small measure in reducing the number of viable operational flying days during 1917. Indeed only in the summer did they have a handful of suitable days for bombing raids.

Forecasting the weather was essential if the squadron was to be successful. As a result, Lieutenant Cloessner, who was an accomplished meteorologist and a former officer on an airship, took charge of the meteorological station at Ghistelles. It was his responsibility to interpret weather reports received on a daily basis from Bruges, Hamburg, Frankfurt and Ostend. In order to support them he also carried out his own weather observations, notably releasing balloons in the area to check for wind speed.

Weather conditions over the British Isles were, of course, somewhat different from those over mainland Europe and this caused additional concerns. There were frequent deep depressions coming in from the Atlantic, which the German weather-forecasting team could not predict from the data available from their own observatories. The danger was that south-westerly winds would have a drastic effect on the speed and fuel consumption of the GIVs. This had already been noted during the Zeppelin offensive. But whilst the Germans did have an answer within their grasp, they failed to use it. U-boats were in operation in the Atlantic Ocean and it would have been prudent to order their captains to provide daily – or occasional – weather observations, which would have been of great value to the squadron.

It was not until late 1917 that the Rumpler CIV two-seater, long-range reconnaissance aircraft became available. It was used over the North Sea as a weather-surveillance aircraft. The pilot was seated above the fuel tank and beneath the navigator's seat was a cutout in the floor of the fuselage, which contained an observation camera. It had a machine-gun on a swivel mount for defence and, in addition, a second rigid machine-gun to the right of the engine. It was one of a number of aircraft designed by Edmund Rumpler, who created a number of sea and other reconnaissance aircraft, flying boats, trainers and large combat craft. It was 30ft long and had a height of $10^1/_2$ft with a wingspan of $24^1/_2$ft. It had a maximum speed of 100 mph and a service ceiling of 18,700ft. With a range of 370 miles it could patrol for around five hours.

Setting the vagaries of the weather aside, a five-hour mission, primarily over British-dominated skies, would prove to be an enormous endurance test and a challenge to the nerves of the GIV crew. As they would have to fly at a relatively high altitude to avoid attention, the men would be operating in extremely cold conditions. Consequently, they were given bulky, fur-lined flying suits. Their flying suits were worn over their field uniforms and they were issued with thick gloves and high thigh-boots. They also had crash helmets, although the majority of the men preferred to wear their standard-issue leather headgear, as this was not only considerably more practical but also warmer. Each man had access to a portable tank of liquid oxygen, which they could breathe through a bladder attached to a breathing tube. In practice, however, the men used this on very few occasions.

When the aircraft was not passing over British territory it would be traversing the North Sea. In theory, if it was forced to ditch at sea it should have been capable, according to the manufacturers, of staying afloat for up to eight hours if the vents or other openings in the fuselage had been closed. The aircraft were fitted with water brakes, which had two purposes. First, to slow the aircraft down at the point when it began to glide on the water, and second, to prevent it from turning over. The crews were also issued with air bags, which they were supposed to inflate prior to the aircraft ditching in the sea. In practice, however, in the panic immediately preceding a ditching, the air bags would be one of their last concerns, and many of the crews in the latter months did not even bother to take them onto the aircraft.

If the pilot had coaxed the aircraft down without any damage and the vents or other openings had not begun to let in water, the crew had around eight hours before they began to sink. This, in theory, would allow the navy to find them. Their chances were in fact slight, despite the fact that the navy ensured that U-boats and torpedo boats patrolled underneath the flight path. The crew would have no opportunity to contact either the navy or their base, as they did not carry radios. Only when a search and rescue craft was spotted could the alarm be raised with flares. Radios were ruled out as essential equipment because of their weight and bulk. The alternative was simple: Brandenburg ordered that each crew be issued with two carrier pigeons, although the birds would not be of any use if the aircraft ditched and sank immediately.

Initially, despite the fact that the Germans had already developed parachutes, Gotha crews were not equipped with them; indeed they were not in general issue. Moreover, using them over water would have simply reduced the crews' chances compared with what they would be if the aircraft ditched relatively intact. Numerous ditching incidents, however, soon proved that despite the manufacturers' boast, the crew were lucky if their aircraft had not sunk after thirty minutes.

Whilst the England Squadron awaited the completion of delivery of the GIVs the crews were given the opportunity to hone their skills in hours of practice flying. There was much to learn and very little margin for error. It was not a great surprise that during these practice flights the squadron suffered several casualties.

One of the most important operational aspects was the ability of the observers to cross open sea using dead-reckoning navigation. This was to prove extremely difficult, and would ultimately determine the success or failure of the squadron's overall mission. Brandenburg sent his observers for training with the German navy at Heligoland and Sylt, where they were despatched in seaplanes in order to hone their navigational skills, using lightships to aid their calculations.

The observers were also issued with maps of the North Sea and the Dover Strait. From these maps they determined the departure points from the European mainland and the landfall targets on the British coast. It was decided that either the Belgian/Dutch border, Blankenbergh, Nieuport or Ostend would be used. The target landfall stretch included the North Foreland, Tongue Lightship, Foulness Island, Swin and Clacton.

The squadron determined the normal approach path for an attack on London. They decided that they would leave the mainland via Ostend and head for Foulness Island. They would then head for London using Epping Forest as a major visual clue to their location. In other words, they would attack from the north or north-east. They would then head back to mainland Europe by following the Thames along its northern bank and then head out over its estuary.

Operating in daylight hours meant strength in numbers. They would fly rather as British and American aircraft were to do in the Second World War, in a close, defensive formation. This would allow each aircraft not only to defend itself, but also to provide additional covering crossfire for its partners in the formation. This meant that Allied fighters approaching the formation would have to negotiate interlocking fields of fire, making it a formidable opponent.

Usually the squadron would adopt a diamond-shaped formation, with Brandenburg and the other two headquarters aircraft leading. Brandenburg would signal turns or changes in altitude with flares. It was essential that the men were trained to fly in these tight formations, over both land and sea. In reality however, Belgium had a relatively small airspace, and they could not overlap into neutral Holland's space. There was also the need to avoid the Western Front, where they would draw the attention of both anti-aircraft guns and Allied fighters. At this stage in the proceedings it would have been a huge blow to the squadron's overall chances of success for a Gotha to be shot down in Allied-held territory, since they were working on the premise that the Allies were unaware that the GIVs would soon be unleashed against the capital. For the allies to become aware of the presence, let alone the physical evidence, of a GIV would have been a catastrophic blow. So the tight formations had to be practised over less dangerous and more controllable airspace, and Paderborn, in Prussia, was chosen, some 200 miles east of the squadron's base.

The pilot and crew had a lot to learn, and quickly. Evasion tactics and instant response to commands had to be ingrained in their operational activities. It is probably during this period of intense training that Brandenburg developed the concept of breaking the formation apart when necessary. If it flew into an area of concentrated anti-aircraft fire, it would split into two distinct groups, flying at different altitudes, to avoid the formation itself from being shattered and dispersed whilst evading the gunfire.

In order to qualify and be accepted as a GIV pilot each man had to make twenty landings, half during the day and half by night. The reason behind Brandenburg's insistence that his pilots should be able to land in both sets of conditions was that the GIV was considerably lighter when returning from a mission. The slab-sided fuselage was amongst several aspects of the aircraft that left it prone to problems if there was a crosswind. It was not terribly stable when lightly loaded, which was not the case if it was fully loaded, as it could glide for considerable distances with the engines turned off.

Brandenburg also intensively trained his crews in sending and understanding commands using the flares. He used a mixture of red, green and white flares for a variety of purposes. For example, each target would be given a number. Then when closing in on a target, Brandenburg would be able to signal the shift from one to another by firing off the appropriate number of flares

By April 1917 Brandenburg had prepared his squadron as best he could for the first air raid against Britain. When they returned to Belgium it was decided that Allied aircraft had been paying too close attention to the air base at Ghistelles. Therefore two flights, Nos. 13 and 14, and Brandenburg himself, with the headquarters aircraft, would transfer to Melle-Gontrode and the other two flights, Nos. 15 and 16, would be based at St Denis Vestrem.

The squadron was still not ready to launch the first raid, however. There were considerable mechanical difficulties with the engines and the petrol pipe works, and the 70 gallon reserve petrol tanks still needed to be installed. Brandenburg took the opportunity during this period to continue to train his observers in navigation skills and to provide other crew members with machine-gun practice.

It took the entire month of April to deal with all the problems with the aircraft. The bearings in the engines were replaced, the petrol pipe work was modified and the reserve petrol tanks were installed. This considerably delayed the operational readiness of the existing GIVs and, of course, delayed the arrival of the new production models, as they also needed to be brought up to the new specification.

CHAPTER FOUR

The Gotha Bombers

Gothaer Waggonfabrik (Gotha or GWF) was originally a manufacturer of railway rolling stock based at Warnemünde, but during the First World War it manufactured a series of bombers originally designed by Oskar Ursinus in 1914.

The numbers manufactured were never huge, but there were several different types (GI, GII, GIII, GIV, and GV). The GV was the most numerous – up to thirty-six were available for squadron service at any one time – but the GIV was also seen over Britain at various stages of the war.

The Gotha LE2 was a very early attempt to produce a large combat aircraft. Following on from this attempt, efforts were made in 1914 to identify appropriate engines and develop the key design features of what would become the Gotha GI.

Gotha LE 2
Reconnaissance and training aircraft, 1913

Wingspan	14.4m
Wing area	28sq m
Max. take-off weight	1,053kg
Weight empty	690kg
Max. weight carried	363kg
Max. speed	102km/h
Cruising speed	90km/h
Wing load	38kg/sq m
Range	600km
Engine	Mercedes D I
Power rating (max.)	104hp
Number of Engines	1
Total power rating (max.)	104hp
Crew	2

Gotha G I (GUH)
Large combat aircraft, 1914

Total length	12.9m
Maximum height	4m
Wingspan	22m
Wing area	82sq m
Max. take-off weight	2,800kg
Weight empty	1,800kg
Max. weight carried (payload)	240kg
Max. speed	125km/h
Ceiling	2,750m
Wing load	34kg/sq m
Range	540km
Engine Type	Benz BzIII
Power rating (max.)	148hp
Number of engines	2
Total power rating (max.)	296hp
Crew	3
Armament	2 × MG 7.9mm
	200kg bomb

Oskar Ursinus, a civil engineer, carried out most of the early work, and he created the Friedel-Ursinus *Kampfflugzeug* ('battle plane'). In August 1914 he proposed that it should be built and Gotha signed the production licence in March 1915. In April 1915 an initial contract was given for six GI aircraft. Five of them were to be powered by two Benz BZIII 150hp engines and one by a pair of Mercedes DIII 160hp engines.

The aircraft were to be capable of carrying a 200kg load and would incorporate 150kg of armour for protection. They were to be crewed by two men and have a maximum speed of 125km/hr. The aircraft were delivered between 27 July and 8 September 1915, designated as G9 – G14/15.

A second series of six aircraft were ordered in July 1915, with the same specifications, but with the proviso that they should have an increased performance. They were delivered between 22 September and 5 November 1915.

The final series of the GI aircraft, with Mercedes DIII 160hp engines, were ordered in October 1916. These were to have the capacity to carry 350kg of bombs and have three crew members. Five of these aircraft were delivered between 24 January and 20 March 1916.

In all, just fifteen GI aircraft were constructed and their lifespan was relatively short.

Gotha B (Type LD 1)
Reconnaissance and training aircraft, 1914

Total length	8.28m
Maximum height	3.45m
Wingspan	14.5m
Wing area	46sq m
Max. take-off weight	982kg
Weight empty	590kg
Max. weight carried	392kg
Max. speed	115km/h
Wing load	21kg/sq m
Range	520km
Engine	Mercedes D I
Power rating (max.)	104hp
Number of engines	1
Total power rating (max.)	104hp
Crew	2

The Germans experimented with several versions of the Gotha B reconnaissance and training aircraft, primarily the LD1, the LD2 and later the LE3. Experience with these early variants allowed the Germans to identify many of the problems associated with aircraft of this type. Bearing in mind that the bombers at this time were virtually unknown, this experience, limited though it was, proved to be invaluable, and many lessons were learned that would aid the development of the more numerous later versions of the Gotha bombers.

Gotha B (Type LD 2)
Reconnaissance aircraft, 1914

Total length	8m
Maximum height	3.25m
Wingspan	12.55m
Wing area	36sq m
Max. take-off weight	935kg
Weight empty	525kg
Max. weight carried	410kg
Wing load	26kg/sq m
Range	450km
Engine	Mercedes D I
Power rating (max.)	118hp
Number of engines	1
Total power rating (max.)	118hp
Crew	2

Gotha LE 3
Reconnaissance and training aircraft, 1914

Total length	10m
Maximum height	3.15m
Wingspan	14.5m
Wing area	33.5sq m
Max. take-off weight	1,062kg
Weight empty	690kg
Max. weight carried	372kg
Max. speed	96km/h
Wing load	32kg/sq m
Range	385km
Engine	Mercedes D I
Power rating (max.)	104hp
Number of engines	1
Total power rating (max.)	104hp
Crew	2

Gotha GII
Large Combat Aircraft, 1915

Total length	9.1m
Maximum height	3.49m
Wingspan	16.2m
Wing area	59sq m
Max. take-off weight	2,470kg
Weight empty	1,450kg
Max. weight carried	280kg
Max. speed	140km/h
Service ceiling	3,000m
Wing load	42kg/sq m
Range	700km
Engine	Benz BZIII
Power rating (max.)	148hp
Number of engines	2
Total power rating (max.)	296hp
Crew	3
Armament	2 × MG 7.9mm and 200kg bomb

The GII which was simply a staging post between the early versions of the GI and the far more successful and numerous GIII, GIV and GV, entered service in March 1916. It was plagued by unreliable engines, but nonetheless fifteen of them were used in the Balkans until they were finally withdrawn.

Flugzeugbau Friedrichshafen, a part of the Zeppelin Airship Company, who had been involved in the development of the GI, manufactured the majority of the GIIIs, which had a fairly conventional construction, being made of wooden frames strengthened by wire braces and covered in plywood. The aft of the fuselage was also made of wire-braced wood, but here it was covered with fabric. At the centre of the fuselage was the cockpit. There were also six cells to hold bombs and, of course, the fuel tanks. The pilot sat next to the bombardier and the flight controls were fairly rudimentary, with rudder pedals and a yoke.

Steel tubes and plywood ribs reinforced the upper and lower wings and in order to improve the load bearing, the centre section of the lower wing was clad in plywood, whilst the rest was covered in fabric. The central struts were made of ash and the vertical and horizontal tail surfaces were constructed of steel tubing covered in fabric.

The landing gear was fairly rudimentary with a pair of wheels mounted on struts on either side. Sometimes the aircraft was also fitted with a fifth wheel on the nose to prevent it from tipping over if it landed on soft ground. The liquid-cooled Mercedes DIVa, 260hp engines had rear-mounted propellers. The entire engine and radiators were fixed to V-shaped struts fixed to both lower and upper wings.

For defensive protection there were a pair of 7.92mm machine-guns, one mounted on the nose and the other behind the cockpit on the fuselage. Some aircraft also had a third machine-gun mounted at the bottom of the aft compartment. It was capable of carrying 1,587kg of bombs. The larger ones were carried under the fuselage or close to it on the lower wings. The smaller ones were carried on racks inside the fuselage.

There was a variant of the GIII, the GIIIA, which had slightly altered wing tips. It also had what became known as the Gotha Tunnel, situated in the lower aft fuselage, which was designed to improve the field of fire of the machine-gun positioned there.

The GIV, or to be more precise the AEG GIV, was a natural development of the GI, GII and GIII. The company primarily involved in its development was Allgemeine Elektrizitäts Gesellschaft (AEG) which had produced an early single-seat GI in 1915. It had also produced GIIs and in December 1915 had introduced the GIII.

The AEG GIV was very similar to the GIII. It was primarily built from steel tubing, wood and fabric. The nose area was covered in plywood, whilst the rest of the fuselage was covered in fabric. The crew were housed in a nose compartment, a rear compartment and the cockpit. Importantly, any member of the crew could get to any other area of the aircraft whilst in flight. It was therefore possible for a reserve pilot to replace the original pilot if that pilot was killed or injured.

The leading edges of the wings were made of wood, although steel tube bars provided the main strength, and were covered in shrunken fabric. AEG chose to use the Mercedes DIVa, a liquid-cooled, 260hp, six-cylinder engine. It was a natural development from the one that they had used in the GIII, the Mercedes DIV 220hp engine. The engines had their own radiators and often the side panels were removed on the engines to cut down on weight. For landing two sets of two wheels were mounted under the engine's nacelles.

The effect of using so much steel in the construction of the aircraft meant that it was comparatively heavy. This in turn meant that once fuel had been taken into account it was only capable of carrying 400kg of bombs. It usually carried up to three × 45kg bombs under the central fuselage, another one under each lower wing and 11.3kg bombs inside the fuselage.

The GIV weighed 2,395kg when empty and 3,222kg fully loaded with bombs, fuel and ammunition. The defensive armament consisted of a pair of 7.9mm machine-guns, which were air-cooled. The forward-facing gun was on a 360-degree ring mount, whilst the other was on a U-shaped mount in the aft compartment.

Although the GIV was used over Britain, its primary use was against Allied targets behind the lines. This meant that, as the targets were within fighter range, attacks could be made during both the day and the night. The GIV saw service in Macedonia from February 1917, but it was mostly used over France.

The aircraft remained in production until 1917 and in all 542 G-type airframes were produced, the majority of which became GIVs. When the armistice was signed on 11 November 1918 there were still fifty in service. By then, AEG had produced a GIVb with an increased wingspan of 24m and were in the last stages of producing a GIVk, which was designed to be a ground-attack aircraft with a quick-firing cannon mounted in the nose. Five were produced, but by the time of the armistice none of them had reached operational units.

Gotha GIV
Large Combat Aircraft, 1915

Total length	12.4m
Maximum height	4.3m
Wingspan	23.7m
Max. take-off weight	3,966.kg
Weight empty	2,734kg
Max. weight carried	300kg
Max. speed	140km/h
Service ceiling	6,498m

Range	486km
Engine	Mercedes DIVa
Power rating (max.)	260hp
Number of engines	2
Crew	3
Armament	2 × MG 7.92mm and a 300lb bomb

The GIV was replaced by the GV in August 1917. It had several structural changes and, above all, it was more robust and had more powerful engines. A notable addition was the ventral tunnel, which allowed the gunner to fire to the rear and below, a hitherto dangerous blind spot for the earlier bombers.

The vast majority of the attacks against London and the rest of the British Isles during 1917 and 1918 were undertaken by GV bombers. Whilst the GIV had become, in effect, the world's first strategic bomber, the GV, of which around 100 were built, formed the backbone of *Bogohl* 3's offensive arm. By April 1918 their total strength of around thirty-six aircraft included GIVs, GVs and GVbs.

The GV's fuselage was built of wood with wire braces and covered with plywood sheets. The fuel tanks were placed immediately aft of the cockpit, which meant that the access to the aft gunner's compartment was blocked, so a gun tunnel was necessary, in the form of a triangular section, that allowed the gunner to get in and out of his position.

The GV was not dissimilar to the GIV in many respects. Both had a wingspan of nearly 24m, both had Mercedes DIVa, liquid-cooled 260hp engines turning two-bladed wooden propellers with a 3m diameter. With the fuel tanks moved to the centre of the fuselage, the engines had new streamlined nacelles. There was a pair of gravity fuel tanks mounted on the top of the centre section of the upper wing. The GV was also capable of carrying around 500kg of bombs, although more usually in attacks against Britain they carried six 50kg ones.

The GVa was a slight improvement, as it had twin vertical fins and rudders and biplane horizontal stabilizers. This meant that its engine performance was slightly better. There was even a GVb, which was exactly the same as the GVa, except that it had a pair of wheels in front of the main undercarriage.

Gotha GV
Large Combat Aircraft, 1917

Total length	11.86m
Maximum height	4.3m
Wingspan	23.7m

Wing area	89.5sq m
Max. take-off weight	3,975kg
Weight empty	2,740kg
Max. speed	140km/h
Service ceiling	6,500m
Range	840km
Engine	Mercedes DIVa
Power rating (max.)	250hp
Number of Engines	2
Crew	3
Armament	2 × MG 7.9mm and a 500lb bomb

Although the GVb was the last operational version, strictly speaking, there were still further developments. The GVII was designed with a slightly shorter nose, but was still powered by the Mercedes DIVa. Both it and the GLVII had biplane tail assemblies. Only a handful of GVIIs, GVIIIs and GLVIIs were produced. Maybach MBIV 245hp engines powered later models, including the GVIII, GLVIII, GIX and GX.

Bogohl 3's, the Gothas made twenty-two night attacks on Britain. They lost twenty-four aircraft, either to British or French fighters or to anti-aircraft defences. A further thirty-seven were lost in landing accidents, largely caused by the weather conditions, damage caused by defensive sorties or anti-aircraft guns, shortage of fuel or pilot miscalculations.

In addition to the Gothas that were deployed against Britain and those that were used against ground targets on the Western Front, a further thirty GIVs were supplied to Austria-Hungary in 1917 and were used in a series of bomber attacks against Italian cities.

CHAPTER FIVE

The First Gotha Raid: May–June 1917

Brandenburg and his squadron were still kicking their heels in May 1917. Brandenburg was mindful of von Hoeppner's memorandum, which had stated that in his opinion any technical oversight, negligence or impatience would bring about the ultimate failure of the squadron's mission. He and his men oversaw the replacement of the engines and hoped that the new ones would be far more reliable. It was a vain hope, however, as around 12 per cent of the bombers that set out on missions during 1917 and 1918 were forced to turn back with engine difficulties.

Brandenburg still needed to give his men practice in taking off, flying and landing with full loads. The new aircraft in particular had still not been fitted with the reserve fuel tanks, but the squadron was now champing at the bit and desperately wanted to prove themselves as an effective offensive arm. A compromise was arrived at, which meant that the bombers would lift off from their airfields and fly directly to Nieumunster, on the Belgian coast, around 30 miles from Ghent. This would allow the GIVs, which had not yet been fitted with the 70 gallon tanks, to be topped up with 20 gallons, which would be sufficient for them to cross the North Sea, approach London, deliver their payload and then return home. There were huge assumptions in all of this and there was little margin for error should there be any serious detours, or if the GIVs had to fight against strong headwinds.

Towards the middle of May, Brandenburg considered that his squadron and the aircraft had reached operational readiness. Consequently, he contacted von Hoeppner, who arranged for the Commander in Chief, *Feldmarschall* Paul von Hindenburg, to conduct an inspection. A few days later von Hindenburg arrived. He was impressed, and eager for the squadron to begin operations at the earliest possible opportunity. He, too, was acutely aware of the importance of this relatively small band of men and aircraft and how important their success was in terms of overall German strategy.

As it was, however, whilst the squadron was ready, the men willing and the machines technically capable, the weather was not prepared to abate on their behalf. The next few days were typified by high winds and thunderstorms. It was not until 24 May that the weather conditions seemed to be right to launch the squadron on their mission. An anticyclone had centred itself over France and whilst it was known that mainland Europe had acceptable flying conditions, it was not entirely clear whether this applied to south-eastern England.

Despite the threat of thunderstorms over the British Isles, Brandenburg and the squadron forged ahead in their preparations for their first raid, which they still intended to launch on 25 May. As a precautionary measure a series of subsidiary targets were identified, should London be inaccessible. Unfortunately for him, however, the Allies had also taken advantage of the break in the weather and even whilst the GIVs and their crews were finally being prepared, an air-raid warning sounded at St Denis Vestrem, and a flight of de Havilland DH4s, operating out of Dunkirk, appeared over the airfield. They dropped sticks of bombs that came perilously close to the eight operationally ready GIVs, which were parked close to the runway. At the very least this should have warned the Germans that despite their elaborate attempts at secrecy over the GIVs, the Allies were perfectly well aware of their existence and considered them to be a potential threat. As it was, however, the attack, which was launched by the RNAS, caused little damage and did not seriously impair the squadron's ability to prepare the aircraft for their own mission.

At around 1400 hours, twenty-three GIVs lifted off from the two airbases and headed for Nieumunster. One of them soon experienced engine trouble, however, and was forced to land on the airfield at Thielt. The remainder reached Nieumunster for refuelling. For an hour the squadron would have been helpless prey had there been Allied aircraft overhead.

At approximately 1530 hours the remaining twenty-two GIVs were airborne once more and for the first time heading across the neutral, but hostile, North Sea, making for the Essex coast. They were soon to stir up a hornet's nest, with no fewer than seventy-seven sorties being launched by the RNAS and RFC.

With Brandenburg's red-painted GIV in the lead, the bombers rose to 10,000ft and adopted their diamond-shaped formation. Not long after achieving this height, however, one of the bombers began to fall behind. The crew signalled to Brandenburg that they would have to return to Belgium. The aircraft was suffering from fuel problems, but it managed to negotiate the turn and the trip back to Ghistelles, which was now serving as an emergency landing field.

At approximately 1645 Brandenburg's squadron passed over the Tongue Lightship and was immediately spotted. The lightship telephoned a message to be passed on to the Admiralty. Unfortunately, there was a delay in sending the information from the Admiralty to the London Warning Controller, which lost fifteen minutes of response time. Ten minutes later the squadron was approaching Swin Middle Lightship and here, acting on a predetermined order, it split into two. They were now at around 16,000ft and crossed the Essex coast somewhere between the River Crouch and the River Blackwater.

It was scant consolation to the British that the squadron had approached the coast in almost precisely the direction that had been predicted. By now the RNAS coastal stations, stretching from Dover to Felixstowe, had been given the order to scramble their aircraft. The messages were sent in stages according to information and sightings received, but most of the stations had aircraft aloft within an hour and a half.

By 1655 the RNAS at Felixstowe and Westgate had fifteen seaplanes hunting for the invaders and a further ten fighters had been scrambled from Manston. The next stage of the British response was systematically to warn potential civilian and military targets on the supposed flight path. This meant that innumerable people had to be contacted across the London and Essex regions. All the warning districts were gradually being informed from around 1700.

The next layer of response came from the home defence Squadrons. BE and FE fighters were aloft by 1714, having been scrambled by Nos. 37, 39 and 50 squadrons. All available aircraft made for their defence patrol areas. No. 37 Squadron was responsible for protecting a line between Detling and Goldhanger, for which they had sent eight aircraft. No. 39 Squadron was charged with patrolling the eastern edge of London with eleven aircraft. Meanwhile, to the south, No. 50 Squadron had scrambled thirteen aircraft to cover a line stretching from Throwley to Bekesbourne and all the way to Dover. Amongst the first up were Lieutenant L. P. Watkins and Lieutenant L. F. Hutcheon, who both left Goldhanger in BE12As as part of A Flight, No. 37 Squadron. They were joined aloft by Captain C. A. Ridley, of B Flight out of Stow Maries and two aircraft from C Flight flying from Rochford, commanded by Lieutenants W.R.S. Humphreys and Orr-Ewing. Humphreys was forced to land at Goldhanger with engine trouble just fifteen minutes after taking off. No. 39 Squadron initially scrambled Captain S.R. Stammers of A Flight from North Weald, in a BE12A, but he was forced to return at 1719, to take to the sky again in another BE12A at 1730. No. 39 Squadron's C Flight from Hainault initially scrambled Captain W. H. Haynes and Lieutenant G. T. Wix. No. 50 Squadron's A Flight, scrambled Second Lieutenant W. R. Oulton from Detling, Second Lieutenant A. J. Arkell from Throwley and Lieutenant R. W. Le Gallais, Second Lieutenant L. Lucas and Second Lieutenant N. E. Chandler from Bekesbourne.

The RNAS was, of course, already aloft, with aircraft out of Felixstowe, Grain, Manston, Westgate and Walmer. Although the RFC home defence squadrons were charged with immediate defence of the British Isles, the Admiralty, largely owing to its excellent communication and co-operation with the War Department, was able to throw up an initial line of defence.

Meanwhile, Brandenburg and his men were crossing the estuary of the River Crouch. Here they came under fire from the 13th Mobile Anti-Aircraft Battery based at Highland Farm, Burnham-on-Crouch. The Germans were fortunate as the battery only managed to get off one shot. This was to be the only anti-aircraft shell fired at the squadron until it reached the coast once again on its return home. As far as Brandenburg was concerned, he could almost discount the defensive ability of the RFC aircraft. They were just too slow, sluggish and un-manoeuvrable to pose any threat to his aircraft, as they were far more attuned to dealing with Zeppelins. The crews of the RNAS, in their faster and more deadly aircraft, posed a far more serious threat.

As if to reinforce his dismissal of the RFC, Brandenburg's squadron passed over the airfields of No. 37 Squadron at around 1715. Below, he could see the BE aircraft based at Stow Maries and Rochford desperately trying to climb to his height. He knew that they would not be within range for at least another thirty minutes and that by the time they had, he would be thirty-five miles away.

When passing over the Crouch estuary Brandenburg correctly estimated that he would be over London in about forty minutes. Only the aircraft of the RNAS, notably the Sopwith Camels, Sopwith Pups and SE5s, had any chance of catching him.

As it happened it was not defensive aircraft or anti-aircraft fire that stopped Brandenburg and his men from raining bombs down onto the capital. The Gothas, still at 16,000ft, could see an immense layer of cloud 9,000ft below them. They simply could not see the target. It would have been suicidal to lose height and to bomb from beneath the cloud layer. His squadron was still heading towards the centre of London at 70mph but Brandenburg had to make a decision. By this time he had reached Tilbury and it was around 1730 hours. He lit flares and ordered his squadron to turn about and head south into Kent.

The Gothas probably made their turn somewhere over Gravesend, with the two wings of the squadron approximately 3 miles apart. The Thames estuary and Kent were a target-rich environment. There were the RFC's airfield at Lympne, railway lines, the Royal Navy base at Dover and the army's rest, recuperation and embarkation centre at Folkestone, all of them seemingly powerless to prevent their destruction.

The British, meanwhile, were still labouring under the mis-apprehension that the Gothas were heading for central London, and the skies above the capital and the Thames Estuary were full of RFC and RNAS aircraft, all hunting for the Germans. Here lay an even deeper problem with the potential defence of London and the Home Counties. Even if the warning controller and the headquarters were aware of the direction and speed at which the Germans were flying, there was no way of informing the pilots who were already aloft of any abrupt change in their direction. With the British aircraft and ground spotters looking in the wrong direction, Brandenburg's squadron managed to elude their hunters and, in fact, disappear for upwards of twenty-five minutes. They reappeared over Wrotham and here they were spotted, but communication to potential ground targets along their new flight path failed.

Brandenburg ordered his men to begin dropping 50kg bombs on Harvel and Linton. Five were dropped, but mercifully there was little damage and few casualties. Not only were these two villages not warned, nor were the next batch of targets pinpointed by Brandenburg. More bombs were dropped on transport centres near railway lines at Bethersden, Kingsnorth, Marden, Mersham, Pluckley and Smarden. Targets along the Royal Military Canal between Rye and Hythe were also picked out at Bilsington and Ruckinge. These targets were near the RFC airbases at Detling and Harrietsham. Three RFC BE12s were scrambled at around 1800 from Telscombe, but this was over 40 miles away and the aircraft had little chance of intercepting Brandenburg's squadron.

Brandenburg now attacked Ashford, with his primary target being the railway works. Two 50kg bombs and four 12.5kg bombs were dropped here, and the casualties were one killed and three wounded. It was during this time over Ashford that the squadron could claim its first Allied aircraft kill, although more accurately, the pilot of the Bristol F2B was forced to make a landing at the RFC's Lympne airfield. The pilot, Lieutenant Baker, was in the process of ferrying the aircraft from its factory to France when a machine-gun burst from one of the GIVs hit him. No sooner had Baker managed to nurse his aircraft down than Brandenburg's squadron hit the airfield. Little damage was actually inflicted by the three 50kg and nineteen 12.5kg bombs they dropped.

Lieutenant G. Gathergood, in a de Havilland DH5, left the No. 8 Aircraft Acceptance Park at Lympne at 1840, in pursuit of Brandenburg, but it took him upwards of twenty minutes to reach the height at which the GIVs were operating.

The next available target was Hythe. Here all the seven 50kg bombs and nine 12.5kg bombs managed to achieve was to kill the verger of the parish church and one other person and wound the vicar and his wife. Panic set in at the RFC's School of Aerial Gunnery at Hythe. None of the school's aircraft had been scrambled and indeed none of them was in a position to take off. All the men could do was scatter.

The first nearby Folkestone learned of the attack were the explosions caused by the bombs being dropped at Hythe. Few people took any notice, because it was common to hear the Royal Navy's firing practice out to sea and the British Army's coastal batteries testing the ranges.

Having come in over their targets of Harvel and Linton, spaced out over a 5 mile front, Brandenburg brought his aircraft closer together into a diamond formation about 1 mile wide. It came into view at about 15,000ft at around 1820, according to eyewitness accounts at Folkestone that day. There had been no air-raid warning and the immediate assumption, as the aircraft were coming from inland, was that they were Allied aeroplanes. Certainly, according to Harry Reeve, the Chief Constable of Folkestone, he had had no prior warning from the London Warning Controller, nor from the British Army's Eastern Command.

The first five 50kg bombs hit the Sandgate area. Mercifully three of them exploded prematurely, which gave a number of people a chance to seek cover. The aircraft on the right flank of the formation made this initial attack, while the others waited for the opportunity to drop their bombs on the Shorncliffe and Cheriton army camps.

Canadian infantrymen occupied the camps, and Brandenburg's aircraft ranged freely over them, unmolested by Allied aircraft and unthreatened by anti-aircraft fire. In total the Germans dropped six 50kg bombs and twenty-one 12.5kg bombs. One company of Canadian infantry was preparing for an evening exercise when a bomb dropped amongst them, killing seventeen and wounding ninety-three.

The next target was Folkestone itself, where around twenty-one 50kg and thirty 12.5kg bombs were dropped. Most of them fell not on military targets but on residential and commercial buildings. Twelve failed to make any impact on their targets, as ten failed to explode and two exploded prematurely in the air. Neither Sandgate nor Folkestone had any anti-aircraft gun protection; the nearest anti-aircraft unit was based at Dover, where the army had six shore batteries. The only anti-aircraft fire drawn by the German aircraft was the 12-pounder based at West Hougham and the 18-pounder at Cauldham, some 2 miles to the east of Folkestone. Nonetheless, they both engaged the GIVs as soon as they were in range. This was probably the only warning that the rest of the Dover batteries and the naval gunners had that the GIVs were in the area.

Brandenburg's attack on Folkestone was truly devastating. It was a Friday evening and there were many people still shopping for the Whitsun weekend; in fact some of the shops were so busy that there were queues outside. A Canadian sergeant, who was recuperating after having been wounded on the Western Front, said of the attack on Tontine Street, the main shopping area:

> The whole street seemed to explode. There was smoke and flames all over, but worst of all were the screams of the wounded and dying, and mothers frantically looking for their kids. A couple of minutes before, those of us who were on the street were like innocent kids ourselves, as we watched those swine in the sky.

In the narrow streets of the old part of Folkestone, the people were caught between bursting shop windows, falling masonry and flames. In just ten minutes Brandenburg's bombers had claimed ninety-five dead and 195 injured. Speaking later, the Chief Constable, Harry Reeve, said:

> I saw an appalling sight which I shall never forget till my dying day. Dead and injured persons were lying about; several horses were lying dead and a fire had broken out in front of premises which had been demolished. Several of the business premises were very seriously damaged; others had their plate-glass windows blown out.

It was not just the Tontine Street area that was devastated. Casualties were also inflicted on Bouverie Road and Cheriton Road.

The Pleasure Gardens Theatre, the railway station and several hotels, shops and houses were also hit over a 1 square mile area.

Brandenburg was still not content, some of the Gothas still had bombs onboard. He now headed for what could be the most important target: the Royal Navy base at Dover. By now, however, the hornet's nest had been well and truly stirred and in the space of a few minutes the Gotha squadron was shot at no less than 358 times by the army batteries based around Dover. As the Gothas approached, the Royal Navy vessels in the area joined in, firing 9.2 in shells at the small targets in the air. Allied aircraft were now also beginning to pinpoint the formation.

Flight Sub-Lieutenant R.F.S. Leslie took off in his Sopwith Pup at 1820. He had to put down shortly afterwards due to engine trouble, but scrambled a Sopwith Camel, taking off again at 1840. Already in the air was Flight Sub-Lieutenant L.C. Pincott, who had been up in the air since 1725 and had landed at 1805 in his Short 830. He took off again at 1815 and remained aloft until 1950. From Walmer, Flight Sub-Lieutenant W. H. Chisam, on board a Bristol Scout, and Flight Lieutenant S. Kemball, in a Sopwith Pup, had both taken off at 1830.

Leslie caught up with the rear Gothas at about 1830. By now Brandenburg had given up any hope of launching a successful attack on Dover. He later claimed that they had in fact attacked Dover and had hit the Mole, but the British categorically denied that any such attack had happened.

In all probability the British anti-aircraft fire was bursting far too low to have any chance of hitting the Gothas. Nonetheless, it did sufficiently deter them. At that point in the war the anti-aircraft gun crews had been used to firing at relatively slow moving Zeppelins. This was also a problem with the searchlights, which in later night attacks proved unable to keep up with the faster-moving aircraft.

Author A. Gathorne-Hardy left a seafront hotel and walked along the esplanade at Dover and sat down close to the Victoria Pier. In his account of the attack in the *Folkestone Herald*, he said:

The nearest bomb fell and I saw it splash into the sea just below me. As it fell I heard it hurtling through the air quite close. I could see little clouds, probably shrapnel, bursting round the aeroplanes, but they were really too high up to be in much danger. The heavy guns from Dover began to roar, and went on for some time. I watched the raiders passing in a south-easterly direction over the Straits, and long after I could no longer see them I observed little clouds shining in the air.

Whilst the anti-aircraft fire was clearly missing the Gotha formation, Leslie was having far better luck. Having caught up with the Gotha stragglers at about 11,000ft, he positioned his aircraft about 150 yards behind and above them. He then dived to attack. His first burst of machine-gun fire passed harmlessly ahead of the target Gotha. Leslie increased his dive and fired 150 rounds at about a range of 50 yards. At this point the Gotha returned fire. Leslie pulled away and looked behind him to see that the Gotha had also entered a steep dive and that smoke and steam were coming out of the centre of the fuselage. At this point he had to break visible contact with his first target, as he had come under fire from two other Gothas. He over-compensated in his banking manoeuvre, to avoid the stream of machine-gun bullets and, as a consequence, lost several thousand feet of altitude. He now reasoned, having come out of the banking manoeuvre, that the Gothas had gained too much ground for him to catch up. He was convinced that he had shot down one and returned triumphant to Dover. Although his kill was never officially confirmed, as he had tackled the Gotha squadron single-handed, he was awarded the DSC.

Shortly afterwards Lieutenant G. W. Gathergood, who had left Lympne in his DH5 at 1840, was cruising at an altitude of 14,500ft. He may well have encountered the Gotha that had been attacked by Leslie, as he described the GIV as trailing the main formation and belching black smoke. He came in for an attack, but his guns jammed. He had come close enough to the Gotha to receive defensive fire whilst he was trying to guide his DH5 with his feet and using his hands to release the jam on his Vickers machine-gun. He fired a handful of shots at long range, but by then he had realized that the DH5's compass was unserviceable and that he had lost sight of land. Reluctantly he turned about and headed back for the coast.

Sopwith Pups of RNAS squadrons Nos. 4 and 9 had been scrambled out of Dunkirk. Nine were aloft and hunting for the Gothas about 30 miles out from their base. Brandenburg's aircraft were heading for the Belgian coast at 18,000ft. No. 4 Squadron found them first and piled in for a combined attack. One of the Gothas was shot down and ditched into the sea to the north of Westende. Another was claimed to have been hit several times and spun out of control and into the sea. The Germans only ever admitted one loss, but the pilots of No. 4 Squadron were certain that a second had been dealt with. No. 9 Squadron now intercepted the Gotha formation. At the very least, they riddled one of the GIVs sufficiently to force it to crash land near Beernem, near Bruges. There is no clear indication whether it was badly damaged from the attacks from No. 9 Squadron or whether it suffered from engine failure, or indeed whether it was simply a pilot landing error. In any event, the whole crew was killed. There was speculation that it crashed as a result of the pilot having a heart attack.

A third Gotha was hit, but managed to land safely back at base.

The Germans claimed three kills: Leslie's aircraft, Gathergood's, and a third one, which was probably Captain C. B. Cooke's BE12A of C Flight, No. 37 Squadron, which had lifted off from Rochford at 1722 and had landed back at base as a result of an engine fire at 1815.

Both sides learned many lessons from this first bombing raid. As far as the British were concerned, it was clear that aircraft based at Dunkirk were far more able to respond to the Gothas by attacking them on their return trip. There were many reasons for this, principal among which was the fact that by this stage they were running short on fuel and would not be able to afford the increased fuel loss involved in taking evasive action. It was also readily apparent, despite the heroics of Leslie and Gathergood, that individual aircraft attacks on the Gotha formations were not only ineffective but also highly perilous for the solo pilot. A concerted attack by several Allied aircraft was the only way of dealing with the formations and their interlocking fields of fire. Perhaps the most stark lesson, however, was that the aircraft that had been allocated to the RFC home defence squadrons were woefully inadequate, in terms both of armament and performance, and that it was only the more modern and superior aircraft flown by the RNAS that had any prospect of dealing with the raiders.

As far as Brandenburg was concerned, he was dismayed by the losses at take-off and landing. He was also concerned at the continued unreliability of the GIVs' engines, which had forced two of his aircraft to turn back. The aircraft also had design flaws that were not easy to correct. Their instability and the relative flimsiness of the undercarriage were issues that would have to be dealt with in the longer term. In any event, the squadron had suffered more casualties at take-off and landing than the British had been able to inflict in aerial combat or in anti-aircraft action. In response to the successful attacks by the RNAS aircraft out of Dunkirk, Brandenburg requested that von Hoeppner allocate German fighters to cover the bombers on their return trip. Von Hoeppner agreed, realizing that whilst the Gothas had the element of surprise on their side when they approached the British Isles and also had an advantage if they abruptly changed direction, the element of surprise was lost on their return and that the British would respond as vigorously as possible at the very point when the Gothas were most vulnerable.

Von Hoeppner was sufficiently impressed with Brandenburg's first raid that he decorated Lieutenants Elsner and Reulner and Sergeant Helger for their contribution to the effort.

The British government and the civilian population were incensed, not only by the slaughter of non-military personnel, but also by the relative ease with which the German aircraft had over-flown one of the most densely populated and well defended parts of the British Isles, carried out their mission and escaped relatively intact. Initially the Government suppressed information about the raids and did not mention the number of casualties or the actual targets hit. All they admitted to was that attacks had taken place against targets in the south-east of England. Thousands of people therefore made desperate telephone calls to establish whether their relatives were safe.

On the following Monday, working from a report from the German news agency, *The Times* finally named Folkestone and Dover as the targets of the attack. This forced the government finally to give full details of the raid. What further angered civilians was the inability of the home defence squadrons to intercept and destroy the German raiders. They were also castigated for the fact that the RFC could not launch a retaliatory attack on a German city and that only the RNAS, using a small number of Handley Page and Short bombers based at Dunkirk could strike back against Germany.

The immediate British response was to try to use the RNAS aircraft to deal a knockout blow against the Gothas directly, by launching another raid on St Denis Vestrem on 28 May 1917. Although the airfield was damaged, however, it appears that none of the Gothas were actually hit.

Being targeted by the German bombers particularly outraged Folkestone. The town had felt a sense of kinship with the Germans since 1878, when fishermen had braved the English Channel in order to rescue the crew of the *Grosse Kurfürst*, a German battleship that had been involved in a collision at sea and was foundering off the coast. A delegation visited Field Marshal Lord French on 30 May and demanded that he give the region assurances that they would be protected from enemy aircraft attacks in the future. He promised that he would do everything in his power to prevent a reoccurrence, but obviously he could offer no absolute guarantees.

There was a meeting the following day at the War Office, chaired by Lieutenant General Sir David Henderson. Representing the home forces were Major General Shaw and Lieutenant Colonel Higgins. Rear Admiral G. Hope and Commodore Paine represented the Royal Navy. The chairman opened by reiterating the decision made in February 1916 that the navy, principally the RNAS, would be responsible for dealing with enemy aircraft or airships approaching the coast. Once they had crossed into British airspace, it was then the responsibility of the RFC. In essence, the navy was to provide a tripwire or early-warning system in order to give the RFC sufficient notice to get aircraft up into the air and at a sufficient altitude to deal with the raiders. In addition, the RNAS aircraft stationed at Dunkirk were charged with the task of intercepting the raiders on their return journey.

The Royal Navy was roundly criticized for not having given the home defence sufficient warning, particularly for wasting fifteen minutes once the first alert had been received from the Tongue Lightship. It was proposed that, as far as was practicable, warnings should be immediate and that to supplement the lightships in their warning role, aircraft spotters should be transferred from the Western

Front and allocated to each of the seven lightships dotted around the Thames Estuary and the east coast.

Greater cooperation was called for between the RNAS and the RFC. Henceforth, however, the RNAS aircraft based at Dunkirk would be assigned an additional role. They were regularly to overfly the German airfields at St Denis Vestrem and Ghistelles and report the numbers of aircraft and any significant movement in or out of the airfields. It was also suggested, although no serious work was ever done on this, that RNAS aircraft should be fitted with radios at the earliest opportunity.

The role of the RNAS seaplanes and flying boats operating in the North Sea was also reviewed; they were now also to provide another link in the early warning chain against German raiders.

The greatest problem that had arisen on 25 May was that only a limited number of aircraft from the RFC home defence squadrons had been available to deal with Brandenburg's attack. Higgins suggested that only twenty-two aircraft had actually been available on that day, which accords with the number of aircraft that actually scrambled in response to the attack. It was decided that as an interim measure training squadrons would be prematurely activated in order to assist the RFC's efforts. All training squadrons, from Southwold in Suffolk to Rottingdean in Sussex and as far as Bury St Edmunds and Brentford, would be activated. No. 65 Squadron, based at Wyton, Cambridgeshire, which was in the process of changing over to Sopwith Camels, would also be called upon in the event of another raid.

This meant that theoretically the RFC could provide forty aircraft to cover London (primarily the role of No. 39 Squadron), seventeen to cover the Thames Estuary (mainly No. 37 Squadron's area), eight to cover the Hastings and Romney area (No. 78 Squadron) and a further sixteen to cover the area from Throwley to Dover and Sandwich (mainly No. 50 Squadron). The weak point in this defensive line was the aircraft covering the Thames Estuary, BEs which had already proved to be less than adequate in terms of their climbing ability and speed. Immediate attention was to be given to reinforcing this part of the line.

The most serious issue was that any immediate action to reinforce or improve the quality of the defence aircraft would be to the detriment of aircraft cover over the Western Front. For the time being all that could be hoped for was an aerial response of some kind wherever the Germans probed, regardless of the actual quality or value of that defence. In many respects what could be achieved in the short term would be token but visible.

Both the RFC and the RNAS would now have to mount patrols during the day and the night, although it was argued that this would be to the detriment of aircraft defences against German airships. The British, however, were determined to be ready for the next Gotha attack and this time the Germans would not be able to avoid an aerial confrontation.

At this stage of the war there were obviously competing demands for equipment and personnel. It had already been decided that in July 1917, No. 101 Night Bomber Squadron would be created and in August No. 102 Night Bomber Squadron. These would need around 420 trained personnel, which would serve as a further drain on the men available to man the twelve home defence squadrons. These squadrons needed 197 pilots, but at that time they could muster just 107. Lieutenant Colonel Higgins implored the Deputy Director General of Military Aeronautics, based at the War Office, a Major General Brancker, to delay the creation of the two new night bomber squadrons until August and October 1917.

On 1 June 1917, the RNAS DH4s began their bombing campaign against the Gotha airfields in Belgium, which would continue through to July. On 4 June No. 5 Naval Squadron, together with the RFC's No. 27 Squadron, hit St Denis Vestrem. This heavier attack was part of the overall plan, wrapped up in both the conclusions made at the conference in London and the renewed ground offensive in the Flanders region, on the Western Front. It was also planned that another major attack would be made on 7 June.

Meanwhile, however, the weather conditions and reports were favourable for the Germans to consider a new attack on London. Lieutenant Cloessner predicted that there would be a light wind from the south-west, which would actually aid the return flight. In any case, Brandenburg was under intense pressure to launch an attack on London.

Brandenburg ordered twenty-two Gothas to take off at 1600 on 5 June 1917. By this stage there was no need to refuel at Nieumunster, as they had all now been fitted with the reserve fuel tank. The Kentish Knock Lightship and the vessel *The Clacton Belle* spotted the raiders at around 1810. Just an hour before the Gothas had lifted off, the home defence squadrons had launched a practice alert and at 1530 about thirty aircraft were in their areas around London. Their orders were to patrol for two hours and then return to base for refuelling.

Meanwhile, the Gothas had climbed to around 10,000ft. The Kentish Knock Lightship had spotted them initially at about 1740, some 30 miles from the Essex coast. This time the Admiralty was immediately informed.

By this time the bulk of the Royal Flying Corps aircraft which had been scrambled for the practice raid had already landed and were in the process of being refuelled. No. 50 Squadron was the first to get some of their BEs back in the air, lifting off from Bekesbourne, Detling and Throwley. By a few minutes after 1800, around thirty aircraft from four home defence squadrons (Nos. 37, 39, 50 and 78) were all aloft. Two Sopwith Camels from No. 65 Squadron, based at Wye, had also taken off, as had three Bristol Fighters of No. 35 (Training) Squadron, Northolt. Nine other aircraft from the aircraft parks at Lympne and Hendon had also joined in the defence.

The RNAS had also managed to launch fighters out of Dover, Eastchurch, Manston and Walmer, as well as several seaplanes based at Grain and Westgate.

Meanwhile, Brandenburg's squadron, now flying at 1,500ft, crossed the River Crouch at 1815. He had been fortunate because they had actually been spotted by a patrol of the RNAS, No. 4 Squadron, just off the Belgian coastline, but the three Sopwith Pups, under the command of Flight Commander J. D. Newberry, had no means of alerting anyone to their discovery. They had given chase, but as the Gothas had reached the Thames Estuary Newberry had peeled off as his aircraft were getting low on fuel and they landed at Manston. One of his men had tried to engage the Gothas, but his machine-guns had jammed.

The response of the RNAS was quite impressive: they managed to launch twenty-two aircraft in the fifteen minutes after 1805. Once again, however, the Royal Flying Corps had been caught flatfooted. Even as the pilots of No. 37 Squadron at Rochford were attempting to climb to a reasonable altitude, the Gothas passed tantalizingly above their heads. The 13th Mobile Anti-Aircraft Battery, based at Highland Farm, Burnham, however, delivered ineffective fire.

The raiders had crossed the British coastline close to Foulness Point, but then turned south and began bombing at around 1825. Their initial target was Great Wakering and then the gasworks at North Shoebury. The formation now headed towards the British Army's gunnery school at Shoeburyness. They dropped no fewer than twenty-one 50kg and three 12.5kg bombs there. They only managed to kill two soldiers, and then came under heavy and accurate anti-aircraft fire. There was a pair of operational 3in anti-aircraft guns in the school itself and a third stationed on the gun range. Brandenburg ordered his formation to break to provide a less compact target. He had already been informed that there was the likelihood of thunderstorms over London and now indicated with flares that the formation should move towards its secondary target, Sheerness.

No sooner had he made the signal than two of his aircraft signalled back that they were experiencing difficulties with their engines (an alternative explanation is that they had already dropped all their bombs on Shoeburyness). These two turned and headed east, whilst Brandenburg and the rest of the squadron headed across the Thames Estuary towards the Isle of Sheppey.

One of the first RNAS aircraft to get aloft was Flight Sub-Lieutenant J. E. Scott's Sopwith Pup. Flight Sub-Lieutenant R. H. Daly and Flight Sub-Lieutenant A. C. Burt accompanied him in Bristol Scouts. Flight Sub-Lieutenant De Wilde also took off, but was forced to return to base with a broken gun sight. Scott encountered the Gothas at around 15,000ft over Southend. The Bristols were struggling to gain altitude and had probably already reached their operational ceiling. Scott, in his Sopwith Pup, climbed to 17,000ft, hoping to have a height advantage in his attack on the Gothas. By this time he was over North Foreland, however, and he was unable to catch up with them. Daly meanwhile had managed to climb to 16,000ft and he attacked one of the trailing Gothas, only to come under fire from another four close by.

Squadron Commander C. H. Butler, also of the RNAS, out of Manston, caught up with the Gothas to the east of the Kentish Knock. He continued to chase them as best he could, but then lost sight of them. Another Bristol Scout, out of Eastchurch, flown by Flight Commander J.C.P. Wood, attacked one of them at around 11,000ft, somewhere over the Thames Estuary. It is not clear whether he scored any hits.

Shortly before 1830 the remaining Gothas approached Sheerness. The air-raid sirens were already sounding, but there were hundreds of people on the seafront, holidaymakers oblivious to the danger. About 2 miles out, the aircraft came under anti-aircraft fire from the position at Barton's Point. Over the next few minutes it fired off ninety-three rounds, causing one of the Gothas to drop to 9,000ft and engage the battery by dropping four bombs. The aircraft, GIV/660/16, received a close hit, which caused the right-hand engine to seize, and crashed into the sea around 2 miles out from Barton's Point. The pilot, Erich Kluk was drowned, the observer, Lieutenant Hans Francke, was picked up but died later, and the gunner, Georg Schumacher, suffered a broken leg. In all probability shrapnel, having shredded the propeller, caused the damage to the engine. Shortly after 1830 the rest of the squadron began circling over Sheerness. They dropped thirty-two 50kg bombs and thirteen 12.5kg bombs in an area bounded by Barton's Point, Garrison Point and Queenborough.

Up until the point when the Gotha had been shot down, upwards of 320 rounds of anti-aircraft fire had been targeted at the German formation. Yet this did not stop the Germans from pressing home their attack. The coastal battery at Ravelin Bridge was attacked; five 50kg bombs, one of which caused a fire in the Grand Store, hit the dockyard. The Germans also managed to damage a dry dock and destroy a goods shed at the railway station. Some of the bombs strayed a little further afield and one hit Sheerness high street, wrecking the Crown, Anchor and Pier Hotel; an outfitter's shop was also destroyed by a direct hit, killing a Royal Navy officer and the shop manager. In total the British armed forces suffered ten killed and twenty-five wounded, while civilian casualties had amounted to three killed and nine injured.

The German raiders were under constant fire during their short attack on Sheerness but, having dropped all their bombs, they turned for home. Most headed straight down the Thames Estuary, but some made for Whitstable. These aircraft came under fire from the Eastchurch anti-aircraft gun, along with HMS *Blazer*, a gunboat stationed in the mouth of the River Swale. With the exception of the RNAS aircraft from Manston, none of the British defenders had got anywhere near the raiders. But now, with the Germans heading home, the naval squadrons at Dunkirk, having been alerted by Dover, would be waiting for them.

No. 4 (Naval) Squadron had managed to get seven aircraft aloft and three from No. 9 (Naval) Squadron joined them. As the Germans headed towards the Belgian coast, they rendezvoused with their own fighter escort just as the RNAS aircraft closed in. There was a running dogfight between Nieuport and Ostend at around 18,000ft. There is no consensus as to precisely what happened. The British claimed at least one Gotha and up to three fighters. Flight Commander A. Shook of No. 4 (Naval) Squadron, flying a Sopwith Camel, claimed two German fighters. Flight Sub-Lieutenant Enstone, flying a Sopwith Pup and also from No. 4 (Naval) Squadron, claimed the third. The Germans admitted to having lost one Gotha, although there was confusion as to who could claim the kill. In all likelihood it was one of the RNAS pilots flying at Dunkirk.

In all sixty-five (although some sources say sixty-two) RFC and RNAS aircraft had been scrambled. Only five of these, all from the RNAS, had positively engaged the Gothas. There were still many lessons to be learned.

The first major change to take place was that anti-aircraft batteries could now engage German raiders flying over Britain during daylight hours. The men manning the guns were reinforced and retrained.

On 9 June 1917 the RNAS bombers based at Dunkirk attacked St Denis Vestrem once again and on the same day the home defence squadrons carried out another practice alert, this time managing to get thirty-two aircraft to operational height in around twenty minutes.

Although Brandenburg had by now lost the element of surprise and the British were slowly reorientating their defensive network to deal with his incursions, he still eagerly awaited the opportunity to launch a raid on the capital itself. On 12 June Cloessner eagerly collected weather reports from various German stations and continued his own weather prediction at the airfield. It seemed likely that the next day would provide Brandenburg with the opportunity to launch his long-awaited assault on London. Weather reports predicted light sea winds running easterly up to 14,000ft and then westerly winds above that altitude. This would ideally match the squadron's approach and return. There was a possibility that some time after 1500 there could be thunderstorms.

This news probably prompted Brandenburg to consider a much earlier take-off than usual. He ordered the squadron to be ready to be airborne at around 0900, which would mean that they would be over London by noon and back to base before any chance of encountering a thunderstorm.

In order to offset his lack of surprise, Brandenburg ordered that two diversionary targets should be selected: Margate and Shoeburyness. To add to the confusion, he ordered one Gotha to carry out a photoreconnaissance sweep of the Thames Estuary and the Medway area. In anticipation of a hostile reception, he asked for naval fighters and seaplanes to be scrambled on his return towards Belgium and for the German navy to step up their search-and-rescue patrols off the Belgian coastline.

There are conflicting reports of how many Gothas set off from Melle-Gontrode and St Denis Vestrem at 0900 – either twenty-two or twenty. The figures are probably confused because two aircraft almost immediately turned back with engine trouble. To add to the confusion, it is also clear that a third Gotha also turned back with engine problems and a further three were not part of the squadron's formation as they had lagged behind for various reasons.

The squadron was about 10 miles north of the North Foreland, just north of the Tongue Lightship, at around 1030. Almost opposite the lightship, one of the Gothas peeled off and headed towards the Isle of Thanet to make the planned diversionary attack on Margate. Brandenburg hoped to draw away the RNAS aircraft based at Manston. The aircraft appeared over Margate station at a height of about 14,000ft, immediately drawing anti-aircraft fire from guns at St Peters and Hengrove. In a matter of minutes the two 12-pounders fired off at least twenty-four rounds, without even scratching the Gotha. It proceeded on target and dropped four 50kg bombs, which did little more than injure four people and break a number of windows.

Despite the lack of damage, Brandenburg's ruse was paying off. An alert was immediately sent out, stating that Margate was under attack. The Edinburgh Lighthouse had just sent a message saying that around nineteen Gothas were heading towards Foulness Island. Despite this, the British took the bait and aircraft from Manston and Westgate were sent to deal with the raid on Margate, diverting them from the main German threat.

Meanwhile, warnings had been sent out across London and Essex and the anti-aircraft units stationed in the area were now prepared for the formation, which crossed the mouth of the River Crouch at around 1050. At this point Brandenburg detached three more aircraft: two were sent to launch a second diversionary attack, this time on Shoeburyness, and the third peeled off to carry out its photoreconnaissance mission, taking in the south bank of the Thames Estuary and heading as far west as it dared. In all probability it had been lightly loaded and did not carry any bombs. One of the detached aircraft dropped a solitary 50kg bomb on Barling. Just short of Shoeburyness the two aircraft detailed to attack took the same route used just six days earlier. As they came within range, a 3in anti-aircraft gun began firing. It loosed off thirty-eight rounds to no effect. The Gothas managed to drop five 50kg bombs, which fell near the village of Shoeburyness but only managed to injure two civilians. They then peeled off and headed for home. There is a confusing description of one of these three aircraft (including the photoreconnaissance aircraft) as having attacked the Royal Victoria Docks with at least one bomb.

Meanwhile, Brandenburg and the rest of the squadron were heading for London. They were intent on hitting the docks and Liverpool Street Station. As they approached about 14,000ft the right-hand flank of the squadron passed over Brentwood and the left over Upminster. It was around 1123. As they continued on they came under fire from anti-aircraft guns at Abbey Wood, Rainham, Romford and Shooter's Hill. Visibility was poor, however, and there were layers of cloud protecting the raiders at around 5,000ft. Gun crews at Chadwell Heath and Ockendon reported hearing them overhead but not being able to see them.

The Germans were probably somewhere over Regent's Park when Brandenburg ordered the attacks to begin. At around 1130 a single 50kg bomb fell on Barking and then seven more on East Ham, which killed four and injured thirteen. Two more bombs were dropped on the Royal Albert Docks, destroying railway equipment and killing eight dockworkers. The aircraft now closed up once more and flew at around 16,500ft, with their primary target, Liverpool Street Station, dead ahead of them. The anti-aircraft guns at Blackwall engaged them and by 1140 the Gothas were also spotted by Captain C. W. E. Cole-Hamilton and Second Lieutenant J. Chapman, who had been scrambled from Northolt in their Bristol fighters shortly after 1118.

Brandenburg fired another flare and the Gothas dropped upwards of seventy-two bombs in and around Liverpool Street Station. Many fell off target, the worst-hit area was Hoxton, close to Shoreditch. Only three actually penetrated the station, destroying two trains and killing sixteen. Two 50kg bombs, killed twenty and wounded fourteen, and demolished a large four-storey building in Fenchurch Street. Another bomb hit Aldgate High Street, killing thirteen and injuring twenty-two and a 50kg bomb hit Beach Court, where eight foundry workers were killed and ten injured. The most fortunate civilians were the children at the Cowper Street Foundation School in City Road. One 50kg bomb smashed through the roof and penetrated five floors before causing a crater in the basement, but it proved to be a dud.

The Gothas split up to make individual attacks. Those in the northern group dropped bombs on Dalston, Stepney, Limehouse and Poplar before heading north-east to attack Bow and Stratford. The southern group crossed the Thames close to Blackfriars Bridge and came under fire from an anti-aircraft gun in the Tower of London.

The worst event of the day occurred in Poplar, which received five 50kg bombs. One of them had hit the Upper North Street School and exploded three floors down, in a room in which sixty-four children were sheltering. Eighteen were killed and thirty badly injured. This incident radically changed air defence policy.

The Gothas in the southern half-squadron dropped half a dozen bombs on Southwark and Bermondsey. One of those that fell on Southwark, a 50kg, hit the British and Bennington Tea Company, killing three and wounding twenty-four. A jam factory in Staple Street, in Bermondsey, was hit by a 12.5kg bomb, which killed three workers on the roof.

The two groups were now under fire from artillery positions at Abbey Wood, Beckton, Chadwell Heath, Grove Park, Ockendon, Rainham, Romford, Shooter's Hill and Tilbury. The formation was still not together and various British pilots met scattered groups until the squadron reached the British coastline.

Brandenburg and his men flew towards Southend and at around 1200 anti-aircraft guns based at Bowers Gifford and Hawkesbury Bush engaged them. Members of No. 37 Squadron, including Captain C. B. Cooke, Lieutenant G. D. F. Keddie and Lieutenant G. E. R. Young, now engaged them. These men of C Flight, No. 37 Squadron, had been scrambled shortly after 1100 hours in their Sopwith $1^1/_2$ Strutters. Captain W. Sowrey of A Flight, No. 37 Squadron, who had scrambled at 1104 from Goldhanger, joined them in his RE7, together with Captain T. Grant of A Flight, No. 39 Squadron, who had scrambled at 1032 in his BE12 (Grant was actually Tryggve Garn, a Norwegian).

Several attacks were made on the formation around Maidstone, but eventually the Gothas outpaced the British aircraft. There was still anti-aircraft fire coming in from Shoeburyness and Captain Grant's aircraft was hit, forcing him to land at Rochford. Meanwhile, Flight Lieutenant F. M. Fox, piloting a Sopwith Pup from the RNAS base at Grain engaged a Gotha over Southend at around 14,000ft. He was certain that he hit the fuselage, but then his gun jammed and he had to pull out of the attack.

The photoreconnaissance Gotha was flying at around 13,000ft and had almost reached Maidstone when Grant and two other pilots, Captain I. T. Lloyd of No. 98 Depot Squadron, flying out of Rochford, who had scrambled at 1110, and another whose identity is unclear, attacked it.

At some point Captain C.W.E. Cole-Hamilton and Second Lieutenant J. Chapman, both flying Bristol Fighters of No. 35 (Training) Squadron, caught up with Captain S. R. Stammers, flying a BE12 from North Weald's A Flight and engaged three straggling Gothas somewhere over Ilford. Cole-Hamilton's observer, Captain C. H. Keevil, was shot and killed and the aircraft's front gun jammed. They all reported that one of the Gothas had been hit and was clearly in trouble, but all three had to peel away because of engine difficulties. Cole-Hamilton had got to within 600ft of the tail of the trailing Gotha of the three and had fired nearly 100 rounds, but just as he had turned away to allow Keevil to fire his Lewis gun, they had come under fire. Keevil got off over 150 rounds before he was hit in the neck and killed.

Other attacks were made against the raiders, including one by Captain James McCudden. He had reached a height of about 15,000ft in his Sopwith Pup and was somewhere near the Girdler Lightship. He fired off three drums of ammunition from a position around 500ft below the Gotha at the rear of the formation.

Despite these scrapes with the RNAS and the RFC, Brandenburg's aircraft continued home. Not a single bomber had been claimed by the fighters or the improved anti-aircraft defences. They had been over British soil for ninety-minutes, during which they had dropped the majority of their 4 ton payload on London. They had killed 162 people and injured 432. It was a far more impressive performance than even the devastating attack on Folkestone, but now they faced having to cope with the aircraft of No. 4 (Naval) Wing at Dunkirk.

Flight Commander Shook and six other aircraft (one Sopwith Pup and six Sopwith Camels) hastened to intercept them when they spotted them in the distance. No. 9 (Naval) Wing also had a patrol up, consisting of Sopwith Pups and Triplanes. The aircraft of No. 9 Squadron flew as far as the Thames Estuary, but failed to encounter the Gothas. The weather conditions were deteriorating and visibility was poor, but just half an hour before a heavy hailstorm broke at 1430, the Gothas had landed safely at their bases.

The day after the raid, on 13 June 1917, on the instructions of the Kaiser, Brandenburg left Melle-Gontrode in an Albatros two-seater aircraft, piloted by Lieutenant von Trotha. They made for Kreuznach, where the Kaiser decorated Brandenburg with the Blue Max. With von Trotha piloting the aircraft, the Albatros headed back on their return journey on 19 June but very early on in the flight the aircraft's engine failed and it stalled, spinning towards the ground. Von Trotha died in the crash, but Brandenburg survived, although his legs were severely damaged. Clearly he was in no condition to resume command.

On the recommendation of the Chief of Staff, Hermann Thomsen, Captain Rudolf Kleine, already a distinguished pilot at the age of thirty, was selected to replace him. Kleine was recovering from wounds, so probably did not officially assume command until 25 June 1917. This meant that the England Squadron was idle during the remainder of June.

Meanwhile the RNAS No. 5 (Naval) Squadron, in conjunction with the ground offensive of the third battle of Ypres, launched another raid against St Denis Vestrem on 15 June. The following night two German navy Zeppelins, the L42 and the L48, were launched against London. Originally six airships had been earmarked to attack, but two did not leave their sheds because of strong winds and a further two turned back with engine problems.

They sighted the Suffolk coast at 2130, and the L42 aimed for Dungeness. At around 0200 it attacked Ramsgate. Meanwhile the L48 was seen off Harwich at 2334 and crossed the Suffolk coast at Orford Ness at a height of around 18,000ft at about 0145 on 17 June. It attacked Harwich at 0250, but its bombs fell at least 5 miles to the north. Shortly after the attack it encountered engine problems.

Lieutenant E. W. Clarke in a BE2C and Lieutenant F. D. Holder in a FE2B lifted off from the experimental station at Orford Ness at 0150. Clarke engaged the L48 near Harwich to no effect and Holder attacked after the airship had dropped its bombs, but after firing a few shots his front gun jammed. By 0310 the L48 was near Aldeburgh, where Holder attacked again, firing four more drums of ammunition. He attacked again near Leiston and as the L48 tried to evade him he saw it fall towards the ground in flames. It had been hit by Captain R. H. M. S. Saundby, also from the experimental station at Orford Ness, who had taken off at 0255 in a DH2. He had approached it at 0310 and fired three drums at it. Partway through the third drum the L48 caught fire and it began to burn. It had also been attacked by Lieutenant L. P. Watkins of A flight, No. 37 Squadron, Goldhanger, who had left the airfield at 0206 in a BE12 and had approached the L48 when it was near the coast at a height of about 14,000ft. Although he was 2,000ft below it he fired 2 drums of ammunition and then climbed to within 500ft and began firing at it with short bursts and reported seeing a fire start at the tail. It came down at Hollytree Farm, Theberton at around 0330. Three of the crew survived, although one died of his injuries several months later.

The L42 had aimed to bomb Dover and Deal, but it was actually seen by five aircraft out of Great Yarmouth. Flight Sub-Lieutenant G. H. Bittles in a Sopwith Baby left Great Yarmouth at 0325 and encountered it about 30 miles to the east of Lowestoft, flying at around 11,000ft. He approached to within 100ft and unleashed a drum of ammunition at it. Flight Sub-Lieutenant H. B. Brenton, who had left at the same time as Bittles, continued the attack. He chased the airship for over an hour without ever being able to get within range. Later, Lieutenant E. Cadbury and Flight Lieutenant G. W. R. Fane were in the vicinity in time to see the L48 go down and then located the L42 at a height of 16,000ft. Both of them failed, for various reasons, to get anywhere near it.

Flight Commander V. Nicholl, who spotted it 45 miles to the east of Great Yarmouth, trailed it for an hour and a half, but could not reach its altitude.

CHAPTER SIX

The Raids Continue:
July–August 1917

Whilst the British had effectively dealt with the attacks by L42 and L48, the next raid by the England Squadron would prove to be an altogether more difficult task. The RFC home defence squadrons were, as promised, gradually being reinforced and re-equipped with better aircraft. No. 37 had already received some Sopwith Pups and 1½ Strutters and No. 39 SE5s and Armstrong Whitworth FK8s. No. 50 Squadron was also receiving Sopwith Pups and Armstrong Whitworth FK8s. The RNAS was also being reinforced; instead of five Sopwith Camels being transferred to Dunkirk they were instead sent to Eastchurch.

There was a significant meeting in London on 17 June, when Field Marshal Haig and Major General Trenchard presented a series of plans to the War Cabinet, several of which related specifically to the air defence of Great Britain. They particularly emphasized the importance of the capture of the Belgian coast as a primary objective. This would force any German aircraft to cross Allied-held ground before being able to get to the North Sea and launch an attack on Britain. They also emphasized the importance of launching as many bombing raids as possible on the Gotha airfields and increasing the number of combat air patrols over the Western Front to give as much notice as possible of the Gothas leaving their bases. They also suggested improving the communications between combat air patrols and reconnaissance aircraft on either side of the Channel and the North Sea. Finally they warned against launching reprisal raids against German towns and cities. They felt that at this stage the Allies' ability to launch successful bombing raids against German civilian or military targets beyond the Western Front zone was limited and would only encourage the Germans to launch an even greater offensive against the British Isles.

These suggestions should not have come as any great surprise. The primary concern of the military planners was the ground offensive in Europe and they would not countenance any weakening of that effort, even to protect the British homeland. Indeed, had they had their own way they would have suggested denuding the British home defence squadrons even more and reinforcing combat air patrols over the Western Front. Haig desperately needed as many aircraft and personnel to be transferred into the Flanders region as possible. He was due to launch a major air offensive on 5 July.

A further meeting on 20 June saw Prime Minister Lloyd George suggest a raid against Mannheim, but Haig was adamant that the RFC could not carry out such a raid successfully, nor could he afford to divert their efforts from the main purpose of a land offensive on the Western Front.

A compromise of sorts was reached in relation to the improvement and co-ordination of combat air patrols either side of the Channel. Henceforth No. 56 and No. 66 Squadrons, based at Liettres and attached to the Western Front, would take on responsibility for patrolling the Channel. No. 56 Squadron would be sent to Bekesbourne and No. 66 to Calais. It was also suggested that the number of anti-aircraft guns around the Thames Estuary and indeed to the east of London was insufficient. Lieutenant Colonel Simon, who was in command of the anti-aircraft batteries, claimed that he needed an additional forty-five guns, but his pleas for reinforcements fell on deaf ears.

The problem of air-raid warnings was also discussed and it was felt that in the long run warnings to civilians would be counterproductive. It was felt that they would simply flood into the streets in order to see the German aircraft and that any air-raid warning would add to their danger and not to their protection. Moreover, air-raid warnings would unnecessarily disrupt war production and since this was the primary aim of the German raiders, the Government would not compromise it.

Meanwhile, in Belgium, Captain Kleine had taken command of the England Squadron. Weather reports suggested that 4 July would provide suitable weather for another raid. The Germans were aware that No. 56 Squadron had been reassigned to Bekesbourne and to Rochford, which probably prompted Kleine to consider an attack on the Suffolk coast, rather than the primary target of London.

He planned to launch his Gothas early in the morning of 4 July. By sheer coincidence the RNAS's, No. 7 (Naval) Squadron, attacked Nieumunster and Ghistelles on the night of 3/4 July, but not Melle-Gontrode or St Denis Vestrem. Kleine's squadron set off at 0530, but within minutes seven of the Gothas had to return to base with engine problems. Kleine led the remaining eighteen to the north in order to avoid being spotted by the British lightships in the Thames Estuary or encountering patrols from the RNAS squadrons at Dunkirk.

The Gothas were heard off Orford Ness at 0655 and at 0700 they crossed the coast at Bawdsey. They attacked Harwich at 0720, coming under fire from anti-aircraft guns at Felixstowe. The gunners fired 135 rounds and managed to destroy a German H12 flying boat and damage a second.

On the mistaken assumption that the raiders' primary target was London, none of the home defence squadrons was ordered aloft until 0726. The only RFC aircraft in the air was on a routine engine-testing flight, out of the testing squadron at Martlesham Heath. Captain Palethorpe and Air Mechanic James Jessop were flying a DH4 when they spotted the Gothas moving south-west across the coastline at about 14,000ft at around 0705. Palethorpe made straight for the formation and attempted to fire as he came in, but his gun jammed and several of the Gothas opened fire on him. Jessop managed to fire one drum from his machine-gun at about 100 yards, but he was hit and killed instantly by a stream of enemy fire. Palethorpe swung away and landed back at Martlesham Heath, but he was aloft once more by 0740 in a second DH4, this time accompanied by Lieutenant Hoffert. He was later awarded the MC for his brave attempts.

By now the Gothas were at about 14,000ft and they banked towards the south-west to cross the River Deben. One flight headed across the Rivers Orwell and Stour to attack Harwich, whilst the other headed east to attack Felixstowe. By now it was around 0710 and the seven Harwich anti-aircraft guns sighted on the Felixstowe side of the Orwell estuary opened fire. They managed to get off around 135 rounds, but this did not prevent the Gothas from dropping sixty-five bombs, primarily 12.5kg, but the majority of them fell into the sea. Just two hit the RNAS air station at Felixstowe, destroying one flying boat and damaging a second. Nine men were killed and nineteen wounded. Three more naval ratings were killed at Shotley balloon station and five soldiers were killed and ten wounded when bombs hit the Suffolk Regiment's camp.

By 0715 the raid was over and the Gothas were heading back out to sea, and would reach the Belgian coast in around ninety minutes, but it was not until 0820 that No. 66 Squadron at Calais had Sopwith Pups aloft, hunting for them. Around half of them were sent to search the area between Dunkirk and the North Hinder Lightship, while the rest looked further west. By the time they reached their patrol positions, however, the Gothas were very close to Belgium and home and safe.

Aircraft of No. 4 (Naval) Wing of the RNAS, a patrol consisting of eight Sopwith Camels and two Sopwith Pups led by Flight

Commander Shook, left Bray Dunes at 0800. They encountered the Gothas just 30 miles from Ostend. Flight Sub-Lieutenant Ellis attacked one of them, riddling it with 300 rounds and claimed to see smoke issuing from it. Ten aircraft from No. 6 (Naval) Squadron, also at Bray Dunes, were also scrambled, but they found no sign of the enemy.

No. 56 and No. 66 Squadrons were now due to return to their home bases on the Western Front; as it happened, the next German attack would coincide with their redeployment. Thundery weather threatened to prevent them from launching another attack, but a break allowed Kleine to order a new attack on 7 July. He decided that although London would be the primary target, he would carry out a diversionary attack on Margate with one of his Gothas. He also assigned two or three to carry out further photoreconnaissance over London. Kleine also decided to reduce the 300kg bomb load in order to be able to maintain an altitude of 16,000ft and an average speed of 80mph. Once again, on the night before the impending raid, RNAS bombers attacked the Gothas' airfields, but once again they failed to do any lasting damage. Twenty-four Gothas lifted off from their air bases at 0800, and gradually climbed to 10,000ft and adopted a V-formation, heading for the River Crouch as their entry point into British air space. As was becoming something of a feature of these raids, two of the Gothas were forced to return to base with engine problems. The weather was sufficiently clear for the Kentish Knock Lightship to spot and count the Gothas at around 0914 hour. The Admiralty was immediately informed and the RNAS at Chatham was aware of the raid by 0916.

The warning had also gone out to the London Warning Centre, and aircraft from the home defence squadrons were given the patrol order at 0924. Twenty-one minutes later the Gothas approached the mouth of the River Crouch. As had already been arranged, one of them peeled off and made for Margate. It crossed the Isle of Thanet and was spotted by anti-aircraft crews at St Peters and Hengrove at 0930, flying at a height of around 12,000ft. It managed to drop three 50kg bombs, killing three and wounding three. It now ran into even greater problems. The RNAS station at Manston scrambled two Sopwith Camels, one Sopwith Pup and three Triplanes shortly before 0930, and they were already climbing to engage. The airfield's pair of anti-aircraft guns opened up on the Gotha and shortly afterwards another gun at Cliffsend opened fire. The German was now in danger from six aircraft and five anti-aircraft guns, the latter having fired 115 rounds in five minutes. The Manston aircraft did not follow the solitary Gotha but instead raced to engage the main formation. It failed, however, and within an hour was back at Manston.

By 0930, forty-six aircraft from the RFC's defence squadrons were aloft, together with thirty-four from various training squadrons and depots. There was a mixed bag of Sopwith Pups, Camels and $1\frac{1}{2}$ Strutters, several Armstrong Whitworth FK8s, a pair of SE5s, some BE2s and BE12s and a scattering of DH4s, DH5s and Bristol Fighters.

Captain E. B. Mason of B Flight, No. 37 Squadron, in a Sopwith Pup, caught up with the raiders over Billericay. His engine was misfiring but he continued to shoot into the formation, concentrating on one of the rear trailing aircraft. He closed to within 100 yards, having fired eight bursts at the aircraft but was then forced to break off because of continuing problems with the engines. When he landed he found the cause: four German bullets lodged in various parts of his aircraft. Captain E. S. Cotterill, also piloting a Sopwith Pup, closely followed his attack. He fired ten bursts at two of the Gothas before his Vickers machine-gun jammed. He then resorted to his Lewis gun, but began receiving return fire. This gun also jammed so he was forced to land at Hainault. With the machine-guns fixed, however, he was back aloft just eight minutes later, but could not intercept the Gothas for a second time.

Second Lieutenant G. A. Thompson, also of B Flight, was suffering from engine problems, but managed to reach an altitude of 8,000ft. Bursts from his Lewis gun cut through the wings of one of the Gothas. He then wheeled around and attacked the nose of a second, only to discover that his Vickers machine-gun had jammed after just one shot. The Germans got away and Thompson landed to discover several bullet holes around his aircraft seat.

Captain W. Sowrey of A Flight, out of Goldhanger, intercepted the raiders over Romford in his BE12A. He emptied two drums from his Lewis gun into the one at the rear of the formation, but was unable to match the Gotha's climb to bombing height.

Meanwhile, Lieutenant Ernest M. Gilbert, flying a BE12A of No. 39 Squadron's A Flight from North Weald, was on patrol between Joyce Green and Hainault. He intercepted the formation over Ongar. He began firing but his Vickers machine-gun jammed. He desperately tried to clear the stoppage and managed to catch up with them again over the City of London, firing all his remaining Lewis gun drums.

Lieutenant E. S. Moulton-Barrett, in an SE5, spotted and overtook the formation somewhere over north London at around 1015. He fired at three of the aircraft, then concentrated on one Gotha, which had strayed from the squadron and seemed more vulnerable. He emptied all his Lewis gun drums into its fuselage and then tried to force it towards the Shoeburyness anti-aircraft guns. It was probably one of those given the photoreconnaissance mission.

Meanwhile, Captain W. H. Hayne of C Flight, No. 39 Squadron, accompanied by Lieutenant G. T. Stoneham in an Armstrong Whitworth FK8, had scrambled at 0935. They tracked the Gothas from Epping and desperately tried to close with them, but they only managed to get off thirty-seven rounds.

Shortly before 1000 the Gothas rose to their ideal operating altitude of 16,000ft after receiving the attention of anti-aircraft fire. They headed for Epping Forest and then approached the City of London from the north-east. Shortly after 1015 new anti-aircraft units came into range from Chingford, Enfield, Epping, Higham Hill, Lambourne End, Newmans, Parndon, Temple, Theydon Bois, Warlies Park and Woodford. At around this time, they were also being attacked by five RFC aircraft and two Sopwith Camels out of the RNAS at Eastchurch (flown by Flight Commander C. Draper and Flight Lieutenant S. R. Watkins).

The first bombs fell on Chingford, but mercifully they landed in a field. The gasworks at Tottenham was the next target, although the four 50kg bombs dropped there also missed. Five more bombs were dropped on Stoke Newington and Dalston, killing several people. The raiders now turned their attention to Islington, Clerkenwell and Hoxton. A zinc mill, several houses and a timber yard were damaged here. The anti-aircraft fire had now been reinforced by further guns, which were based at Finchley, Highbury, Kenton, Palmers Green, Parliament Hill, the Ridgeway and Wanstead.

At around 1030 Second-Lieutenant N. E. Chandler, of B Flight, No. 50 Squadron, out of Throwley, caught up with the raiders. Not only did he have to brave their defensive fire, but he was also in peril from his own anti-aircraft fire. His aircraft, a Sopwith Pup, suffered from a gun jam and engine problems, added to which he could barely see because his goggles were covered in oil.

Kleine and his men dropped around thirty bombs on the City of London, hitting various targets in Aldgate and the Barbican. They killed thirteen and injured twenty-six civilians. One 50kg bomb hit the Post Office's central telegraph office on St Martins-Le-Grand and the building was virtually gutted. Several warehouses and buildings were hit close to St Bartholomew's Hospital at Smithfield and more casualties were caused when bombs hit Lower Thames Street and Billingsgate Fish Market. Buildings were also hit on Fenchurch Street, a bank was damaged close to the Bank of England and a dud bomb fell near Moorgate railway station.

New anti-aircraft units were now in range at Acton, Hanwell, Hyde Park and Tower Bridge. Captain Palethorpe from the testing squadron at Martlesham Heath also attacked again in his DH4. Both his Vickers machine-guns jammed and his aircraft was hit several times, wounding him in the hip and forcing him to land at Rochford. Second Lieutenant R. Martin, in a Sopwith Pup from No. 40 (Training) Squadron, Croydon, pumped fifty rounds into one of the Gothas and saw the enemy aircraft spin out of control, but he could not finish it off as he came under fire from others.

The Gothas swung over the Isle of Dogs, heading for the River Crouch and Foulness. They were now coming under fire from Beckenham, Blackwall, Dulwich, Grove Park, Norbiton and Richmond. Somewhere over Southend, they were also intercepted by Captain James T. B. McCudden, who was flying in a Sopwith Pup belonging to No. 63 (Training) Squadron. He was at around 16,000ft when he saw the formation flying east. He attacked the rear-most aircraft, firing a whole drum at it at close range. 'I put on a new drum', he reported, 'and dived from the Hun's right rear to within 300ft, when I suddenly swerved, and changing over to his left rear, closed to fifty yards and finished my drum before the enemy gunner could swing his gun from the side at which I first dived'.

He only had three drums with him and after he had used his last one, all he could do was to harass the formation by buzzing it. He figured that if he could attract fire from the Gothas it would give other incoming British aircraft a free route to attack. Finally, after buzzing them for around twenty-five minutes, his aircraft was hit; one bullet went straight through his windscreen.

As the Gothas crossed Essex they came under fire from anti-aircraft guns at Chadwell Heath, Ockendon, Rainham and Romford. It is probably in this area that Second Lieutenant W. G. Salmon of No. 63 Training Squadron attacked them. He was hit in the eye by an enemy bullet and attempted to return home to Joyce Green airfield. Unfortunately he lost control of his aircraft 100ft from the ground and was killed in the crash.

The raiders were now in range of Bowers Gifford, Hawkesbury Bush, Asheldham, Burnham-on-Crouch, Great Stambridge and Heybridge anti-aircraft guns. They also ran into four Sopwith $1^1/_2$ Strutters from C Flight, No. 37 Squadron, Rochford, piloted by Captain C. B. Cooke, Captain C. E. Holman, Second Lieutenant H. A. Edwardes and Second Lieutenant J. E. R. Young. Cooke and Young had been involved in an attack on the Gothas on 13 June and made attacks from above. Major B. F. Moore, piloting a Vickers FB12C from No. 198 Depot Squadron, Rochford, joined them. Also, joining them was a Sopwith Camel flown by Captain H. T. Tizard from the testing squadron at Martlesham Heath. The Gothas were now in a tighter formation and Young's aircraft was badly hit. He came down in the sea, was trapped in the wreckage and despite the prompt arrival of a naval vessel, he drowned. His gunner, Air Mechanic C. Taylor was wounded but was plucked out of the sea. Cooke's aircraft was also damaged and he was forced to land at Rochford.

At around 1100 hours Lieutenant F. D. Holden, flying a Bristol Fighter, BF2A, from the experimental station at Orford Ness, encountered the bombers. Captain C. A. Ridley, flying a Sopwith Pup of B Flight, No. 37 Squadron out of Stow Maries, joined him. He attacked from below and almost immediately his target hit his aircraft several times.

Around this time Second Lieutenant F. A. D. Grace, accompanied by Second Lieutenant G. Murray in an Armstrong Whitworth FK8 of B Flight, No. 50 Squadron, Throwley, spotted a damaged Gotha near the North Foreland. It was flying at low altitude. Grace pounced on the stricken aircraft. It ditched into the sea and he could see two of the crew on the wings. He fired off flares, but the aircraft sank and the crew drowned.

Meanwhile, the Sopwith Pups out of Manston, which had been scrambled at around 0927 hours, had landed, refuelled and were airborne once more at around 1100. There were six of them, accompanied by three Bristol Scouts. Squadron Commander, C. H. Butler, in a Sopwith Triplane, riddled one Gotha at close range and then attacked a second. He claimed that he saw the first aircraft plummet towards the sea and sink about 20 miles to the west of Ostend. Butler had been leading his aircraft north of the Tongue Lightship and had spotted them close to the Kentish Knock. He had given chase for nearly half an hour before attacking. Flight Sub-Lieutenant R. H. Daly, also piloting a Sopwith Triplane, launched a second attack against the bomber stream. He attacked a German aircraft, probably not a Gotha, about 15 miles off the Belgian coast at an altitude of 17,000ft. He shot it down in flames then attacked a second nearer to the coast, but his guns jammed.

Flight Lieutenant J. E. Scott, also from Manston, in a Sopwith Pup, fired off 475 rounds into a solitary Gotha about 35 miles off the coast of North Foreland, at an altitude of 8,000ft. It hit the sea and Scott could see at least one of the crew swimming away from the wreckage.

Another Manston pilot, Flight Sub-Lieutenant A. H. Loft, chased three Gothas for some time. He caught them up just short of the Belgian coast in his Sopwith Camel and fired nearly 200 rounds straight into the fuselage of one. It dipped as if it was going to crash land, but when he tried to fire once more his guns jammed. He peeled off to deal with the stoppage and lost sight of the aircraft. He headed back towards Manston, but 40 miles out his engine failed; fortunately he survived a crash landing at Manningtree.

The remaining Gothas arrived back at their airfield at 1300, but four of them were badly damaged in landing crashes. The British had lost two aircraft during the raid and the Germans had effectively lost five of the twenty-two that had managed to make it to the British Isles.

A year later Lieutenant S. R. Schulte, a Gotha captain, was captured. He said that he had had to make a forced landing on the Ostend beach and that his aircraft had no fewer than eighty-eight bullet holes. Whether the other German aircraft that crash-landed on their return to Belgium had been as badly damaged by aerial combat is unknown, but this may have been a significant factor in their inability to make a safe landing.

The British counter to this raid had been far more effective. Thirty-six RFC and RNAS aircraft had engaged the Gothas of the ninety-one that had been scrambled. It was the most effective scramble to contact ratio that the British would achieve during the war against the raiders.

Despite the fact that over a third of the aircraft had actually engaged the Gothas, however, there were still serious deficiencies. Many had suffered from engine problems and the jamming of their guns whilst literally on the verge of making an attack had hindered them even more. Solo attacks had been beaten off fairly easily, but multiple attacks had been far more successful. The new rules of engagement for anti-aircraft batteries had also proved effective: they had broken up the formation and forced the Gothas to seek safety at a higher altitude. The batteries based in London alone had fired off around 2,000 shells, whilst those outside London had fired another 1,000.

If the Germans had hoped that bombing and terrorizing the British civilians would bring calls for peace then they had been seriously mistaken. The civilians did want improved protection, but the most dominant cries were for immediate and devastating retaliation against German cities.

There was a War Cabinet meeting on the afternoon of 7 July and it was decided that strenuous steps needed to be taken to improve the efficiency of the defensive fighter cover over Britain. The second key decision was to approve counter-strikes against German towns and cities. It was further agreed that at least one squadron, earmarked for eventual movement to the Western Front, be retained in Britain and, significantly, that two fighter squadrons be brought back from the Western Front and posted in Britain. Lloyd George's earlier suggestion to launch a raid on Mannheim was also approved, provided Field Marshal Haig could scrape together enough aircraft and that the allocation of these aircraft would not hinder his strategic operations on the Western Front.

Haig still believed that the most effective counter to the Gotha raids would be to seize their air bases around Ghent and that all efforts should be concentrated on an offensive in the Flanders area. He still firmly believed that his fighter squadrons on the Western Front would be providing a far more effective defence for Britain if they remained where they were and dealt with German aircraft threatening the front.

The redistribution of squadrons began in the next few days. No. 39 Squadron's aircraft at Suttons Farm were moved to Hainault Farm. Here they would be merged with No. 39 Squadron's C Flight in order to create a new fighter squadron, No. 44, which it was hoped would eventually be equipped with Sopwith Camels. No. 66 Squadron was moved from the Western Front to Suttons Farm. This redistribution, however, only served to reinforce the fact that Britain did not yet possess enough aircraft to cope with the dual demands of offensive operations on the Western Front and defensive operations over Britain. Production figures were improving, but there was still a distinct lack of aircraft engines. The Government was desperately trying to balance three key demands of war: first for aircraft to be available to support infantry attacks on the Western Front, to defend against German counter-offensives and to provide air cover for reconnaissance, as well as regular combat patrols, second, to carry out tactical and strategic air raids against German military and industrial targets; and finally to defend the British Isles against raiders.

For the time being it was decided that military operations needed to be given priority. This decision was made in the certain knowledge of what the Germans were trying to achieve by sending Gothas to attack British towns and cities. To some extent that purpose had been acheived by making the Government move fighter squadrons from France back to Britain. Although the decision had been made to give military operations the priority, it was the earnest wish of the British government that the Germans should not be aware of this.

On 10 July, No. 66 Squadron was re-posted back to France and their place at Suttons Farm was taken by No. 46 Squadron's Sopwith Pups, commanded by Major P. Babington. Having operated on the Western Front for some time, they were, comparatively speaking, far more efficient and able to respond. Indeed, within five minutes of an alert they could have eighteen aircraft in the air. However, it was soon to become abundantly clear that the Germans knew of the move and that Kleine and his squadron had been informed. Meanwhile, at Hainault Farm, No. 44 Squadron was beginning to be formed.

The War Cabinet also decided on 10 July to provide the civilian population of London with a five-minute warning of an air raid. They lacked the means to warn such a large number of people over a huge distance, however, so as a temporary measure policemen were to walk around the streets with a placard stating 'Police Notice – Take Cover'.

Haig was in the last stages of preparing for what would become the third battle of Ypres. The offensive was to get underway towards the end of July. As a part of the preparations, four fighter squadrons were moved from the Western Front to Dunkirk. No. 6 (Naval) Squadron was equipped with Sopwith Camels, No. 48 with Bristol Fighters, No. 9 (Naval) with Sopwith Camels and Triplanes and No. 54 with Sopwith Pups.

On 11 July the War Cabinet approved the creation of the Committee on Air Organization and Home Defence Against Air Raids, which was initially charged with making recommendations to improve the air defence of London and, more generally, examine the organization of aircraft and operations. Leading the committee was Lieutenant General Jan Smuts, who co-opted a number of key figures to assist him, including Lieutenant General Henderson, Lieutenant Colonel Higgins, Major General Shaw, Lieutenant Colonel Simon and Commodore Paine.

While Smuts brought together as much information and as many views as possible, the RNAS's Nos. 5 and 7 (Naval) Squadrons, hit the Gotha airfields on the night of 11/12 July. The following day it was decided that twenty-four Sopwith Camels and four DH4s would be made available to the home defence squadrons. The Camels would be sent directly to Hainault Farm.

Haig was incensed, as he had been counting on these aircraft to support his forthcoming offensive. On this occasion, however, Lloyd George and the War Cabinet ignored him. On 15 July, twelve Sopwith Pups were delivered to Nos. 37 and 50 Squadrons. However, as Haig was eager to point out, this meant that Nos. 43 and 45 Squadrons on the Western Front were still using obsolete $1^1/_2$ Strutters.

Smuts, meanwhile, had completed his document and presented it to the Prime Minister on 19 July. He made four key recommendations: first, that any effective air defence system, or indeed offensive system, would have to be under a single command; second that a more effective anti-aircraft screen be established around London; third, that the creation of the three day-fighter squadrons, Nos. 44, 61 and 112, be accelerated; and fourth, that a reserve force be created, which could deal with diversionary attacks such as those made on Margate, so that the front-line defence aircraft could deal with the main threat.

Meanwhile work was also underway to improve the air-raid warning systems. Henceforth London's County Hall would be informed of an impending air attack, and it would be their responsibility to contact eighty fire stations within a 10 mile radius of

Charing Cross. Each would then fire off three rockets at fifteen-second intervals.

Across the Channel in Belgium, Kleine's squadron had been restricted by adverse weather conditions after their last attack, to bombing attacks against targets in Belgium and France. On the morning of 21 July weather reports suggested more favourable conditions the following day, but Kleine decided not to risk his aircraft on another assault against London. This was partly due to uncertainty over the weather, but more to the fact that No. 46 Squadron now lay in their path to the capital. He therefore decided on a coastal raid against Felixstowe and Harwich, and once again opted for an early start in order to take full advantage of the better weather.

Either twenty-three or twenty-two Gothas lifted off from their two airfields at 0630 on 22 July. It is unclear whether one or two Gothas turned back, but certainly it was reported that twenty-one were actually involved in the raid. At a height of 14,000ft they approached the Hollesley Bay area at around 0800 in their familiar V-formation. The conditions were hazy and the sun was behind them. The Sunk Lightship, about 9 miles off the Naze, immediately informed Felixstowe and the warning went out across the district.

Eighteen Sopwith Pups of No. 46 Squadron began lifting off at 0813 and took up their patrol area at 16,000ft in a line from Joyce Green to Hainault Farm. No. 37 Squadron's B Flight at Stow Maries scrambled eleven Sopwith Pups, lifting off from 0823. No. 39 Squadron's C Flight at Hainault sent up ten Sopwith Camels, lifting off from 0824. Elsewhere BE12As of No. 37 Squadron's A Flight at Goldhanger had started lifting off at 0823, No. 50 Squadron scrambled Sopwith Pups from Detling, BE12 and BE12As were aloft from Bekesbourne and a solitary Armstrong Whitworth FK8 was up from Throwley. No. 39 Squadron's A Flight scrambled some BE12s and 12As and an FK8 from North Weald. Other aircraft came from Nos. 78, 46, 62 (Training) Squadrons, No. 2 Aircraft Acceptance Park, Hendon, No. 8 Aircraft Acceptance Park, Lympne, the Experimental Station at Orford Ness and the Testing Squadron at Martlesham Heath. In all, the home defence squadrons scrambled around 122 aircraft.

Kleine and his squadron headed south-west, straight for Felixstowe. As soon as they crossed the River Deben they came under fire from seven anti-aircraft batteries belonging to the Harwich command. In twelve minutes the guns fired 273 rounds. The artillery fire forced Kleine's raiders to seek greater altitude and to break up into two groups. Nonetheless they continued on their bombing run and dropped fifty-five bombs in and around Harwich and Felixstowe.

Harwich did not suffer any casualties, but the RNAS station at Felixstowe seemed to be the main target. A 50kg bomb hit the engineers' workshop, killing one and injuring three others. The Suffolk Regiment came under attack and their barracks was hit, killing eleven and wounding twenty. A bomb also hit the Ordnance Hotel, killing a barman and damaging six houses and two churches.

Having carried out their attack, the squadron headed east. It was around 0815 and the first and only British aircraft to engage the Gothas appeared on the scene, a Vickers FB14D flown by Captain Vernon Brown and Captain B. M. Jones from the Experimental Station at Orford Ness. Jones, the observer, was testing his own design, a periscopic sight, which he had designed to improve the firing of guns and which made allowances for the relative speed of the firing aircraft and the target aircraft.

Brown and Jones chased the Gothas for around 50 miles before they got to within range of two which were lagging behind the others. Jones managed to fire around 100 rounds, but Brown was forced to peel off when the other aircraft turned to help beat them off.

The aircraft of No. 46 Squadron had the task of chasing the Gothas over the North Sea. It was wrongly reported that they were heading for Southend and indeed the anti-aircraft guns around the Thames Estuary did begin shooting at something from around 0845. However, what they were firing at was a formation of No. 37 Squadron's Sopwith Pups. Captain Claude A. Ridley, the leader, had his engine cowling shot away at 14,000ft over Shoeburyness. He managed to land safely at 0942. Other aircraft were also hit and Lieutenant G. Barrett, in an Armstrong Whitworth FK8 from the Experimental Station at Orford Ness, was forced to land at Rochford as he had two enormous holes caused by shrapnel in one of his wings. There was obviously a serious problem here, the anti-aircraft gunners were literally firing at anything in the sky, despite the fact that Ridley himself had flown a Sopwith Pup over the batteries only the day before so that the gunners knew what the aircraft looked and sounded like.

Just as the Gothas were leaving Harwich the RFC's 14th Wing at Dunkirk was informed. They immediately sent up a number of Bristol Fighter F2Bs of No. 48 Squadron, which left their base at around 0830 and headed east, gaining a height of 16,000ft. Also despatched were Sopwith Camels of the RNAS's Nos. 3 and 4 (Naval) Squadrons, but these missed the bombers, as did the RFC's No. 55 Squadron's DH4s.

At around 1040 Captain Brian E. Baker and Second Lieutenant G. R. Spencer, in a Bristol Fighter, were at 16,000ft, about 8 miles to the north-west of Ostend when they spotted five Gothas and dived down to intercept them. Baker fired at one that was flying at an altitude of about

3,000ft. He then attacked it again at 2,000ft, hitting it several times. At the same time Lieutenant R. D. Coath and Second Lieutenant A. D. Merchant, also in a Bristol Fighter, engaged it from the rear. Between them they managed to shoot it down and it crashed into the sea just off Ostend.

It was clear that there were deficiencies in the air-raid warning system. Instead of the warning being cancelled when it was clear London was not under attack, it was transmitted to County Hall at 0830. Consequently, seventy-nine of the fire stations fired off their rockets. Thousands of people headed for shelter and the transport system ground to a halt. The all clear was not finally given until 1000, when hundreds of policemen were sent around the streets on bicycles, carrying placards. The failure to cancel the warning had also caused the various batteries to fire on the RFC aircraft; the anti-aircraft batteries did not let up until 0945, by which time they had fired nearly 300 rounds. Luckily none of the British aircraft was lost or crews killed.

After 22 July the weather deteriorated once more, with high winds and heavy rain. On the 24th, No. 44 (Home Defence) Squadron was officially formed, and No. 39 Squadron would now be based at North Weald.

On 29 July Handley Page and DH4 aircraft of No. 7 (Naval) Squadron, Dunkirk, launched an early-morning air raid on Ghistelles. Kleine had determined to launch another raid on the same day. His squadron took off and began to cross the North Sea, but the wind was strong and it was clear that poor weather was imminent. With great reluctance Kleine fired the signal to return to base.

On 30 July No. 112 (Home Defence) Squadron, with Sopwith Pups, was formed at Throwley in Kent from No. 50 Squadron's B Flight. On the 31st the first of Smuts' recommendations were put into effect with the creation of the London Air Defence Area (LADA), which covered a huge area from Southwold to London and then to Rottingdean. It would ensure that the anti-aircraft units and nine home defence squadrons (Nos. 37, 39, 44, 50, 51, 61, 75, 78 and 112) co-operated. Additionally a series of observation posts manned by the Royal Defence Corps were incorporated, running from Grantham to Portsmouth. The person responsible for co-ordinating the entire effort was Brigadier General Edward B. Ashmore.

On the same day the British 5th Army, supported by the 2nd Army and the French 1st Army, launched their Flanders offensive. They managed to advance 2 miles in a day, but then, in dreadful weather, ground to a halt and just 7 miles from Ypres the appalling slaughter of Passchendaele took place.

Whilst the appalling weather at the beginning of August ruined Haig's plans to burst through the German front and overrun the Gotha airfields in Belgium, it also meant that this was a frustrating time for Kleine and his squadron. Indeed for the first three weeks of August there was almost continuous rain and at times severe gales.

Ashmore officially took command of LADA on 5 August, with the rank of Major General. He immediately recognized that in deploying the forces available to him he had three key concerns. The first, a renewed Zeppelin offensive, was relatively unlikely, indeed, he could almost discount it. He had, however, to assume that the Germans would continue their daylight attacks on Britain and his defensive network needed to be ready. His third concern was the possibility of being too successful in dealing with the daylight threat. This would force the Germans, if they wished to continue their raids against Britain, to switch to night attacks, which would bring about an entirely new set of problems.

The first step in preparing the defences was the establishment of a ring of anti-aircraft batteries to the east of London. Lord French, amongst others, had suggested that a minimum of 110 guns would be required. On 9 August the War Cabinet did approve the establishment of this eastern ring, but they only approved the movement of thirty-four guns (ten from London and twenty-four from the counties). The War Cabinet still believed that the main priority would be to protect British ports and shipping, and they would therefore not allow the wholesale movement of anti-aircraft units, which would leave the ports vulnerable to attack.

The defensive ring was set up at a range of up to 25 miles from Hyde Park. The most northerly site was Ware and the most southerly was Oxted. In order to avoid anti-aircraft guns firing on British aircraft, an inner circle was established, which would become known as the Green Line. The anti-aircraft guns would be the primary defence against incoming aircraft therefore the guns would have priority at this point in the attack. Once the raiders had crossed the line, British fighters could then engage and would be given priority.

Improvements were also made in ground-to-air communications. Anti-aircraft units were supplied with large, white arrows which would be pointed in the direction in which the Gothas had flown away from the battery. It was believed that they could be seen from a height of 17,000ft. An operations room was also set up, which could plot the flight path of the Gothas and mark the position of any British fighters that were intercepting. BE aircraft fitted with radios would now patrol both sides of the Thames and four would be made available by the end of August.

Although Ashmore had operational command of all of the aeroplanes within his zone of command, he did not have any control over the RNAS aircraft. It was agreed on 11 August that RNAS fighters operating out of Eastchurch, Manston and Walmer would remain responsible for coastal patrolling, but would not operate inland towards the capital.

On 10 August the RNAS once again hit Ghistelles, once more with little or no effect. On the 12th, with the weather slightly improving over Belgium, Kleine decided to order a raid for that very afternoon. The weather reports, however, were not optimistic and in any case, after many days of sitting around waiting for an opportunity, a large number of the Gothas and their crews were not ready to launch an attack that same day. Kleine nevertheless ordered all available aircraft to take off at 1430. Thirteen were scraped together and Kleine delegated the leading of this attack to the commanding officer of Flight 15 at St Denis Vestrem, Richard Walter. The primary target would again be London and the secondary targets naval bases along the River Medway.

Reports vary, but either two or three of the Gothas suffered engine difficulties soon after lift-off and only ten or eleven headed for the Essex coast. The first sightings of the enemy formation may have been made either by Flight Lieutenant H. Beamish, leading four Sopwith Camels of No. 3 (Naval) Squadron, or the Sunk Lightship. Certainly the LADA control room received a warning at about 1700. The RFC was alerted at 1709 and told to begin patrols at 1714. Beamish, meanwhile, had tried to follow the Germans and had made a few attacks, but the four Sopwith Camels were forced to break off because of a lack of fuel. Beamish landed at Rochford and the other aircraft landed at Manston and Eastchurch.

The wind drove the Gotha formation further north than they had anticipated; indeed they were 20 miles off course. To compensate Walter ordered them to head south-west for the River Blackwater. Meanwhile, the RFC was scrambling 110 aircraft. No. 46 Squadron had Pups airborne by 1715 and Nos. 44 and 112 were airborne by about 1730. Walter's bombers passed Clacton at 1720 and were over Bradwell at 1735. As they approached Rochford one broke off to make a diversionary attack on Margate.

They were making very poor progress, in fact little more than 50mph, and Walter realized that soon the skies would be full of British aircraft. He fired a signal cartridge to indicate that they should turn east to attack Southend. A few bombs fell on the airfield at Rochford.

The single Gotha heading for Margate may well have peeled off because Beamish or one of his men had hit it. Be that as it may, it managed to draw off nine RNAS fighters. Other British aircraft were now aloft, including twenty-one from Nos. 37, 39, 50 and 78 Squadrons, with a further thirty from various experimental, depot and training establishments of the RFC. The RNAS had also sent up twenty-four aircraft from Eastchurch, Manston and Walmer.

At 1730 the main force was flying in a triangular box, heading generally in the direction of Gravesend, then Canvey Island; they seemed to be going towards London. The weather was deteriorating over the capital, however, and Walter gave instructions to head towards Southend again. The bombers began dropping their bombs along a line from Leigh-on-Sea to Southend, dropping around thirty-four, half of which were duds. They claimed thirty-two dead and forty-three injured. The worst casualties were caused when a 50kg bomb exploded in Victoria Avenue, near the railway station, killing fifteen people, whilst a second hit the area around Milton Street and Guildford Road.

No. 61 Squadron at Rochford was initially ordered not to scramble, but the commanding officer, Major E. R. Pretyman, disobeyed orders and began launching his aircraft from 1718. In the record books all the take-off times were amended later by hand, giving them as from 1738. As it happened, No. 61 the only squadron in a position to deal with the Gothas as they returned home. By the time the Gothas headed home they had reached a height of 15,000ft and the ten pilots of No. 61 Squadron chased them up to 50 miles out to sea.

By 1800 the bombers were heading towards Sheerness and the River Medway. They now came under fire from the anti-aircraft guns on Canvey Island, Grain and the Isle of Sheppey, and it was at this point that No. 61 Squadron's Sopwith Pups attacked. The Germans were in a quandary. If they stayed in a tight formation they would make an excellent target for the anti-aircraft guns, but if they split up they would be easy prey for the British fighters.

Walter took the only choice available to him and that was to break off the raid and head for home. He fired a flare and the formation swung east, pursued by No. 61 Squadron and by fire from the anti-aircraft guns. The guns around the Thames Estuary had fired around 300 rounds.

The Gotha that had attacked Margate managed to destroy an empty house and wound one person. Five RNAS fighters then assailed it. In addition it had to brave the fire from anti-aircraft guns at Broadstairs and Cliffsend. Before it could get away it came under fire from ten RNAS aircraft and one RFC aircraft which made attacks over a distance of around 80 miles. One of the Gotha's engines was hit, but it continued, descending at a rate of about 200ft per mile, still under fire.

Despite the continued attacks the experienced pilot managed to put his aircraft down on the beach at Zeebrugge.

One of the pilots, who had chased the solitary Gotha, Flight Lieutenant H. S. Kerby, flying a Sopwith Pup from RNAS Walmer, turned to see the main formation being chased by sixteen British aircraft. Walter could not afford to head along the Dutch coast, in an attempt to avoid running into RNAS aircraft from Dunkirk, as his petrol reserves were far too low. By 2000 the Gothas were still an hour from home and the sun would be setting in around half an hour. Four Sopwith Camels were scrambled from No. 3 (Naval) Squadron and began patrolling the Scheldt Estuary. They did not encounter any covering German fighters and engaged the Gothas until all four suffered gun jams. The Germans now cut across Holland and four had to crash land in the poor light. It was an extremely high-cost operation. Six Gothas had been lost, either shot down or seriously damaged. Had the weather been slightly better and the British machine-guns less temperamental then the entire force could have been lost.

The Germans now knew that the British had seriously improved their air defences and that any more daylight attacks would be extremely hazardous. To make matters worse the RNAS sent DH4s and Handley Pages to attack the base at Ghistelles on both 14 and 16 August.

There was an extremely important meeting between Smuts and the War Cabinet on 17 August, at which he made eight recommendations that would culminate in the creation of the Royal Air Force. First, he suggested that an Air Ministry be created and that air staff should control operations. He further suggested that the RNAS and the RFC be amalgamated and all their personnel transferred into a new force. He strongly recommended that there should be close liaison between the army, navy and air staffs and that it should be the role of the air staff to provide aircraft to assist the army and navy. In order to achieve an understanding between the army, the navy and the new force, officers from the two senior services should be seconded for periods of time. He also suggested that officers and other ranks from the navy and the army should be allowed, if not encouraged, to apply for transfer to the new force. The War Cabinet formally approved the report on 24 August 1917 and eight months later the Royal Air Force (RAF) was established.

Meanwhile, Kleine was contemplating another attack on Britain. He had pencilled in 18 August, but weather reports suggested that there would be unsettled weather over Britain and that there was a possibility of gale-force winds sweeping across the country. He ignored these reports, however, and at 0630, fifteen Gothas left from St Denis

Vestrem and thirteen from Melle-Gontrode. The wind was strong and the aircraft were blown close to the Dutch frontier, where they received the attention of Dutch anti-aircraft batteries. Nevertheless, Kleine pressed on, although the bombers were now flying straight into the wind and were only achieving a speed of about 50mph. They climbed above the cloud level and continued for three hours towards the British coastline. Kleine had hoped to approach Britain over the Isle of Thanet, but he was 40 miles north and heading for Harwich.

The difficult weather had seriously drained his fuel reserves and he realized that there was every possibility that the Gothas would run out of fuel before they could get home. He therefore reluctantly ordered his aircraft to turn about. As they turned, the wind rose to 90mph and it began to rain. They jettisoned their bombs and began to head for home, but it was too late, several aircraft were running out of fuel. At least two were lost at sea, one of which may have landed on the beach at Zeebrugge.

The wind was still driving the survivors north towards Holland. Two were 60 miles north of their usual inbound flight path and crossed the Hook of Holland. One landed in a field and the other, having had an engine knocked out by a rifle shot, came down. The Dutch captured both crews. Dutch anti-aircraft guns fired at the remaining aircraft as they crossed Holland towards the Belgian coast, and one bomber may have been shot down and crashed on the Belgian side of the border. At least five of those that remained ran out of fuel and had to crash land. Those that did arrive at the airfield found that the strong wind made it incredibly difficult to land and four more were damaged on landing.

Kleine had lost at least thirteen out of twenty-eight aircraft to no purpose; all he had managed to achieve was to anger the Dutch government, who demanded compensation from the Germans for the bombs jettisoned over Dutch soil. Von Hoeppner severely reprimanded Kleine and ensured that from now on he would only order attacks if the weather was favourable.

Kleine was still convinced that daylight raids best served the German war effort, and he eagerly awaited another opportunity to launch an assault. This came on 22 August, and he ordered all fifteen available aircraft to be ready to take off at 0900. Once again London was the primary target, but Southend, the Medway River installations and Dover were all earmarked as secondary targets. He proposed to head straight for the North Foreland and then proceed west to London.

There was only a moderate breeze, Kleine was eager to avoid aggravating the Dutch once again and the Gothas made for the Isle of

Thanet, but during the flight five, including Kleine himself, had to turn back with engine problems. This left Walter in charge of the operation.

The Kentish Knock Lightship spotted the remaining Gothas at 1006, and they immediately came under fire from a destroyer and an armed trawler. They took another half hour to reach Margate; there were now two groups, flying at between 14,000 and 16,000ft.

At around 1037 they approached Margate and came under fire from anti-aircraft guns, which managed to get off 1,000 rounds in ten minutes. Almost immediately one Gotha began spinning down from a height of 14,000ft and crashed into the sea about a mile off Margate. One crew member was later rescued. It is not clear how the aircraft was shot down or by whom but Flight Lieutenant H. S. Kerby, flying a Sopwith Pup, Flight Commander J. E. Hervey from Dover, also in a Sopwith Pup and several other RNAS pilots had opened fire on it. It was also under fire, of course, from the anti-aircraft guns.

Walter now fired some flares to indicate that the bombers should turn and attack Dover. The signal was misunderstood, however, and some attacked Margate. At least one dropped five bombs on the town, but despite some damage to buildings, nobody was killed or wounded. It may have been one of these that was now hit and set alight by anti-aircraft fire. The pilot tried to coax the aircraft down to land, but it broke up and fell into three pieces, which landed on Hengrove Golf Course. All the crew were killed.

The remaining eight bombers headed over Ramsgate, dropping twenty-eight bombs and killing nine people and injuring twenty-one. One 50kg bomb fell on a store near the inner harbour, killing seven and another fell on the railway platform.

Walter now led his bombers out to sea, still harassed by anti-aircraft fire and RNAS aircraft. One gun at Deal managed to get off sixty-one rounds. The Gothas came into range of the artillery based at Cauldham Citadel, Frith Farm, Langdon Bay, River Bottom Wood and West Hougham at 1100. The Gothas managed to drop about fourteen bombs in and around Dover naval base. Two nearly hit Dover Castle, three more fell near Dover College and the Admiral Harvey pub was badly damaged.

Flight Lieutenant Arthur F. Brandon of the RNAS, Manston, arrived on the scene and in a Sopwith Camel engaged a Gotha on the left-hand side of the formation. He fired at 200 yards, continuing until he was just 20 yards away. He made two more attacks and the bomber began to spin out of control. Brandon then had to break off as he had run out of ammunition.

Simultaneously his squadron commander, C. H. Butler, supported by Flight Sub-Lieutenant C. H. FitzHerbert, Flight Sub-Lieutenant E.

The last picture of the England Squadron key figures in Frankfurt-an-der-Oder just after the end of the war. From left to right are Leutnant Stoehr and Leutnant Georgii (HQ Staff), Hauptmann Brandenburg (centre), Leutnant Radke (Brandenburg's former pilot) and Leutnant Genthe (his former observer).

Members of the England Squadron at Chateau Drory in the spring of 1917.

This is a GI Prototype that made its maiden flight on July 27 1915. Note the serial number, G13/15.

This photograph shows an AEG GII. The three men closest to the aircraft are the crew: the pilot and two gunners.

This is a photograph of a GIII belonging to Bombengeschwader III, taken by another low flying Gotha. The photograph is believed to have been taken through the lower gun tunnel. It is probably dated 1917 and taken at Nieuwmunster in Belgium.

This GIV clearly shows the 260hp Mercedes DIVa engines, which turn the twin-bladed, wooden propellers. Note the radiator mounted at the front of the engine nacelle. They were equipped with shutters that aided the pilot in maintaining ideal engine temperature.

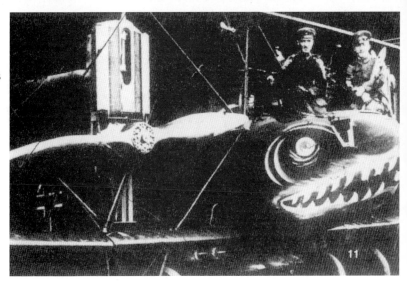

An example of the Gotha GV.

This photograph clearly shows the ventral gun position on a Gotha. The machine gun was mounted here in order to give protection to the rear and below the aircraft.

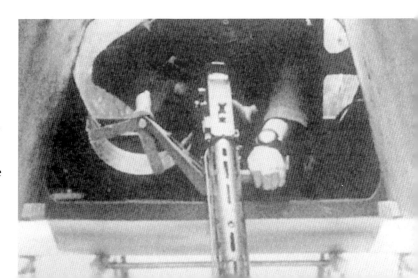

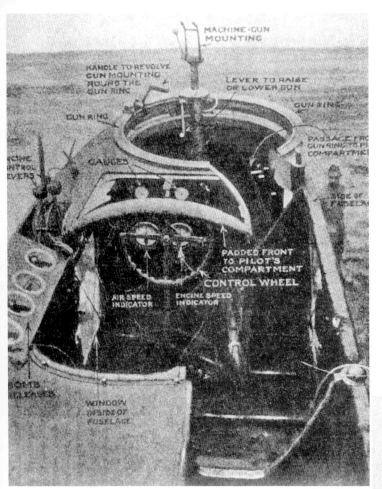

Annotated illustration of the forward crew positions in a Gotha.

Labels on illustration:

MACHINE-GUN MOUNTING

HANDLE TO REVOLVE GUN MOUNTING ROUND THE GUN RING

LEVER TO RAISE OR LOWER GUN

GUN RING

GUN RING

GAUGES

PASSAGE FROM GUN RING TO PILOT'S COMPARTMENT

CONTROL LEVERS

SIDE OF FUSELAGE

PADDED FRONT TO PILOT'S COMPARTMENT

CONTROL WHEEL

AIR SPEED INDICATOR

ENGINE SPEED INDICATOR

BOMB RELEASE

WINDOW IN SIDE OF FUSELAGE

A 300kg bomb, as used by the Gothas and Giants. Note the fins, which were angled to create a spin when the bomb was dropped, which in theory improved its accuracy.

A Gotha gunner/observer sucking on an oxygen tube. Note the the pilot's rear-view mirror and windscreen.

German ground crew demonstrating the range of different bombs used by a Gotha. The bomb on the extreme right is a 300kg weapon.

An illustration showing the internal compartments of the Gotha. Note the bomb racks inside the fuselage.

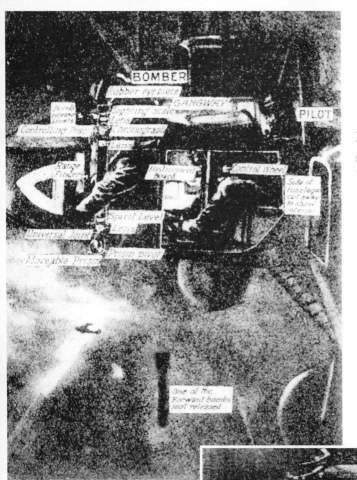

A detailed and captioned view of the Goerz bomb-sight. Note the falling torpedo shaped bomb.

Gothas of Kagohl 3 at Nieuwmunster, Belgium. The aircraft on the right is about to take off.

Gothas and men of Kagohl 3 at Ghistelles, Belgium.

Gothas parked in front of the Zepplin hangar at Melle-Gontrode.

Feldmarschall Hindenburg seen inspecting a Gotha GIV at Melle-Gontrode in May 1917.

An RNAS anti-aircraft gun team going through a practice drill.

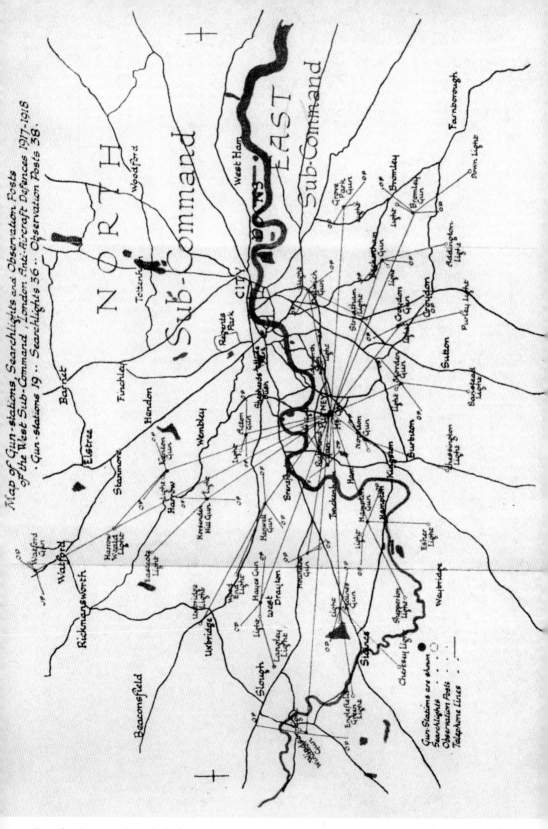

London's anti-aircraft defences.

A variety of mobile RNAS anti-aircraft units being inspected at Kenwood House by Admiral Sir Percy Scott in December 1915.

The Royal Naval Anti-Aircraft Mobile Brigade in the Lord Mayor's show in November 1915. Note the mobile searchlight unit to the rear of the five leading anti-aircraft guns.

An RN Mobile double gun pit and dugout designed by Colonel Rawlinson (centre of picture) for use on cliff tops.

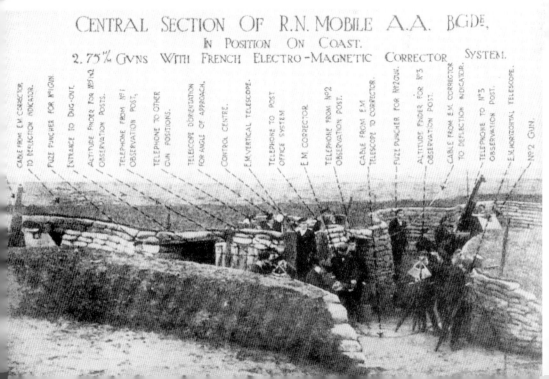

CENTRAL SECTION OF R.N. MOBILE A.A. BGDE,
IN POSITION ON COAST.
2.75″ GUNS WITH FRENCH ELECTRO-MAGNETIC CORRECTOR SYSTEM.

CABLE FROM E.M. CORRECTOR. TO DEFLECTION INDICATOR.
FUZE PUNCHER FOR Nº1GUN.
ENTRANCE TO DUG-OUT.
ALTITUDE FINDER FOR Nº1 & Nº2 OBSERVATION POSTS.
TELEPHONE FROM Nº1 OBSERVATION POST.
TELEPHONE TO OTHER GUN POSITIONS.
TELESCOPE DEMONSTRATION FOR ANGLE OF APPROACH.
CONTROL CENTRE.
E.M. VERTICAL TELESCOPE.
TELEPHONE TO POST OFFICE SYSTEM.
E.M. CORRECTOR.
TELEPHONE FROM Nº2 OBSERVATION POST.
CABLE FROM E.M. TELESCOPE TO CORRECTOR.
FUZE PUNCHER FOR Nº2 GUN.
ALTITUDE FINDER FOR Nº3 OBSERVATION POST.
CABLE FROM E.M. CORRECTOR TO DEFLECTION INDICATOR.
TELEPHONE TO Nº3 OBSERVATION POST.
E.M. HORIZONTAL TELESCOPE.
Nº2 GUN.

The Oldhams Printing Works in Long Acre, London showing the devastation caused by a single 300kg bomb on the night of January 28-29 1918.

The effect of the first 1000lb bomb dropped on Britain during the war. The shattered remains of part of the Royal Hospital, Chelsea in the aftermath of the raid on February 16 1918.

Three civilians were killed in a passing tram when a 50kg bomb hit the Embankment on the night of September 4-5 1917.

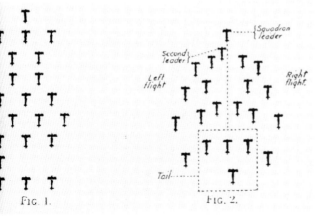

FIG. 1.

FIG. 2.

Squadron leader

Second leader

Left flight

Right flight

Tail

Two different types of Gotha formation as presented by the Air Ministry. In practice, it was rare for the Gothas to adopt any formation other than the duck formation as seen on the right. The figure on the left purports to show the formation as the bombers crossed the coast and the one on the right of the formation adopted to approach London. The date for these figures refer to the raid on July 7 1917.

An illustration of the Gotha Duck formation adopted by the incoming bombers on their attack on July 7 1917. The formation consisted of 21 bombers.

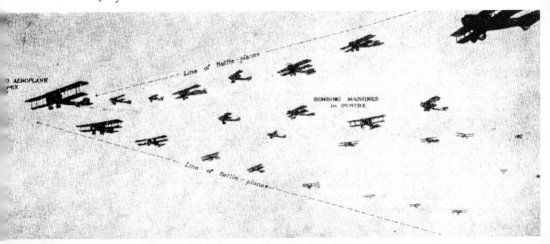

AEROPLANE

Line of Battle-planes

BOMBING MACHINES in CENTRE

Line of Battle-planes

Lieutenant A.S.C. Irwin (No 112 Squadron) at Throwley with his two dogs (Tinker and Tip) and his Sopwith Camel.

Captain Willliam Harold Haynes (No 44 Squadron). He was awarded a DSO after engaging a Gotha on the night of September 30 – October 1 1917. Haynes unfortunately died when his Sopwith Camel over-turned whilst taxiing on the night of September 26 1918.

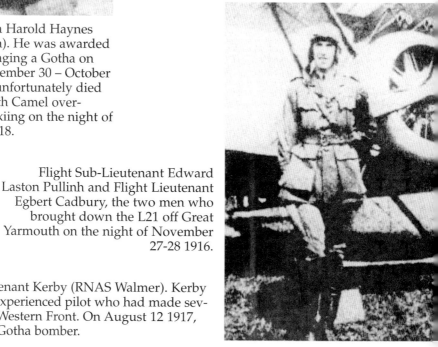

Flight Sub-Lieutenant Edward Laston Pullinh and Flight Lieutenant Egbert Cadbury, the two men who brought down the L21 off Great Yarmouth on the night of November 27-28 1916.

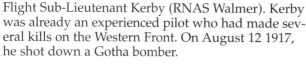

Flight Sub-Lieutenant Kerby (RNAS Walmer). Kerby was already an experienced pilot who had made several kills on the Western Front. On August 12 1917, he shot down a Gotha bomber.

No 141 Squadron at Biggin Hill.
Lieutenant E. E. Turner can be seen
bareheaded near the rear cockpit.

Major Egbert Cadbury and
Captain Robert Leckie
photographed in Great Yarmouth
after their destruction of the L70
on the night of August 5-6 1918.
These ranks were RAF ones, but
the two men still wear their old
Flight Commander insignia of
the RNAS.

The Sopwith Camel D6435 flown by
Captain C.J.Q. Brand of No. 112
Squadron on March 7-8 1918, the first
Camel to be delivered to the squadron.

Lieutenant A.J. Arkell and Aircraftman A.T.C. Stagg at the site of the Gotha they destroyed on the night of May 19-20 1918.

A Neame sight (on the centre of the wing section) on a Bristol Fighter of No 141 Squadron, Biggin Hill.

A Bristol Fighter, probably of No. 141 Squadron, Biggin Hill. The picture was taken in early 1918 shortly after the formation of the squadron.

London as photographed from a Gotha on July 7 1917. St Paul's Cathedral can be seen to the left of the picture.

The Lo-Ri 2 at Melle-Gontronde airfield. The airfield was bombed and the aircraft was badly damaged after a near miss which caused the crater.

The crew of the Lo-Ri 3, Leutnant Kurt Küppers, the commander is in the lighter coloured great coat.

A stunning photograph of a Gotha over Belgium, probably taken by another Gotha in the formation.

A view of the R12's twin Mercedes 160hp engines. The noise and vibration was an enormous problem for the crew. Note the radiator above the engines.

The seemingly indestructible R12. It hit a balloon apron on the night of February 16 1918, but continued on its mission. By the end of the war the R12 had dropped 25,000kg of bombs on Britain. The aircraft is seen here just after the end of the war.

The gunner/mechanic of the R12 perilously perched whilst the aircraft is aloft. He could carry out routine maintenance and checks during flights.

The R13 cockpit. The two pilots are sitting in a very forward position. Behind them is the commander of the aircraft. The ladder leads to the gun position on the upper wing.

The R13 of Rfa 501, the squadron became operational in December 1917.

The Staaken RIV R12 which took part in the last raid on Britain on the night of May 19-20 1918.

The Staaken RVI R39, note the operations marked on the fuselage including three against London.

A Staaken RVI.

The Staaken RVI R25 that was delivered in June 1917. It made a solo attack on London on the night of February 17 1918.

The wreckage of the Gotha GV/925/16 at St Osyth shot down on the night of May 19-20 1918. Note the name Pommern, perhaps signifying that the crew came from Pomerania.

The Gotha GV/979/16 brought down at Frinsted by the combined attacks of SE5As from No 143 Squadron and Bristol Fighters of No 141 Squadron on the night of May 19-20 1918.

The wreckage of GV/906/16 hit over Canvey Island on the night of December 5-6 1917. The aircraft attempted to land at Rochford, but overshot the runway and crashed on a nearby golf course at 0445.

Gotha wreckage following a night landing accident in Belgium.

The Staaken RV4 R12, that was downed by No 39 Squadron on the night of 28-29 January 1918

The wreckage of one of the Gothas lost over Britain on the night of May 19-20 1918.

Another shot of the wreckage of a Gotha destroyed over Britain on the night of May 19-20 1918.

B. Drake and Flight Sub-Lieutenant M. A. Harker, roared in to engage the formation. Butler's aircraft was hit but he still managed to fire and chase the Gothas. Drake focused on one aircraft, seeing it burst into flames. By the time he peeled off he had fired 632 rounds. FitzHerbert and Harker, firing 600 and 300 rounds respectively, made further attacks.

Brandon, meanwhile, had flown back to Manston and immediately jumped into another Sopwith Camel. He caught up with the Gothas about 30 miles from the British coast and continued attacking them until they reached the Scheldt Estuary, during which time he fired over 1,000 rounds.

With the Germans heading home, the RNAS and RFC squadrons from Dunkirk could now pounce. Ten Sopwith Camels of the RNAS's No. 4 Squadron raced to engage twenty-five German fighters that had been sent out to cover the Gothas, whilst two from No. 3 Squadron hunted for the bombers with no success. The RFC No. 66 Squadron scrambled six Sopwith Pups and No. 48 Squadron had six Bristol Fighters aloft.

Captain J. H. T. Letts led the Bristol Fighters and encountered the Gothas at a height of approximately 15,500ft about 30 miles out of Nieuport. He opened fire at a range of about 200 yards and then made several more attacks. His observer gunner, Second Lieutenant H. R. Power, had been firing into them but when Letts turned to make a last attack Power was shot and killed. Letts fired a green flare to signal that he was returning to base; the other pilots in the area took this as a signal to break off and also headed home.

Seven German survivors landed at around 1230. In August alone Kleine had lost twenty-two bombers and forty experienced crew members and he now knew that the British aircraft and anti-aircraft guns combined were perfectly capable of breaking up and then dealing with his formations. Von Hoeppner took note of the losses and demanded that the situation be completely reviewed. It was clear that the Gothas would have to fly at a minimum of 19,000ft in order to avoid the British aircraft and guns, but this would be impossible. It was hoped that the new GV would allow daylight raids to continue, but the Giant Staaken RVVI could also now be used for night raids.

CHAPTER SEVEN

The Giants

The Germans classified their new aircraft as *Riesenflugzeug*, literally 'giant aircraft'. Many of the aircraft which were later classified as R Types were classified as Standard G Types, or bombers, until late 1915.

It was normal practice for the Germans to classify specific models by first stating the manufacturer's name then using the classification type, followed by the model or design. Hence Staaken RIV denoted the manufacturer as Staaken, the classification as Giant aircraft or bomber and the version or model of the aircraft as IV.

In looking at the German bomber offensive against Britain, we will primarily focus on the Staaken range of bombers. Many other different types of aircraft were used in other theatres of the war, including Allgemeine Elektrizitäts (AEG), Ago-Flugzeugwerke, Ostdeutsche Albatroswerke, Automobil und Aviatik, Daimler, Deutsche Flugzeug-werke, Dornier, Junkers, Linke-Hofmann, Mercur-Flugzeugbau, Neuber, Poll, Roland (Luft-Fahrzeug-Gesellschaft), Schütte-Lanz, Siemens-Schuckert, Ssw-Dynamowerk, Union-Flugzeugwerke and Zschach, but by far the most successful and relevant to this book were the R aircraft, built by the Zeppelin-Werke Staaken factory. They were built in much larger numbers and were the only R aircraft to see action on the Western Front.

Back in 1913, Hellmuth Hirth, then one of Germany's most famous pilots, proposed the construction of a six-engined seaplane. It was planned to be ready for an attempt at a trans-atlantic flight by the summer of 1915. Rather like an airship, the engines could be serviced in flight and if the aircraft had to make a forced landing at sea, it could operate as a powered lifeboat.

It was Graf Zeppelin who saw the enormous potential of the aircraft as a weapon of war. Even though he was very much involved in the development of the airship and its deployment, he soon realized its limitations. Shortly after the outbreak of war, he instructed Alfred

Colsman, the director of Luftschiffbau Zeppelin, to begin planning the construction of an aircraft with a range of 600km, capable of carrying a 1,000kg bomb. From the start the project was beset with problems. Colsman believed that the company should be concentrating on speeding up the production of airships: it had absolutely no experience in the building aircraft, nor was there space in the factories to divert effort away from airships.

Early on in Hirth's seaplane project, Gustav Klein of the Robert Bosch Werk had provided financial backing. Now Zeppelin brought him onboard. Klein was released and was joined by engineers, purchasing experts and craftsmen. The German war office at this stage disapproved of the project. But ultimately the Chief of Field Aviation, Major Thomsen and the Chief of the Naval Construction Bureau, Admiral Dick, both gave their support. They also offered trained workmen and the German navy even placed a provisional order for two aircraft.

Work began on the Gotha airfield and in August 1914, Professor Alexander Baumann was engaged to design and supervise the construction of the bomber. He ultimately became the head of the Design Department of the Zeppelin-Werk Staaken until 1918.

Work on the first bomber, named the VGOI (Versuchsbau, Gotha-Ost) began in September 1914, with the final plans ready in December. Construction was delayed in January 1915, as the Maybach 240hp engine had not yet been delivered. Thomsen and Dick had to work around the lack of support from the German war office. Finally, however, Hirth himself piloted VGO1 on its maiden flight on 11 April 1915. Three Maybach engines powered it, one in the fuselage and the other two on the wings.

On 6 June 1915, the aircraft flew from Gotha to the Maybach factory at Friedrichshafen. There the navy carried out a series of test flights. The aircraft returned to Gotha on 16 December 1915. It ran into bad weather, two of the engines cut out and it was forced to make a forced landing near Geroldsgrün. Despite heavy damage, the crew walked away without injury. The aircraft was retrieved and rebuilt with several new features. At the same time the VGOII was also nearing completion.

The VGOI flew again on 16 February 1916 and in June of the same year it was despatched to the Eastern Front for evaluation. It made its first bomb raid on 15 August 1916. It was now flying in the guise of RML1 (*Reichs Marine Landflugzeug* 'Imperial Navy landplane'). It took part in an attack on a rail terminal on 15 August, an air station the following day and a troop camp on 17 August but was not involved in another raid on 24 August because of radiator problems.

Some time around 1 September 1916 the RML1 suffered a near catastrophic disaster. At about 160ft from the ground, fully loaded, having just taken off, two of its engines exploded. The pilots managed to coax it down into a pine forest. Nearly seventy trees were destroyed and all that was salvageable was the fuselage, which was sent back to Staaken for refitting. It was clear that the aircraft was underpowered and five Maybach 245hp engines were fitted, one in the nose and two on each wing; it was a huge improvement.

The VGOI was ready for its new maiden flight on 10 March 1917, but it was another disaster. One of the engines on the left wing stopped and the aircraft did not respond to rudder controls. Hans Vollmöller, the pilot, was killed instantly, Gustav Klein died shortly afterwards from his injuries and the third crew member, Carl Kuring, was badly injured, but survived. This was just two days after the death of Graf Zeppelin from natural causes. The combined losses of these three key individuals could have ended the R-plane forever.

The VGOI

Type	VGOI/RML1 3 engine	VGOI 5 engine
Manufacturer	Versuchsbau, Gotha-Ost	Versuchsbau, Gotha-Ost
Engines	3 Maybach 240hp HS	4 Maybach Mb IVa 245hp
		2 Mercedes DIII 160hp
		or
		5 Maybach Mb Iva 245hp
Span	42.2m	42.2m
Length	24m	24m
Height	6.6m	6.6m
Wing area	332sq m	320sq m
Empty weight	6,520kg	7,450kg
Loaded weight	9,520kg	11,485kg
Wing loading	29.7kg/sq m	37.4kg/sq m
Maximum speed	110km/h	130km/h
Climb	2,000m in 39 minutes	3,000m in 60 minutes
Ceiling	3,000m in 79 minutes	Unknown
Duration	Unknown	Unknown
Fuel	1,500 litres	Unknown
Defensive armament	Dorsal, ventral and nacelle machine-guns	Dorsal, ventral and two Nacelle machine-guns
Service	Eastern Front, August 1916	None

The VGOII was developed taking into consideration many of the problems that had plagued the VGOI. It was to prove to be the first of many Staaken aircraft to be used by the German army. In February

1916 it was also delivered to the Eastern Front for evaluation. Its first fully documented raid took place on 13 August 1916, when it was involved in an attack on the Russian-held rail junction at Schlok. When, later, R planes became available, the VGOII was relegated to a training role. It made its last flight in the summer of 1917, when it crashed and broke its back at Staaken.

The VGOII and III

Type	VGOII	VGOIII
Manufacturer	Versuchsbau, Gotha-Ost	Versuchsbau, Gotha-Ost
Engines	3 Maybach HS or Mb VI, 240hp	6 Mercedes DIII, 160hp
Span	42.2m	42.2m
Length	23.78m	24.5m
Height	7m	6.8m
Wing area	332sq m	332sq m
Empty weight	6,637kg	8,600kg
Loaded weight	10,203kg	11,600kg
Wing loading	30.7kg/sq m	Unknown
Maximum speed	110km/h	110km/h
Climb	2,000m in 39 minutes	2,000m in 29 minutes
Ceiling	3,000m in 79 minutes	3,000m in 56 minutes
Duration	Unknown	6 hours
Fuel	1,788 litres	3,500 litres
Defensive armament	Dorsal, ventral and two nacelle machine-guns	Two dorsal, one ventral and two nacelle machine-guns
Service	Eastern Front, 1916	Eastern Front, September 1916–January 1917

In October 1915 the construction of the VGOIII began. Again the 240hp Maybach engines proved to be unreliable and were replaced by six Mercedes 160hp engines, giving it a total of 960hp, compared to 720hp in the VGOI and VGOII. Its maiden flight took place either at the end of May or at the beginning of June 1916. What is clear is that it flew from Gotha to Friedrichshafen on 13 June 1916. Again it was sent to the east for evaluation and delivered on 8 September, along with its crew of seven. It had improved bomb-carrying ability and initially completed seven bombing missions. Its targets were various railway installations and troop camps around the Riga region.

On 24 January 1917, it was coming in to land at Alt-Auz. It landed on soft ground covered in snow and its front wheels struck a hidden obstacle, snapping them off. The undercarriage collapsed and the fuselage broke into two, tearing off the lower wings. The fuel lines ruptured, petrol spewed over the exhaust stacks and it burst into flames, five crew members were killed; only one man survived.

On 1 August 1916 the VGO works was transferred from Gotha to Staaken, near Berlin. Airship construction had begun to be scaled down by 1917 and was stopped in January 1918. The VGO works was, therefore, able to recruit experienced airship workers. The construction of the fourth Staaken aircraft, which would later become known as the Staaken RIV, was begun in February 1916. It had its maiden flight on 16 August 1916 and by the time it had finished its initial tests, the works had fully transferred to Staaken. Officially then, the RIV 12/15, as it was named, was the first Staaken R-plane. It was very similar in many ways to the VGOIII: there were two Mercedes 160hp engines in the nose, but there were slight differences in the radiators and exhaust stacks. It was up-powered by Benz BZIV 220hp engines, which gave it a total of 1200hp. It became the only aircraft with coupled engines to see service on both the Western and Eastern Fronts.

The nacelles were lengthened in order to accommodate the larger engines, there was a clutch built by Mercedes and a new gearbox. Zahnradfabrik, a subsidiary of Zeppelin, constructed the gearbox. The engines had four-bladed propellers built by Garuda, which rotated in opposite directions. The open engineer's cockpit was replaced by a square hatch that had sliding covers and the machine-gun positions were moved in order to give the aircraft a better field of fire. Indeed, machine-gun positions were built onto the upper wings, above the nacelles and behind the rear wing spar. There were two dorsal, one ventral and two forward gun positions, which meant that the aircraft had seven machine-guns. The gunner on the wings could get in and out of his position by using a ladder from the nacelle. The ladder itself was perilously close to the propellers, which must have made it extremely dangerous.

The German army air services accepted the RIV on 5 May 1917. It flew to Alt-Auz from Gotha on 12 June 1917. It took part in raids on Wolmar on the night of 28/29 June 1917 and Oesel on the night of 8/9 July. It was then assigned to the Ghent area, where it was to take part in attacks on London, Essex, the Thames Estuary and various targets in France. This aircraft survived the war and was broken up in April 1919.

Type	Staaken RIV	Staaken RV
Manufacturer	Flugzeugwerft, Staaken, Berlin	Flugzeugwerft, Staaken, Berlin
Engines	2 Mercedes DIII, 160hp 4 Benz BZIV, 220hp	5 Maybach Mb IVa 245hp
Span	42.2m	42.2m
Length	23.2m	23m
Height	6.8m	6.8m
Wing area	332 sq m	332 sq m
Empty weight	8,772kg	9,450kg
Loaded weight	13,035kg	13,010kg
Wing loading	39.2kg/sq m	42kg/sq m
Maximum speed	125km/h	135km/h
Climb	3,000m in 89 minutes	3,000m in 34 minutes
Ceiling	3,700m	4,500m
Duration	6–7 hours	Unknown
Fuel	2,080 litres	Unknown
Defensive armament	6–7 machineguns	1 dorsal, 1 ventral, 1 upper wing and 2 nacelle machine-guns
Service	Eastern Front June– July 1917 Western Front July 1917–November 1918	Western Front 1917– 1918

The Staaken RV was fitted with five powerful high-compression 245hp Maybach engines. Construction began in June 1916 and it was accepted into service on 29 September 1917. By this time the Staaken RV 13/15 had come into service, after the Staaken RVII 14/15 and the Staaken RVI 25/16.

The RV 13/15 had different engine nacelles. They were wooden and covered in plywood, which aimed to reduce vibration. It was far more aerodynamically sound, but more difficult to construct. Aluminium panels covered the engine in the nose and each engine had five large radiators. In terms of the crew deployment, it was very similar to the VGOIII. The flight mechanic had a compartment behind the nose engine, there was a large, open pilot's cockpit, there were dorsal and ventral machine-gun positions and a forward-firing one in a pod, which became known as the swallow's nest, on the upper wing.

For communication between crew members there was a pneumatic tube message system, with six stations around the aircraft. Owing to the level of noise, sirens, speaking tubes and even telephones were all tried, but proved to be ineffective. Ultimately a simple electric telegraph was used, with between ten and twenty pre-determined commands. The RV had eleven crewmen; the commander, two pilots, three mechanics, a wireless operator, three gunners and a fuel attendant.

The RV 13/15 arrived at Ghent on 23 December 1917 and flew its first bombing mission on 25 January 1918, when it attacked harbour installations around Calais. It was only to fly sixteen combat missions over its eight months service. On the night of 7–8 March 1918, carrying 4,771kg of bombs, it was approaching London when one of its clutches failed, but it returned safely home to base. Its end came on 18 October when the crew was ordered to fly to Düsseldorf-Lohausen. It encountered fog over the Rhine and the crew attempted to make an emergency landing, but the aircraft was virtually written off in the attempt.

The most numerous of the Staaken R-planes were the RVIs. A total of eighteen were constructed, not including seaplane variants, although not all were made at the Staaken works, as various other German companies built several under licence. Amongst those involved were Automobil & Aviatik, Luftschiffbau Schütte-Lanz and Ostdeutsche Albatroswerke.

Four 260hp Mercedes or four 245hp Maybach engines variously powered the RVI. They were mounted on both the front and the rear of each nacelle. Unlike the previous Staaken aircraft, it did not have a propeller fitted to the nose, as operational experience had proven that fuel that close to the fuselage was unnecessarily hazardous to the crew. Each of the engines had self-starting mechanisms. The nacelles were covered with aluminium panels, held in place by hinges and leather straps. A flight mechanic's cockpit was situated between the two engines. Garuda made the propellers. The aircraft had eight to ten fuel tanks installed in the central fuselage, each of which could carry 245 litres, which were pumped to 155-litre gravity tanks. It was the fuel attendant's responsibility to monitor the fuel tanks and there was a gangway between them to allow him to do this.

The wings consisted of three parts: two outer panels and a central section. The main spars of the upper wing were made of ash and those of the lower from spruce. The reasoning behind this was that ash had higher compressive strength, whilst spruce had superior tensile strength and was lighter. The spars were covered in layers of plywood, then wrapped in glued cotton cloth. The wings' ribs were made of spruce and there were compression tubes and sets of steel cables to add further strength.

The undercarriage was a strongly built steel tube arrangement. The early aircraft used rubber shock cords, whilst later ones were fitted with bundles of coiled springs. The fuselage was made of a mixture of wood and steel tubes then covered in plywood and, in some areas, fabric. The cabin itself was fully enclosed, with sliding windows. The two pilots would sit either side of the cabin, behind two steering wheels. The aircraft's engine throttle controls were located in between the seats and arranged so that they could be operated by one or both pilots.

Type	Staaken RVI	Staaken RVI
Manufacturer	Flugzeugwerft, Staaken, Berlin	Flugzeugwerft, Staaken, Berlin
Engines	4 Mercedes DIVa, 260hp	4 Maybach Mb Iva, 245hp
Span	42.2m	42.2m
Length	22.1m	22.1m
Height	6.3m	6.3m
Wing area	332 sq m	332 sq m
Empty weight	7,680kg	7,921kg
Loaded weight	11,460kg	11,848kg
Wing loading	34.5kg/sq m	35.7kg/sq m
Maximum speed	130km/h	135km/h
Climb	3,000m in 55 minutes	3,000m in 43 minutes
Ceiling	3,800m in 150 minutes	4,230m in 146 minutes
Duration	7–8 hours	7–10 hours
Fuel	2,115 litres	3,000 litres
Defensive armament	Nose, dorsal, ventral and upper wing machine-guns	Nose, dorsal, ventral and upper wing machine-guns
Service	Western Front 1917–1918	Western Front 1917–1918

Initially the aircraft was fitted with a Ludolph gimbal-mounted floating compass, but a drum-type compass later replaced it. It was still somewhat unreliable and many of the aircraft were later fitted with two small drum compasses and even later a Bamberg repeater compass. The commander of the aircraft had a charting and a bearing compass. Other instruments and equipment fitted in the cabin included altimeters, a variometer (for measuring rate of climb), four tachometers, a pair of airspeed indicators, an engine temperature indicator, a fluid inclinometer and a clock.

There was also wireless sending and receiving equipment, powered by a Bosch petrol generator. When there was radio silence the generator provided heating for the flying suits and recharged the batteries for the lighting system. Two lamps were fitted behind the landing gear in order to provide a shadow on the ground to assist landing.

The commander of the aircraft moved into an observation post located in the nose of the aircraft during a bombing run. This was also fitted with gear to house a machine-gun. There were two machine-gun posts in the dorsal and a ventral one. Some of the aircraft also had machine-gun posts mounted on the upper wing. Officially, the aircraft was to carry three Lewis machine-guns.

Theoretically the aircraft could carry eighteen 100kg bombs, arranged in three rows of six, but the standard operational load was usually between 1,000 and 1,200kg, although on short flights it could carry 2,000kg. If it was carrying any 300kg or 100kg bombs, they would be carried externally.

The normal operational flight length was around seven hours, but with the fitting of additional fuel tanks this could be extended to ten hours. Probably the longest operational raid took place against Le Havre, when the RVIs involved flew 800km. Again theoretically, assuming a bomb load of 750kg and 3,200 litres of fuel, the aircraft could cover 900km.

The standard crew complement was seven: the commander (who also operated as the navigator), two pilots, two flight mechanics, a wireless operator and a fuel attendant. If the upper wings were fitted with machine-gun posts, a further two men would be added.

Of the eighteen RVIs built, eleven were destroyed during the war. The remainder stayed in service until the end of the war and after that several were converted to civilian work.

The Staaken RVII was developed as a result of lessons learned from the RIV. It had the same engines and drive systems, but had several notable differences. It no longer had upper wing machine-gun positions, its radiator positions were reversed, the undercarriage had eight wheels and the engineer's compartment had open cockpits. It was also just over 1m shorter.

The first RVII, R 14/15, was accepted on 26 June 1917 and entered service in July 1917, but unfortunately it crashed the following month. It left Berlin on 19 August 1917 and had reached an altitude of around 60m when its right wing dipped. It made a sharp starboard turn and seemed to be heading for a ravine covered in pine trees. It hit the hill and crashed into the ravine, killing six of the crew.

Type	Staaken RVII
Manufacturer	Flugzeugwerft, Staaken, Berlin
Engines	2 Mercedes DIII, 160hp
	4 Benz BZIV, 220hp
Span	42.2m
Length	22.1m

Height	6.8m
Wing area	332 sq m
Empty weight	8,923kg
Loaded weight	12,953kg
Wing loading	39.0kg/sq m
Maximum speed	130km/hour
Climb	3,000m in 50 minutes
Ceiling	3,850m
Duration	Unknown
Fuel	3,140 litres
Defensive armament	Unknown
Service	None

An improved version of the Staaken RVI was developed towards the end of 1917, called the Staaken RXIV, powered by four Daimler twelve cylinder 350hp engines, which proved to be highly unreliable. The first aircraft, the R 43/17, was almost ready in February 1918. It began its acceptance trials on 11 April, carrying a load of 4,020kg. The following day the connection rod broke in one of its rear engines. The Daimler engines were therefore replaced by four Bass and Selve 300hp ones. It was ready for a new test flight on 10 May, but these engines had problems with piston seizure. They were removed on the R43 and the new R44 and replaced with five Maybach high-compression 245hp engines. Owing to the extra weight of this aircraft an additional engine was needed in the nose section. This modification took two months to complete and the R43, R44 and R45 began their test flights between 3 and 10 July. The R44 was finally delivered in August and the R45 a month earlier. They were slightly different from the R43, as the engines directly drove their nacelle tractor propellers.

By this stage the Germans had perfected a parachute and were issuing them to all aircrews as soon as they became available. The RXIV carried a full complement. It had six machine-gun posts, two in the dorsal position, two in the ventral and one each on the upper wings. This was essential, as there were many more Allied night fighters at this stage of the war.

The R45 left Staaken, bound for Hanover, on 9 August 1918. The following day it headed for Morville, where it was to take part in a bombing raid against Le Havre on 15 September. On its return journey the crew received a wireless message telling them not to return to Morville as Allied aircraft were circling the airfield. The landing lights had been turned off so the crew attempted to land with ground crew using flashlights and flares. The aircraft missed the runway and its wings hit a water tank, a ladder and a house. It had narrowly missed a barracks in which sixty men were sleeping.

Meanwhile, the R43 and R44 had also been transferred to the Western Front. On the night of 10–11 August the British 151st Squadron, flying Sopwith Camels, shot down the R43 over Talmas. The entire crew was killed and the aircraft's bombs exploded on impact with the ground. On 11 February 1919, the British discovered the R44 on an abandoned airfield at Cologne. It had been totally stripped and very little else is known of its operational experiences.

Type	Staaken RXIV	Staaken RXIVa
Manufacturer	Zeppelin-Werke, Staaken, Berlin	Zeppelin-Werke, Staaken, Berlin
Engines	5 Maybach Mb Iva, 245hp	5 Mayback Mb Iva, 245hp
Span	42.2m	42.2m
Length	22.5m	22.5m
Height	6.3m	6.3m
Wing area	334 sq m	334 sq m
Empty weight	10,350kg	10,000kg
Loaded weight	14,450kg	14,250kg
Wing loading	Unknown	Unknown
Maximum speed	130km/h	135km/h
Climb	3,000m in 70 minutes	3,000m in 45 minutes
Ceiling	3,700m	4,500m
Duration	1,300m with 1,000kg of bombs	1,300m with 1,000kg of bombs
Fuel	1,150 litres	Unknown
Defensive armament	Dorsal, ventral and 2 upper wing machine-guns	Dorsal and ventral machine-guns
Service	Western Front August–November 1918	None

The RXIVa was to be an improved version of the RXIV. It was designed to have an improved payload, operating ceiling and rate of climb. Four of the aircraft were ordered, the R69–R72. The R69 was delivered on 19 October 1918 and did not see action, the R70 and R71 were possibly completed towards the end of 1918 or the beginning of 1919 and it is unclear whether or not the R72 was ever finished. Additional RXIVa aircraft had also been ordered, the R84–R86, but none of these was completed before the end of the war.

The Staaken RXV was in many ways identical to the RXIV. Its major difference was the lightening of the airframe to improve its performance. It was designed to carry six machine-guns and the first, the R46/17, had its maiden flight on 25 July 1918 and was delivered into service in August of the same year. The R47 was completed on 3 August and the R48 on 13 August and both were accepted on 1 September. It is possible that at least two of these three aircraft saw operational duties in the latter stages of the war.

Type	Staaken RXV	Staaken RXVI
Manufacturer	Zeppelin-Werke, Staaken, Berlin	Automobil & Aviatik, Leipzig-Heiterblick
Engines	5 Maybach Mb Iva, 245hp	2 Benz BZVI Pusher, 530hp 2 Benz BZIV Tractor, 220hp
Span	42.2m	42.2m
Length	22.5m	22.5m
Height	6.3m	6.5m
Wing area	334 sq m	340 sq m
Empty weight	Unknown	10,400kg
Loaded weight	Unknown	14,650kg
Wing loading	Unknown	Unknown
Maximum speed	Unknown	130km/hour
Climb	Unknown	Unknown
Ceiling	Unknown	3,710m in 76 minutes
Duration	Unknown	Unknown
Fuel	Unknown	Unknown
Defensive armament	Dorsal, ventral and 2 upper wing machine-guns	Nose, dorsal, ventral and 2 upper wing machine-guns
Service	Western Front late 1918	None

Three aircraft fitted with Benz 12 cylinder, V-block, 530hp engines, with the designation RXVI (AV-Aviatik) R49–R51, were developed by Aviatik. Problems with the engines meant that they had to be replaced by the smaller Benz 220hp versions. These aircraft differed little from the RVI, except that they had more streamlined nacelles. The R49 achieved an altitude of 4,300m and carried a bomb load of 4,250kg. It was due to be delivered in June 1918, but during one of its test flights it landed very heavily and its lower wings were badly damaged. It is unclear whether or not it was ever repaired.

The R50 was due to be completed in January 1919 and ready for its maiden flight the following month, but it was never completed as a bomber, and it entered into civilian service. The R51 was nearly finished by January 1919, but records indicate that it was never actually completed.

CHAPTER EIGHT

Night Attacks Start:
September–December 1917

For the Germans the change from daylight raids to night attacks was simple and necessary. The British defensive responses to the daylight attacks had become more effective, but the promised improvements to the Gotha bombers had not materialized. Initially the problem for the Germans was how to launch efficient and accurate attacks on key targets, but this was soon solved by simply striking at Britain without too much regard to a particular target. It was seen as sufficient to represent a constant threat rather than an effective pinpoint targeting tool.

As far as the British were concerned, the switch to night attacks presented a serious new set of problems. Whilst they had been able to deal with the threat of Zeppelins, which were much larger, slower-moving and easier to track, smaller and faster-moving aircraft were quite a new challenge.

The first move in the new phase of operations took place on the night of 3/4 September 1917. The England Squadron (*Kagohl* 3) launched five Gothas, but one soon turned back with engine problems. The target was Chatham and the night was virtually perfect for a bombing raid on the dockyard complex. Despite this, the targeting was poor and the most significant contribution they made to the German effort was killing 130 naval recruits whose dormitory, a converted drill hall, was hit by two bombs.

The first Gotha was spotted over Westgate at 2235 and the remaining three arrived at approximately 2300. They were in position to bring their bombs to bear on the Chatham naval base at around 2310. Owing to a breakdown in communications, Chatham did not receive warning of the attack but nonetheless sixteen defensive sorties were mounted. Of these around eleven aircraft were already aloft on various training exercises and sorties; just five were actually scrambled. Around forty-six bombs fell on the Chatham area, although only half hit the objective, the rest either falling into the sea or hitting Sheerness or Margate. Around 2,900lb of bombs were dropped that night.

Particularly significant was the scrambling of three Sopwith Camels of No. 44 Squadron, based at Hainault, flown by Captain C. J. Q. Brand, Second Lieutenant C. C. Banks and Captain G. W. M. Green (Squadron Commander). Although none of them spotted any of the Gothas, it did at least prove that the Sopwith Camel, up until that point a day fighter, could successfully take off, fly and land at night.

The total casualties inflicted by just four Gothas that night was 132 killed, ninety-six injured and slightly less than £4,000 worth of damage was caused.

The apparent lack of response to this raid was most encouraging for the Germans. British fighters had not intercepted them, nor had they been unduly concerned with the level of anti-aircraft fire. With slightly better regard to the targeting and the bombing runs, the Germans were now certain that they could inflict significant casualties and material damage by launching Gotha strikes during the night.

They were emboldened to the extent that they launched a larger attack on 4/5 September. It was initially anticipated that eleven Gothas would take part, with London as the target. The first aircraft took off from base at around 2030 and at five-minute intervals ten more followed. Two were forced to turn round with engine problems and the rest, became scattered, one of the major problems of night flying, and approached the British coast between 2220 and 0010, at points as far a field as Dover and Orford Ness. This was a problem for the Germans, but it did in fact work in their favour. Each of the aircraft triggered off an air-raid warning and at one point the British believed that the Germans had launched around twenty-six bombers in seven different formations. They were reported as having been seen in a wide variety of different areas and this confusion continued until the last ones disappeared via Deal at 0215.

Five aircraft managed to regroup and launch an attack on London between 2320 and 0050. The rest struck targets as far a field at Aldeburgh in Suffolk, Margate and Dover. As a result of the confusion amongst the British defences they proved to be somewhat elusive. Eighteen defensive sorties were launched by No. 37 Squadron out of Goldhanger and Stow Maries, No. 39 Squadron out of North Weald, Green and his Sopwith Camels from No. 44 Squadron, Hainault and No. 50 Squadron from Bekesbourne and Detling.

One of the Gothas was targeted somewhere over Faversham at a height of just under 6,500ft by Second Lieutenant F. A. D. Grace and Second Lieutenant G. Murray. They were flying the same FK8 in which they had claimed a Gotha kill on 7 July. At first they were unsure of the identity of the aircraft they were approaching; it did not respond to a recognition challenge, nor to a Very signal, so Murray opened fire. He managed to squeeze off a few shots before it disappeared.

Meanwhile, at some point over the Thames Estuary, Second Lieutenant S. Armstrong, flying a BE2E, spotted two Gothas at a height of around 6,000ft. He stalked them for a while and then emptied a whole drum at one of them, but it managed to elude him.

Once again Green and his Sopwith Camel pilots chased around, hoping to encounter a Gotha, but again they drew a blank. There was, however, one confirmed kill of the night. A Gotha passed over an anti-aircraft position at Borstal, near Rochester, and was illuminated by the battery's searchlight at around 2330. The guns began firing at it and according to Second Lieutenant Charles Cendrew, who was in command of the unit, scored a direct hit, and it began to dive. It was believed that it had gone down in the River Medway, but subsequent searches revealed nothing. It may well have escaped and crashed out to sea, as an anti-aircraft battery on the Isle of Sheppey claimed that they saw a German bomber flying low with misfiring engines, and that it crashed out to sea near Eastchurch. The Germans had managed to inflict over £46,000 worth of damage and had claimed nineteen victims, with a further seventy-one injured.

The next major development in the defence against the night attacks was balloon barrages. These were steel wire curtains that were positioned in such a way as to intersect the probable flight paths of the Gotha bombers as they came in towards their targets. The proposal was to create a series of these aprons, held aloft by three balloons moored 500 yards apart. These were linked together by cables, from which, at 25 yard intervals, 1,000ft long steel wires were hung. It was initially proposed that the balloons be positioned at 7,000ft, later this would be amended to 9,500ft. A trial was carried out on 21 September 1917, but it ended in a dreadful accident. Air Mechanic W. J. Pegge, was aloft and working on the rigging when a sudden gust of wind pitched him away from the balloon to fall 1,000ft to the ground.

The first ten balloon aprons became operational during the early part of October 1917. It had been proposed that 20 would be needed to cover the outskirts of London, but only these first ten were fully operational by June 1918.

Judging by the effectiveness of the night raids, the anti-aircraft batteries also needed to be reorganized. Each one was given an assigned area to cover and British aircraft were ordered to stay out of these zones.

A major night-bombing offensive was launched, beginning on 24/25 September, with five raids over the next seven nights against both London and the south-east of England. The first was intended to hit two different targets; the primary one was London once more and the bombers would carry that out, whilst the Zeppelins struck the Midlands and the North-east.

The Gothas began arriving off the British coastline from about 1903; the majority of them had made landfall shortly after 2013. There were to have been sixteen in the raid but three returned to base with mechanical and engine problems. Once again navigation problems caused them to cross the British coast over an area between Dover and Orford Ness. Some had also taken considerably longer to make the sea crossing. Three bombers struck London between 2005 and 2030, whilst another six, beginning at 1915 and ending at 2130, hit Dover. At least four made attacks on various targets such as the Isle of Sheppey, West Malling, Chatham, Tilbury and Southend. In response the RFC launched thirty sorties, including aircraft from Nos. 37, 39, 40, 50 and 78 Squadrons, in addition to three sorties by the Experimental Station at Orford Ness. The Gothas managed to destroy nearly £31,000 worth of materials, killed twenty-one people and injured seventy.

Although the night was unsuccessful for the defending aircraft, one major historical event took place: the first fighter sortie to be flown out of Biggin Hill. Claiming what would be a momentous first was Second Lieutenant Norman Hugh Auret, of D Flight, No. 39 Squadron. His aircraft was a BE12A and he took off at 2020, returning to base at 2210.

Meanwhile, to the north, the German navy had pulled out all the stops to launch the maximum number of Zeppelins. Included in the raid were the L35, L41, L42, L44, L46, L47, L50, L51, L53 and L55. The L52 was to have joined them on this attack but had to return to base. The Zeppelins began arriving off the coast of Britain about 150 minutes after the last of the Gothas had crossed the coastline on their way home. There is confusion as to actually how many of the ten Zeppelins were involved in the attack, but in all probability it was five: the L35, L41, L46, L53, L55. They made landfall at around 2400 at points between King's Lynn and Bridlington, the last crossing the coast at 0125. There was strong wind that night, coupled with patchy cloud and the fact that the Zeppelins were flying in excess of 16,000ft inhibited their navigational accuracy. It seems that Rotherham, Hull and Skinningrove were all hit by the L35, L41 and L55. The L46 and L53 had intended to hit British airfields in Lincolnshire, but they entirely missed their targets. Indeed, the whole group managed to injure just three people and cause just over £2,200 worth of damage. In response the RNAS and the RFC launched thirty-six sorties.

It was a particularly frustrating night; only three of the British aircraft even saw the Zeppelins. The most spectacular of the interceptions was by Second Lieutenant William Wallace Cook of B Flight, No. 76 Squadron, flying his BE2E out of Helperby. He lifted off at 0100 and headed north-east, seeing the L55 illuminated by searchlights to the south of Middlesborough. He took until 0145 to reach the area, flying at a height of 12,000ft. The Zeppelin was by this time at around 16,000ft, well out of the range of the anti-aircraft fire. Cook attempted to climb, but lost sight of the airship, so he headed back towards his assigned patrol line. He was now at 14,000ft and close to Beverley, and above him at around 16,000ft was the L41, also illuminated by searchlights. Unfortunately it then eluded the searchlights and Cook, who now headed off to see if he could find any of the other reported Zeppelins. At around 10 miles from Bridlington he spotted another Zeppelin, most probably the L42, again at a height of 16,000ft. His own aircraft had reached its ceiling of around 14,500ft, but Cook prepared to engage the Zeppelin. He began firing at around 800 yards, emptying four drums of ammunition into its rear, but it simply climbed away and out of range. When it returned home it was discovered that there were at least two holes in one of the gas cells.

By now Cook had been aloft for nearly four hours and he was 60 miles out to sea and flying into heavy winds. It was an hour and fifteen minutes before he could see the coastline once more, by which time there was virtually no petrol left in his tanks. He was forced to land at Flamborough. For his efforts that night the New Zealander was awarded the MC.

The second British pilot to spot the Zeppelins that night was Captain M. B. Barber, flying a BE2E of A Flight, No. 38 Squadron, Leadenham. He left base at 0050 and chased Zeppelins across Lincolnshire by following the fall of their bombs. At around 0300 he spotted the L41 to the north, but he could not catch it and eventually landed at Elsham at 0410.

Shortly afterwards Captain C. W. Mackey, who had left No. 75 Squadron's Elmswell airfield at 0230 in a BE12, saw a Zeppelin just to the north-east of the airfield at around 0320. He chased it for a while and after about fifteen minutes lost sight of it near Bungay. In all probability this was the L44.

There were several problems for some of the British aircraft that night. Second Lieutenant H. J. Thornton and Second Lieutenant C. A. Moore took off from Seaton Carew in an FE2D of No. 36 Squadron at 0150. It is believed that they chased a Zeppelin out to sea, failed to catch it and then ran out of petrol and were lost somewhere off the coast. No. 33 Squadron's C Flight had scrambled three aircraft, one of which was an FE2D piloted by Second Lieutenant C. Pinnock and Lieutenant J. A. Menzies. They had left Elsham at 2340 and on their return at around 0140 hit trees near the airfield. Menzies, a Canadian observer, was killed.

Second Lieutenant C. R. Gaffney, flying a BE12 of C Flight, No. 38 Squadron, Stamford, lifted off at 0047. His last recollections were struggling to get the aircraft up to 9,600ft. He encountered cloud at that height and throttled back, but must have passed out, probably through lack of oxygen or the freezing temperature. His next recollection was being pulled out of the wreck of his aircraft in a field close to the air base.

On the night of 25/26 September, fifteen Gothas were launched; once again the primary target was London. One was forced to turn back and the remaining fourteen crossed the British coast between Dover and Foulness at various times from 1900 to 1945. Only three actually attacked the capital, however, between 1955 and 2010. The remaining eleven concentrated on the stretch of coast from Margate to Folkestone. In response twenty sorties were launched, including the RNAS, Manston (two aircraft), No. 37 Squadron, Goldhanger (two), No. 37 Squadron, Stow Maries (two), No. 39 Squadron, North Weald (four), No. 39 Squadron Biggin Hill (two), No. 44 Squadron, Hainault (three), No. 50 Squadron, Detling (one) and No. 78 Squadron, Suttons Farm (four).

Although there were fourteen Gothas abroad that night the only sighting was claimed by Captain Douglas J. Bell and Second Lieutenant George G. Williams, flying a Sopwith $1^1/_2$ Strutter from No. 78 Squadron's Sutton Farm airfield. They were flying at a height of around 9,400ft to the south of Brentford at around 2015 when they came under fire from an aircraft that was heading east. Bell and Williams challenged it and it failed to respond so they chased it for around fifteen minutes, firing whenever they were in range. Eventually the Gotha, which was almost certainly one of the three that had attacked the capital, slipped away. Their encounter was witnessed by Second Lieutenant L. Taylor in a BE2E, operating as a wireless tracker from No. 39 Squadron, North Weald.

The Germans now planned one of their largest raids, once again targeted on London. Twenty-five Gothas, accompanied for the first time by two Giants, were to be launched against the city. The weather on the night of 28/29 September conspired against them, however. The first Gotha turned back just as it reached the North Sea with engine problems. Over the course of their flight over the sea a further fifteen turned back. Consequently, only three Gothas and two Giants were actually involved in this raid.

A Giant probably struck Ipswich and Harwich at around 2100, and a Gotha, believing it had dropped its bombs on central London, in fact hit Billericay and Meopham. The other aircraft hit a variety of targets in Essex and Kent, although many of its bombs actually fell into the sea. The major attack that night was an abject failure; there was not a single British casualty and they managed to inflict only £129 of damage.

Despite the poor weather, the RFC launched twenty-three sorties, but none of the aircraft spotted the Gothas or the Giants. The ground conditions were extremely poor and several of the aircraft were forced to land at other airfields or abandon their search pattern entirely.

The weather had done more damage to the Germans than the British had been able to do for many weeks. Three Gothas had been lost, but no wreckage was found, despite the fact that HMS *Marshal Ney* anchored off Ramsgate claimed to have shot down one, as did anti-aircraft batteries based at Deal and the Isle of Sheppey. A further six were badly damaged when they tried to land.

Despite this poor showing and the loss of aircraft, the Germans launched another London-focused attack on the night of 29/30 September. This time they mustered seven Gothas, although only three of them were positively identified as having made attacks during the night. Three Giants, the R25, R26 and R39, supported them this time. This attack group represented the sum total of the German bomber strength at that time.

Once again the weather did not favour either the attackers or the defenders. The Germans came in over the British coast between Deal and Foulness at various times between 1955 and 2240. The appearance of the Giants threw ground observers into confusion. Their size made the observers mistake them for formations of Gothas or even Zeppelins. As a result, they believed that they were being attacked by up to twenty aircraft, of which at least fourteen were heading for London. The aircraft that did attack London began dropping bombs at 2110 and ceased at 2145. In all probability there were just four involved, although the Germans suggested that it was just the R39, supported by two Gothas. The remainder hit Sheerness and several other targets in Kent, with more success: forty people were killed, eighty-seven injured and over £23,000 worth of damage was caused.

The British response was hampered by fog, but nonetheless thirty-three defensive sorties were launched. There were two aircraft aloft at the time the first German bombers appeared. These were an RNAS Manston BE2C piloted by Squadron Commander C. H. Butler and a Martinsyde F1 piloted by Captain L. J. Wackett and Second Lieutenant H. H. Hussey out of the Experimental Station at Orford Ness. The majority of the aircraft that lifted off that night from North Weald, Biggin Hill, Hainault, Bekesbourne, Detling and Suttons Farm could only sustain very short flights due to the fog, but at least three of the pilots claimed to have spotted the raiders.

On the Germans' return flight they were intercepted by aircraft of No. 7/7A Squadron, RNAS Coudekerque in Handley Page aircraft especially armed with five Lewis guns, which were undertaking an anti-Gotha patrol at a height of 10,000ft, to the north of Ostend. Three of the returning German raiders were spotted and two were engaged. The first eluded the Handley Pages, but the second was attacked at close range somewhere between Neuport and Ostend. The British aircraft managed to empty three drums into it. At first it appeared that the Gotha (GIV/602/16) would crash into the sea but in fact it crash landed on Dutch soil at Sas Van Gent: all but one of the crew members escaped intact; the remaining man was severely wounded.

Encountering these converted Handley Page bombers off the Belgian coast must have come as a considerable shock to the Germans. Certainly their combined firepower, with each aircraft sporting five Lewis guns, gave them considerable punch. Unfortunately, the British authorities did not approve of using Handley Pages in this way and henceforth they were relegated back to the role of a bomber.

One other unconfirmed incident took place over Dover that night. A German aircraft was pinpointed by one of the searchlights and it was clear it had been hit, probably by anti-aircraft fire. The crew of the searchlight claimed to have seen it spin out of control and crash into the sea some 2 miles out at around 2140.

On the night of 30 September/1 October the Germans launched eleven Gothas and one single-engine unidentified aircraft. Only ten of the Gothas actually crossed the coast at various points between Dover and Clacton from 1845 to around 2015. It was a fairly short raid and all had left British air space by 2145.

Once again the British ground observers misinterpreted the flight paths and numbers of German aircraft involved. At one point it was believed that two groups consisting of twenty-five aircraft in total, were inbound. Other reports suggested that there were three formations, each consisting of nine aircraft, heading for different targets across Britain. However just six managed to make it as far as London itself, and they began their bombing runs at 1940. They had turned and were heading home by 2045.

The remaining Gothas attacked Dover, Chatham, Margate and scattered targets throughout Essex. Dover was also the target of the single-engined aircraft, which managed to drop four 55lb bombs there.

The British launched thirty-seven sorties, involving RNAS Manston, No. 37 Squadron (Goldhanger and Stow Maries), No. 39 Squadron (North Weald and Biggin Hill), No. 44 Squadron (Hainault), No. 50 Squadron (Bekesbourne and Detling), No. 78 Squadron (Suttons Farm) and the Experimental Station at Orford Ness. The British fighters were informed to prepare to lift off at 1840 and the first aircraft were airborne by 1855. Five of the sorties were cancelled because of engine problems.

The most successful interception took place over Lambourne. Captain William H. Haynes (No. 44 Squadron, Hainault, in a Sopwith Camel) encountered a Gotha at 6,000ft and fired 300 rounds at it at a range of 100 yards before losing sight of it. Meanwhile, over Gravesend, Captain F. Billing, accompanied by Aircraftman E. Cooper (No. 78 Squadron, Suttons Farm, in a Sopwith 1^1/$_2$ Strutter) attacked a Gotha at around 10,500ft. Unfortunately it outpaced them after they had managed to fire just a handful of shots at it.

Once again British aircraft came under fire from their own anti-aircraft guns. One incident took place over Dover at 2010. However one of the Dover guns reported having shot down a Gotha and although the Germans never confirmed this, aircraft wreckage was spotted near the Varne Lightship. In total the eleven German aircraft managed to inflict £21,482 worth of damage, claim fourteen lives and injure thirty-eight people.

The Gothas were back once again on 1/2 October. This time eighteen of them lifted off from base, but six turned round for various reasons. The majority of the remainder came in between Ramsgate and the Blackwater River between 1850 and 2050. Six made for London and attacked between 2000 and 2100. The majority of the others could not find the capital in the mist, and subsequently bombed Suffolk, Essex and Kent. There is an unconfirmed report that a Giant was supposed to have joined them on this raid, but it turned back after it realized that the British had heard their wireless transmissions via a listening station.

There were nineteen sorties launched that night, consisting of patrols from Nos. 37, 39, 44 and 78 Squadrons. A Sopwith Camel, flown by Captain W. H. Haynes, made a positive sighting of a Gotha flying at a height of 12,000ft to the south-east of Epping but could not close with it.

The night also saw a major historical event. An experimental sound locator had been positioned at Fan Bay, near Dover, and it picked up incoming German aircraft between 12 and 15 miles out to sea. The results of the use of the device were mixed and they mistakenly reported that the German aircraft were heading towards London via Folkestone, but in all probability what they had heard was gunfire from the continent in the vicinity of Boulogne.

Altogether the twelve Gothas managed to kill twelve people, injure forty-two and cause £45,570 worth of damage.

The night of 19/20 October saw the return of the German navy Zeppelins: the L41, L44, L45, L46, L47, L49, L50, L52, L53, L54 and L55. No fewer than seventy-eight RNAS and RFC sorties were launched in response. The Germans had intended to hit industrial targets in northern England but it was an absolutely disastrous night for them. Not only was their impact comparatively small, but they lost five of their vessels.

The first problem was the weather: two of the airships did not even leave their sheds because of cross winds. Eleven, however, did make it and began leaving their bases at 1115, the last departing at 1254. The initial plan was to gather off Flamborough Head at a height of 16,000–20,000ft. As it was, the north-westerly winds prevented this and the main force of ten crept across the British coast between Happisburgh and the Humber River from 1845, with the last crossing at 2015. The eleventh, the L46, flying at a higher altitude, was severely affected by the wind and did not reach the British coast until 2220.

The heavy winds caused the Germans huge navigational problems; they were so lost that the L41 bombed the outskirts of Birmingham, believing it was Manchester. The rest hit predominantly open countryside around Bedford, Leighton Buzzard and Northampton. The L45 strayed even further south and found itself over London, where it dropped a 660lb bomb on Piccadilly Circus, killing thirty-three and injuring fifty.

The L54 only managed to penetrate as far as Ipswich, where it dropped several bombs and returned home at 0840. The prevailing winds swept four of the Zeppelins into France. The L44 was shot down by anti-aircraft guns in France, the L45 crashed to the ground close to Sisteron and the L49 at Bourbonne-Les-Bains. The L50 crashed near Dommartin; it hit the ground with such ferocity that the forward cabin was broken off and then the ship rose again and drifted out to sea with four men still trapped onboard. The L55, which was heading for Ahlhorn, actually crash-landed at Tiefenort, 200 miles from base. Those airships that did make it home, apart from the L54, arrived back at base perilously close to being out of fuel between 1200 and 1405.

The British became aware of the impending attack at 1600 hours and the squadrons made ready to scramble. Despite the fact that seventy-eight sorties were launched, however, only six British aircraft actually spotted the German raiders. The weather conditions did not favour an effective response. There were seven crash landings, one fatal crash, four premature returns with engine problems and no less than twelve forced landings.

At around 2200 Lieutenant G. H. Harrison, flying an FE2B of C flight No. 38 Squadron, Stamford, who had lifted off at 2125, was flying at a height of 13,500ft close to Leicester. He encountered a Zeppelin, probably the L45, flying at a height of 15,500ft. Harrison began to climb and fired three bursts of machine-gun fire into the tail before his gun jammed. He peeled away and tried to deal with the blockage. When he returned home his FE2B had several holes in the wing, evidence of return fire from the Zeppelin.

Lieutenant C. J. Chabot lifted off in a BE2E at 2030 from No. 39 Squadron, North Weald. At around 2215 he saw bombs dropping close to Waltham Abbey whilst he was flying at a height of around 12,000ft. He spotted the L52 and the L44, or L53, at a height of up to 16,000ft, heading east. He desperately tried to climb and overtake them, but his aircraft stalled. He realized that he had no chance of catching the Zeppelins and was forced to return to base at 2316.

Meanwhile, some time after 2300, Chabot's squadron colleague, Second Lieutenant Thomas B. Pritchard, was in the North Weald area when he spotted the L45 heading south, aiming for London and was about 15 miles from his position. It was flying at a height of around 15,000ft and it took him until 0010, somewhere over Chatham, to get within firing range. By this time he had climbed to nearly 13,000ft but nonetheless he fired at the Zeppelin and continued to follow it across Kent until he began to lose sight of it at 0100. By this time he was desperately short of fuel and began to drop. At 600ft he dropped a parachute flare and discovered to his horror that he was over the sea. Luckily he found land but just as he was coming in a searchlight blinded him. His BE2E stalled as it came into land at Hooe, close to Becks Hill and was badly damaged, but he walked away with a cut over his eye and concussion. Soon afterwards he was awarded the MC, but he died on 21 November 1917 as the result of injuries from a flying accident.

There was another close run thing to the north, involving RNAS pilot Clarence S. Nunn. He had lifted off at 2256 in a BE2C out of Burgh Castle. At 2330 he had reached a point around 10 miles north of Great Yarmouth and it was here he spotted the L54, flying at 5,000ft. Nunn had the advantage of altitude, being at 8,800ft. He dived to attack but the BE2C's poor performance foiled his attempt. His engine began misfiring and then cut out when he was 3,500ft above the coastline. He was forced to crash land at 0004.

Lieutenant H. C. Calvey and Lieutenant R. A. Varley lifted off from Leadenham at 0040 as part of A Flight, No. 38 Squadron. They saw Zeppelins close to Grantham but lost them before they could close. Calvey's aircraft was experiencing problems and he made an emergency landing at Swinstead then lifted off, heading back for base. He ran out of fuel, however, and landed in a turnip field at Great Gonerby, 3 miles to the north of Grantham.

There was yet another crash that night, this time fatal. Second Lieutenant H. P. Solomon of No. 33 Squadron's Headquarters Flight, based at Gainsborough, took off at 1955 accompanied by Second Lieutenant H. Preston. He managed to take off successfully enough, but when he had reached 200ft the FE2B lurched to the right and hit the ground, bursting into flames. Solomon was killed but Preston was thrown clear of the wreckage.

There were more problems to come for the British that night. Lieutenant E. J. Stockman, in a BE12A of No. 39 Squadron, Biggin Hill, was aloft for just two minutes when his aircraft suffered from engine failure and he crashed straight back down onto the airfield. A similar incident occurred to Flight Sub-Lieutenant C. V. Halford Thompson. He took off in a BE2C from RNAS Bacton at 2107 but at 2230 he tried to land at RNAS Holt and crashed. He walked free, but the aircraft was written off.

Poor weather conditions on the night of 29/30 October prevented the Germans from launching a heavy bombing raid on London. As a result, just three Gothas were despatched, planning to attack coastal towns on the south-east coast. In the event only one of the bombers made the attack, dropping eight bombs on Burnham and Southend, in the belief that the target was Sheerness. The other two chose to attack Calais instead of the British Isles. The RFC launched only seven defensive sorties, largely becasue there was not only thick cloud that night but also very strong winds.

The night would have favoured the Gothas considerably as visibility from 2,000 to 6,000ft was very poor due to the thick cloud cover, and most of the airfields to the south of London were unable to launch any aircraft at all. Nonetheless, the alert was sounded at around 2151 and aircraft began lifting off from around 2220. There were only two squadrons involved that night, No. 37 Squadron at Goldhanger and Stow Maries and No. 39 Squadron North Weald. An additional sortie was launched from Rochford, an unrecorded aircraft of No. 198 (T) Squadron. The solitary Gotha did absolutely no damage and it was never spotted by any of the British aircraft, many of which were aloft for barely half an hour.

An unknown number of raiders, probably just two, targeted Dover on the night of 30/31 October. They were seen to the east of Dover at approximately 0430. It is highly unlikely that these were Gotha bombers; they were probably seaplanes on a hit-and-run mission. They dropped seven bombs on the airfield of RFC Swingate Down and four on Dover Harbour. No British defensive sorties were launched and the raiders did just £2 worth of damage, but they received the hot attention of anti-aircraft batteries around the Dover area.

A far more serious attack took place on 31 October/1 November. This time the Germans proposed to drop a new incendiary bomb on London. They launched twenty-two Gotha bombers, the first of whom was seen over Deal at 2237. Others came in over Foulness and the last was spotted coming in over Canvey Island at 0115. The Germans did not press home their attack on London and according to German accounts only ten of the Gothas actually dropped bombs on the city. They sought alternative targets, largely because the wind had driven them to the north and there was patchy cloud, which was causing them navigational difficulties.

Despite the size of the raid just ten people were killed and twenty-two were injured, and £22,882 worth of damage was inflicted.

British aircraft were given orders to stand by at 2238, and for the next five hours a total of fifty defensive sorties were flown. The RNAS scrambled two aircraft that night, both Sopwith $1^1/_2$ Strutters, one from Eastchurch and the other from Manston. RFC No. 37 Squadron was active in greater numbers, scrambling six aircraft from their two bases at Goldhanger and Stow Maries. No. 39 Squadron at North Weald and Biggin Hill scrambled eight aircraft, No. 44 Squadron, Hainault, with their Sopwith Camels, thirteen, No. 50 Squadron, out of Bekesbourne and Detling, nine and No. 78 Squadron, in Sopwith $1^1/_2$ Strutters from Suttons Farm, nine.

Probably the first sighting of the night was by a Sopwith $1^1/_2$ Strutter out of Eastchurch. The crew members are unknown, but they scrambled at 2325 and engaged one or two Gothas shortly after they had reached operational height.

Second Lieutenant H. T. W. Oswell, a wireless tracker lifted off at 2250 in a BE12 from No. 50 Squadron's Bekesbourne airfield. He saw a Gotha to the north-west of Dover, flying at a height of 11,500ft, but was only able to keep it in sight for around thirty seconds, owing to the clouds. Lieutenant L. Lucas, who was fulfilling a similar role with the same squadron, spotted two more over the Thames Estuary, heading in the general direction of London. Lieutenant N. H. Dimmock of No. 78 Squadron was over Joyce Green at a height of 8,500ft when he saw a Gotha flying at 8,000ft. He too lost it in the clouds.

Meanwhile, the RNAS Eastchurch Sopwith $1^1/_2$ Strutter spotted a Gotha between Southend and Sheerness at 2350. They were able to get within firing range and the observer emptied a drum of ammunition at the target. They then lost sight of it, but soon afterwards they saw five Gothas near Whitstable and again they closed to engage and received return fire.

At around 0025 part of the 2nd Mobile Anti-aircraft Brigade at Ightham in Kent heard a Gotha flying close by. It was brought under heavy fire. They believed that they had hit it, but daylight revealed just some copper tubing and machinery which were later identified as being part of the fuel system. It was presumed that the aircraft's main fuel system had been hit and that they had been able to switch over to an emergency supply just in time. The anti-aircraft unit may have been able to claim a belated kill as this may have been one of the five Gothas that crashed on landing when they returned home.

The remainder of November was quiet period; the Germans did not launch any aircraft or Zeppelin attacks, owing to atrocious weather. But they returned with a vengeance on the night of 5/6 December and once again they determined to subject London to their new incendiary weapons. Having been known up until this point as *Kagohl* 3, the squadron was now renamed *Bombengeschwader OHL* or *Bogohl* 3.

Nineteen Gothas and two Giants were mustered for this next attempt. Fairly early on in the mission three of the Gothas returned home with engine problems, but the rest pressed on. The majority of the raiders crossed at various points between Walmer and the North Foreland between 0200 and 0430. In all probability some of them crossed to the north of the Thames, but the numbers are unsubstantiated. Despite the fact that the primary target was London, it was in fact Kent that took the brunt of the raid. Dover, Margate, Ramsgate, Sheerness and Whitstable were all targeted, with the Giants concentrating on Dover and Sheerness. Around six Gothas hit London, dropping their bombs at various points between 0430 and 0540. More than three-quarters of the ordnance they were carrying was incendiary bombs. Although the casualties during the raid were comparatively low, with eight killed and twenty-eight injured, the damage caused was considerable. Just over £103,000 worth of damage was inflicted, over £92,000 of which was in London.

The RFC launched thirty-four sorties that night, with contributions from Nos. 37, 39, 44, 50 and 78 Squadrons. Most of the British aircraft were given the order to stand by at 0200 but there were relatively few sightings. Lieutenant A. F. Barker, in a Sopwith $1^1/_2$ Strutter of No. 78 Squadron, Suttons Farm, encountered an aircraft at 14,000ft but it may well have been British.

At the time the British knew very little about the new Giants but intelligence was beginning to seep through. At 0139 a wireless listening post at RNAS Grain picked up transmissions from a German aircraft, and several ground observers and anti-aircraft batteries reported that some of the German aircraft were coming in far lower than usual. This was beginning to help put flesh on the suspicions that the Germans were using newer and larger bombers.

There was one major success for anti-aircraft guns that night. Gotha GV/906/16 came in over the North Foreland at 0340 and headed up the Thames Estuary. It received a direct hit that shattered a propeller when it was over Canvey Island at 0420. The bomber immediately jettisoned its bombs but it was still losing height so it had no option but to make a forced landing on a British airfield. Quite by luck the crew managed to fire off British recognition signals as it came into land, avoiding being shot out of the sky by the anti-aircraft guns. The Gotha hit a tree and crashed onto a golf course at 0445. Whether by accident or design, the crew, who had got out of the wreck unscathed, fired the aircraft.

There was a second major success that night, once again by anti-aircraft fire. A Gotha was hit over London at 0500 and the shrapnel from the burst wrecked the port radiator, causing the engine to overheat. The crew could not prevent the engine from catching fire and they were forced to make an emergency landing in a field at Sturry, near Canterbury. They managed to destroy most of their instrumentation and jettison equipment, which was later recovered from a gravel pit. The aircraft came down in the field and the crew fired it before surrendering to a special constable who just happened to be the local vicar. The most probable reason for this aircraft's demise was that it had been hit by an anti-aircraft unit at Herne Bay and also by the defence battery at Bekesbourne. It was probably already in trouble when it received its final and fatal hit over London.

There was another lull in the bomber offensive, but it regained its ferocity on the night of 18/19 December. One of the major reasons for the lull had been the fact that the squadron had lost their driving force and commanding officer, Kleine. He was shot down and killed during an attack against Allied troops close to Ypres on 12 December. *Oberleutnant* Richard Walter replaced him.

The fresh attack, again targeting London, involved fifteen Gothas and one Giant. For various reasons two of the Gothas turned back and took no part in the raid. The other thirteen Gothas crossed the British coast between Ramsgate and the Blackwater River at various times between 1800 and 1915. The vast majority of them attacked targets around Canterbury and Margate, but six made it as far as London and carried out their bombing runs between 1910 and 2030.

The Giant, the R12, crossed just to the north of the River Crouch at 2020 and dropped heavy bombs and incendiaries on London at approximately 2110. It was heading back across the coastline by 2200.

Although casualties were mercifully low, with fourteen killed and eighty-three injured, the bombers had managed to inflict slightly less than £239,000 worth of damage.

The RFC launched forty-seven sorties that night, with Nos. 37, 39, 44, 50, 61 and 68 Squadrons all involved. A notable and well-documented kill was claimed by the commanding officer of No. 44 Squadron, Hainault, Captain G. W. Murlis Green. He lifted off in his Sopwith Camel at 1843. At 1915, when he was at an altitude of 10,000ft over Goodmayes, he spotted a Gotha illuminated by searchlights. He closed to within 30 yards but found to his horror that his starboard Lewis gun had frozen. Just then the Gotha began dropping its bombs, so he banked away to avoid them, seeing them fall on Bermondsey at 1925. He had been temporarily blinded by his own gun flashes, but managed to keep the Gotha in sight and made two further attacks, each time losing his night vision because of the gun flashes and the ever- present searchlight. He came around to make a fourth attack, firing another sixty bullets at the Gotha. This time the enemy tried to dive away and Murlis Green found his Sopwith Camel caught in the slipstream. He must have hit the Gotha fairly hard as it was barely over the River Thames when its starboard engine burst into flames. It began to lose height and by the time it was 10 miles out to sea it had already fallen to 3,000ft. The pilot, Lieutenant Friedrich Ketelsen, decided that he had to turn around and try to land. In fact he ditched just off Dover at 2100. Ketelsen himself was drowned and the crew of the armed trawler *Highlander* captured the navigator and gunner. The *Highlander* tried to tow the wreckage of the Gotha back to the British coast, but it began to break up and then exploded. In all likelihood one of the bombs had struck an obstacle.

For his actions that night Murlis Green, who already had an MC, was awarded a Bar.

Other Gothas had close shaves that night. Captain G. H. Hackwill, also of Murlis Green's squadron, took off at 1843 and encountered a Gotha somewhere over Woodford at a height of 10,300ft. It was around 2005 and he came in to attack, only to be caught in its slipstream. He managed to recover and fired a short burst at the bomber before it escaped.

Anti-aircraft guns must have also inflicted some damage. Indeed, both Folkestone and Wrotham claimed kills or close hits. The Germans lost two of their Gothas when they burst into flames after landing and five others were damaged in forced landings, possibly as a result of being hit over the British Isles.

The last raid of the year is poorly recorded and it is not known exactly how many Gothas were involved. What is certain, however, is that two Giants were despatched. The attack targeted coastal towns in the south-east on the night of 22/23 December. It is probable that a considerable number of Gothas were earmarked for the attack, but poor weather over the North Sea forced many of them to turn back. What is clear is that one Gotha was seen approaching Westgate at 1745. Ground observers reported it as being a British flying boat so no alert was sounded and it was only positively identified as a German aircraft when it passed over the anti-aircraft battery at Hengrove.

As it was, it was already in serious trouble. Its starboard engine had malfunctioned and then stopped, and the whole aircraft was vibrating. Just before it reached the coast it jettisoned its bombs and made a forced landing to the south of Margate at Hartsdown Farm. The crew fired the aircraft and surrendered to a group of local policemen who had arrived on the scene in a taxi.

As for the two Giants, the R12 and R39, they were seen off the North Foreland at around 2130. Later they reported that they had bombed British vessels in the Thames Estuary, but in fact the bombs had fallen harmlessly into the sea near Sandwich and Ramsgate.

There were eighteen defensive sorties launched that night, by Nos. 37, 39, 44 and 78 Squadrons. None of the aircraft made any visual contact with the raiders.

CHAPTER NINE

Night Fighters:
January–April 1918

On 3 January 1918 the Air Council was formed as a result of Lieutenant General J. C. Smuts' recommendations back in August 1917. Major General Sir Hugh Trenchard became the first Chief of the Air Staff and Lord Rothermere became the Secretary of State.

From the very beginning there was friction between the two men. Rothermere was committed to a unified British air force, but Trenchard was not. The wrangling came to a head with Trenchard offering his resignation on 19 March. It was a bad time politically for him to do so and his resignation was deferred until after 1 April 1918, when the Royal Air Force came into existence. Ultimately Major General F. H. Sykes replaced him, but the announcement of his appointment was not made until 15 April.

Major General Henderson had seemed to be the obvious candidate to become the First Chief of Air Staff, but he had been passed over in favour of Trenchard. Now obvious qualities and suitability for the post were ignored once again, in favour of Sykes. From the creation of the Air Council, Henderson had been appointed Vice President, but now he decided that he could not work with Sykes and resigned. Lord Rothermere was not far behind him; he resigned on 25 April, and was replaced by Sir William Weir.

The New Year brought mixed fortunes for both the British and the Germans. The first Gotha raid took place on 28/29 January, and it looked as though a corner had been turned when one was shot down. In all there were fourteen Giant and six Zeppelin raids up to April. The British had seriously to reconsider their strategy, particularly in relation to the Giants, despite over 300 fighter sorties, very few of the aircraft came within sight of the raiders.

The Germans had been reorganizing, as *Bogohl* 3 had suffered heavy crew and aircraft casualties in the previous year. Brandenburg had finally returned to the unit, complete with an artificial leg. The unit was not truly operational again, however, until March, and by that time the Germans, under considerable pressure on the Western Front, had decided that targets in France should take priority over the continuing raids against the British Isles. But they were still convinced that continued pressure in the form of aircraft and Zeppelin raids would continue to divert considerable amounts of men and materials away from the continent. They were still committed to continuing the air offensive against Britain.

Supporting the Gotha efforts were the Giants of RFA 501, now operating from St Denis Vestrem and Gontrode. On 7 March they moved to a purpose-built airfield at Scheldewindeke.

There had been considerable improvements in British fighter aircraft, many of which were now far more suited to dealing with Zeppelin raids or night attacks by bombers. There was a definite requirement for a two-seater fighter that could achieve altitudes of at least 20,000ft. It appeared that the NE1 and the FE9 were quite unable to provide this level of performance. As an alternative a new version of the FE2, with a 200hp engine, was proposed.

Meanwhile, the Sopwith Dolphin looked as if it could provide the performance levels sought by the home defence squadrons. It could reach an altitude of 15,000ft in twenty minutes and was still highly manoeuvrable at 21,000ft. The first squadron to be equipped with these aircraft was not part of the home defence network, however, but No. 19 Squadron in France, received the aircraft in January 1918. It was immediately realized that this aircraft could, with minor modifications, be ideal for night flying.

The Sopwith Camel offered another solution. Its 130hp engine was ideal up to heights of 14,000ft, but after that its manoeuvrability was severely impaired, and it only had an operational ceiling of 16,000ft. With a new 110hp engine, however, it performed far better and was probably the ideal solution for the defence squadrons in night operations.

The BE12B was capable of handling Gothas but it was considered to be inferior in the new role as anticipated for it against the better Zeppelins and the newer Giant bombers. The basic problem was its limited visibility from the cockpit and its lack of speed.

So there were several aircraft that were potentially useful to the home defence squadrons in their nighttime roles: the modified Sopwith Dolphin; the SE5, which could prove a useful alternative as it had reasonable performance and was relatively easy to fly at night; the Bristol Fighter, and the modified Sopwith Camel.

No. 141 Squadron was the first to be equipped with Sopwith Dolphins, in January 1918. In February No. 143 Squadron started receiving the same aircraft and in the following month so did No. 78 Squadron. No. 112 Squadron had to wait until May before they became available to it. There were considerable problems with them, however. Many of those that arrived at No. 141 Squadron Rochford in January were unmodified and in any case the squadron was in the process of transferring to Biggin Hill. The pilots encountered major problems with the engines, which were unreliable. The aircraft went into a spin when the pilot tried an acute left turn and generally it was not very stable. Moreover, none had Lewis gun mountings. Generally, however the pilots were pleased with it; it was easy to manoeuvre and provided excellent all-round vision.

One major problem remained: these aircraft required highly experienced pilots to use them at night. There were also servicing issues, not least of which was the fact that the engine had to be virtually stripped down in order to access certain parts that needed to be replaced on an almost daily basis. The defence squadrons still lacked an aircraft with a reliable engine. In addition the crew had to have decent all round vision in a stable aircraft and, above all, the pilots needed to have an even chance of being able to land it successfully at night. It had to have the speed to catch the raiders and also to be able to climb to make attack manoeuvres. The other major concern, of course, was the operational ceiling.

In the end the premature equipping of the squadrons with the Sopwith Dolphins proved to be an operational and financial disaster. The squadrons needed to be re-equipped with better and more reliable aircraft. Consequently, No. 78 Squadron received Sopwith Camels, as did No. 112 Squadron. No. 141 Squadron was re-equipped with Bristol Fighters and No. 143 Squadron, having first received FK8s, was then given SE5As.

No. 44 Squadron had already been using a modified version of the Sopwith Camel, the $1^1/_2$ Strutter, and it was now decided that the Camel would be the preferred option as a single-seat night fighter. It would require extensive modification, such as the removal of the Vickers guns and their replacement with two Lewis guns. Overall, however, the aircraft was far more suitable for the home defence squadrons, although it had a smaller petrol tank, which meant that it was no longer able to undertake long-range patrols. The modified Camel was unofficially dubbed the Comic and it was initially proposed that 204 should be earmarked for conversion.

The squadrons were still looking for a long-term solution, however: an aircraft with the ability to climb to 20,000ft in forty-five minutes, with an operational ceiling of 22,000ft and a Lewis gun for the pilot and a pair for the observer (or a shell gun). A number of different aircraft were looked at and rejected, including a version of the DH10 twin-engine bombers, the FE2, the FE9 and the NE1. They were all considered to be inefficient and even with re-engineering they would not provide the necessary performance levels. In desperation, they looked at the Avro 504K, a variant of the Avro 504 that had been used against Zeppelins in 1915 and after that as a trainer. The 504K had modifications and was powered by a 110hp engine. Even with these changes, it still only had an operating ceiling of 18,000ft, however. Some pilots had managed to get higher, but it was clearly not efficient at that altitude.

The Vickers FB26 Vampire was also considered. It was powered by a 200hp engine, had three Lewis guns, and an operational ceiling of around 17,000ft. It was assessed at Martlesham and at Biggin Hill but it proved to be unstable and slow, and the engine was extremely difficult to service. It was decided that it would be next to useless against Zeppelins and of limited value against bombers.

Despite the problems with the aircraft, one major improvement was created by Lieutenant H. B. Neame of the Technical Directorate. He developed an illuminated ring sight, which became known as the Neame sight, which could be adjusted so that the pilot would see the entire 77ft width of a Gotha at exactly 100 yards. It first proved its value on the night of 28/29 January, when Second Lieutenant C. C. Banks and Captain G. H. Hackwill shot down Gotha GV/938/16 in their Sopwith Camels.

One problem was that when pilots engaged a Giant, with its 138ft wingspan, they fired when it filled the sight, which was of course too far away; probably about 250 yards.

There was also ongoing work by Sir Richard Threlfall to try to develop a bullet that had both explosive and incendiary properties, so that, when it hit an enemy aircraft's fabric, it would cause irreparable damage. Early tests of a prototype manufactured by Albright and Wilson in August 1917 had proved to be promising. It was issued to home defence squadrons in the December, but many pilots discovered that it exploded prematurely, often as far as 100 yards from the target.

The two Sopwith Camels that attacked and destroyed the Gotha on the night of 28/29 January were armed with these new RTS bullets. They did have two normal Vickers guns and a Lewis gun with one RTS bullet loaded every third round. It was difficult to tell whether or not the RTS bullet had contributed to the destruction of the Gotha. Between them the two pilots had fired off over 1,000 rounds, but only thirty-two were RTS bullets. In any case, the RTS bullet was not ideal for a Vickers machine-gun and only Lewis guns would fire them.

Another problem that was under investigation was the loss of night vision when pilots fired their own guns. There were mixed experiences. Some were apparently unaffected, whilst others were rendered temporarily blind by just a few shots. Work was therefore underway to produce a flash eliminator for the Lewis gun, whilst other people were looking at possible solutions for the Vickers.

The Germans, whilst continually modifying their Gothas and Giants, were also developing a far larger bomb, weighing 1,000kg, the largest of its type used in the war. In the event, only three were ever dropped on the British Isles, the first on the night of 16/17 February with devastating effect. In the event, however, only one Giant was ever converted to carry this weapon, the R39. The rest of the aircraft, at the insistence of the crew, still carried smaller bombs, which they believed did greater damage overall.

The Air Council was still labouring under the misapprehension that the German bomber force was far larger than it was in reality. They believed that the Germans had the theoretical capacity to launch up to eighty bombers on any given day during the summer of 1918. To face them the British had eight home defence squadrons, mustering eighty-nine day and sixty-three night fighters. These figures are somewhat confusing, however, as in fact some of the aircraft were both, so the effective strength overall was no more than 100 aircraft, supported by at best twenty-five or twenty-six aircraft from various training units. These figures must be seen against the backdrop of what the home forces assessed they needed in order to defend London. General Headquarters produced a document on 8 February, calling for twelve squadrons of twenty aircraft, supported by four flights of six aircraft with wirelesses. This meant a total of 264 aircraft. At this time, with RFC squadrons Nos. 141 and 143 still being formed, the total strength, if all squadrons were up to strength, would be just 200 aircraft, which was well short of their minimum requirement.

As far as ground support was concerned, the new listening posts were welcomed, but in order to defend the capital they suggested that they needed 349 anti-aircraft guns and 623 searchlights – an increase of 100 anti-aircraft guns and 300 searchlights.

This call for additional reinforcements met with mixed reactions. Whilst Field Marshal Sir Henry Wilson, who had replaced General Sir William Robertson in mid-February 1918, agreed that Britain should have priority over France in terms of anti-aircraft guns, it should be the other way round as far as aircraft were concerned. As the Chief of Imperial General Staff, his views had considerable weight and the War Cabinet ratified his decision on 27 February.

New developments were also underway with regard to the anti-aircraft fire. Rather than tackle German bombers with a seemingly impenetrable line of airbursts in front of them, they would now be faced with a circle around them.

The RNAS had originally helped in the air defence of Britain, but since September 1917 this contribution had been almost negligible, as they had relinquished this responsibility to the home defence squadrons. In any case, any discussion about air defence responsibility was irrelevant as the RFC and the RNAS would soon be a single force. The RNAS was still committed to providing aircraft to chase German bombers on their return to their airfields, however, and both they and the Admiralty were adamant that they lacked suitable aircraft to launch any form of night fighter cover.

One more major problem to be solved was the difficulty in coordinating the work of the searchlights, the anti-aircraft guns, the listening stations and the home defence squadrons; the first part of 1918 was punctuated by several false alarms. A prime example took place on the night of 18/19 February. There were no German aircraft or airships operating over Britain, yet the alert was sounded at 1950 and fifty-five home defence squadron aircraft were scrambled. All across London anti-aircraft batteries responded to the false alarm by firing off in excess of 2,500 rounds. Some of the targets were merely phantoms, whilst others were British fighters. It was more by luck than by judgement that no aircraft were downed by their own batteries that night. The cause of the alarm had been German bombers attacking Calais.

Lieutenant E. F. Wilson, of No. 38 Squadron, had not been so lucky on the night of 3/4 January. He was in his FE2B, undertaking a training flight out of Stamford, when he encroached into the outer anti-aircraft defences around London and could not remember the recognition flares required for that night. He was hit by anti-aircraft guns at Roding and was lucky to survive a forced landing.

Considerable reorganization had been undertaken towards the end of 1917. All the home defence squadrons were under the command of No. 6 Brigade, which consisted of four separate wings. Henceforth No. 50 Wing would consist of Nos. 37, 61, 75 and 198 (T) Squadrons, No. 49 Wing would consist of Nos. 39, 44, 78 and 141 Squadrons and No. 53 Wing would consist of Nos. 50, 112 and 143 Squadrons. The remaining wing, No. 48, based at Gainsborough, was essentially a training wing.

As we have seen, the first German bomber attack on Britain in 1918 took place on the night of 28/29 January. It was notable for several key factors, including the destruction of a Gotha and the biggest reaction by British night fighters, totalling 103 sorties.

Initially the Germans had intended to launch thirteen Gothas and two Giants against London, but only seven Gothas and the one Giant made the attack. This was largely due to fog over the German airfields, but the Giant that turned back, the R35, got as far as the sea to the north of Ostend when its engines began playing up and it jettisoned its bombs.

The Gothas were spotted between 1955 and 2025 between Harwich and the North Foreland. Half of them peeled off to attack Margate, Sandwich, Sheerness and Ramsgate, whilst the other three headed straight for London and dropped their bombs over a period of an hour and a quarter from 2030. The R12, the solitary Giant, crossed Hollesley Bay at 2225 and was over London at 0015.

It was in Long Acre, at the Oldham's Press building, that the worst carnage of the night took place. Two 660lb bombs dropped by the R12 hit the building, killing thirty-eight and injuring eighty-five.

Despite fog at the Germans' home bases, over Britain there was only a small amount of cloud near the coast. Otherwise the night presented ideal flying conditions for the British defenders. Above all, recent attempts to improve the cooperation between the squadrons and their partners manning the searchlights and anti-aircraft guns had proved to be a great success, and this contributed to the demise of Gotha GV/938/16.

Lieutenant Friedrich von Thomsen, operating as the navigator, commanded the aircraft, which crossed the British coast at the Naze at 2000 and approached London by way of Clacton. Instead of heading for the centre of the capital it dropped its bombs on Hampstead at 2145 and was then picked up by the searchlights. Flying in the vicinity were two Sopwith Camels of No. 44 Squadron, Hainault, flown by Second Lieutenant C. C. Banks and Lieutenant G. H. Hackwill, who encountered it flying at an altitude of around 10,000ft over Romford. Both aircraft were upgraded Sopwith Camels with Lewis guns loaded one-in-three with the RTS ammunition.

It was a perfectly coordinated attack. Banks came in just underneath the Gotha on its left-hand side and opened fire. Hackwill then moved to engage on its right. Both pilots jockeyed for position, continually firing at the raider for around 10 minutes, and all the time they were being watched by anti-aircraft batteries based at Billericay, Noak Hill and Shenfield. Banks was the first to break off when his aircraft suffered an electrical fault, causing problems with his cylinders. He took one last look at the Gotha as he peeled away and saw that Hackwill was still firing at it. It then fell to pieces, some of it bursting into flames, and when it hit the ground there was a terrific explosion. It came down at 2210 at Frund's Farm, Wickford, and none of the crew survived. Both British pilots were awarded the MC for their actions that night.

Other Gothas were intercepted and fired at by aircraft from Nos. 39, 50, 61 and 78 Squadrons. The RNAS also reported an attack on one of those that had attacked Sheerness. An unnamed pilot encountered it at 2150 in a Sopwith $1^1/_2$ Strutter which had lifted off at 2115. He made an attack but then lost sight of it.

Meanwhile, the R12 had not proceeded without incident. A Bristol Fighter piloted by Lieutenant J. G. Goodyear and Aircraftman Walter Thomas Merchant first encountered it at around 2300 when it was inbound in the Harlow area, heading for London. Goodyear was at about 10,000ft and positioned his aircraft behind the R12. As he got close, the slipstream buffeted him and the aircraft made an abrupt turn to the right. He came around for a second pass, this time under fire, and turned to allow Merchant to fire at the Giant. Just at that point a stream of bullets hit the Bristol Fighter, wounding Merchant and breaking the petrol tank. Seconds later Goodyear's aircraft spluttered and the engine stopped. Incredibly he managed to guide it back to North Weald, where he landed without incident. Merchant got away with a graze on his arm.

The eventful night was not over for the R12. On its continued progress towards London it hit a barrage balloon apron at Chingford, an incident that was confirmed when a German prisoner was later interrogated.

There was one misfortune for the British that night when a Sopwith Camel of No. 78 Squadron was hit at a height of 11,000ft by anti-aircraft guns based at Woolwich. The pilot managed to nurse the aircraft back towards Suttons Farm but he hit telegraph wires near Hornchurch. The aircraft burst into flames but the pilot escaped unscathed. Remarkably, having crashed at 2130, he was back at base, sitting in another Sopwith Camel and awaiting orders to take off again just forty minutes later.

The results of the German efforts that night were sixty-seven killed, 166 injured and over £187,000 worth of damage caused. The majority of the damage occurred at the Oldham's Press building in Long Acre.

For a variety of reasons, including losses, engine difficulties and other aircraft malfunctions, *Bogohl 3* was unable to launch another assault for a considerable period of time. The effort now fell on RFA 501 and its limited number of Giants.

Four Giants were launched against London on 29/30 January. Only three crossed into British air space, but they stirred up a veritable hornet's nest of night fighters, which launched eighty sorties. This large number was probably the result of misinformation, which suggested that upwards of fifteen Giants and Gothas were abroad that night.

The fourth Giant, the R12, which was meant to be part of the attack, suffered engine problems as it was crossing the English Channel and therefore turned and used its bombs against fortifications at Gravelines. The three remaining Giants, the R25, R26 and R39, continued inland. Two attacked the outskirts of London, whilst the third restricted its activities to an area around Southend.

The first Giant seen that night was the R39, which came in at the mouth of the Blackwater River at 2205. Fairly soon afterwards it was attacked by Captain Arthur Dennis in a BE12B of No. 37 Squadron, Goldhanger. It was flying at a height of 12,000ft and Dennis emptied an entire Lewis gun drum into it whilst under fire, before the slipstream buffeted his aircraft. By the time he had recovered he had lost sight of it.

The R39 carried on. The crew made their first serious mistake when they believed they were above Tower Bridge, when in fact it was Hammersmith Bridge. Consequently, all their bombs fell in Acton and Richmond, killing ten people and injuring ten. Meanwhile Second Lieutenant Robert N. Hall, flying a Sopwith Camel, had spotted the Giants at 11,000ft and followed it over Roehampton, but his aircraft suffered from persistent gun jams and he was unable to engage.

The R39 next encountered a Sopwith Camel piloted by Captain F. L. Ulxmoore of No. 78 Squadron, who was flying at a higher altitude; the Giant was proceeding along at 10,500ft. Ulxmoore dived at it from the rear and managed to get off fifty rounds before turning and firing another fifty, one of which struck his own propeller, part of which broke off and hit him in the forehead. By the time he had recovered the R39 had disappeared.

It soon came within plain view of Captain G. H. Hackwill in his Sopwith Camel, from No. 44 Squadron, Hainault. He closed to within 150 yards, loosing off 600 rounds before his fuel became perilously low. Second Lieutenant F. B. Bryant and his observer, Second Lieutenant V. H. Newton, made another attack in an Armstrong Whitworth FK8 of No. 50 Squadron, Detling, close to Throwley at 0015 hours, but they lacked the necessary speed and manoeuvrability.

The R25 was spotted five minutes after it had crossed the coast at Foulness, at 2250. Second Lieutenant R. F. Kitton, in a BE2E out of Goldhanger, reported it as flying at a height of 8,000ft. He engaged it, emptying an entire drum into it, but then lost sight of it whilst he was reloading.

Bob Hall, who had encountered the R39, now came across the R25. He fired just five rounds before his gun jammed again at 2315 over North Benfleet. Unperturbed, he dealt with the jam and continued to follow the Giant. Ten minutes later, Second Lieutenant H. A. Edwardes of No. 44 Squadron, who had managed to engage it at a range of 40 yards, joined him in shadowing it. One of his own bullets also hit his propeller but he had the forethought to switch on his navigational lights to attract other British fighters. Edwardes and Hall were now joined by Second Lieutenant T. M. O'Neil, who made at least two attacks, one from above and one from below the tail, firing 300 rounds before his gun finally jammed.

Next to arrive on the scene was Major G. W. Murlis Green from the same squadron, but with a Sopwith Camel equipped with two Lewis guns and RTS ammunition. Just as he came in to attack O'Neil launched another dive and Murlis Green took the brunt of the return fire. He quickly fired off a full drum of RTS ammunition and three-quarters of another drum of standard bullets. He then had to peel off in order to sort out his gun jams.

It is not clear exactly who did the major damage to the R25, but in all probability it was Hall or Edwardes who hit one of the port engine's radiators. Despite this it continued to press on towards London, gradually losing height. It now saw the balloon apron from Woodford to Southgate and had to make a long turn to avoid it. The crew then decided to drop their bombs on Wanstead at around 2400. Although the R25 was now lighter, it was still losing height, and with twenty or more British fighters between it and the coast and with Murlis Green rearmed and airborne again after just eleven minutes on the ground, it faced a difficult journey home. In the event the crew were lucky and were only spotted briefly near Sheerness. They eventually left the British coast near Shoeburyness at 0030. When they landed back at base they found that the aircraft had taken 88 hits.

The last Giant, the R26, had come in over The Naze at 2244. The crew believed that they were over Southend, having clearly mistaken the Blackwater River for the Thames Estuary. At around 2320 the aircraft developed problems with two of its engines and began to lose height. It immediately jettisoned its bombs in the Rayleigh area then turned for home. On two engines it was just able to stay at 5,000ft on its approach to Ostend, where it crossed the Belgian coast at 0150.

Britain now had over two weeks' respite from German attacks, until the night of 16/17 February, when five Giants were launched, primarily against London. One had to turn back and three of the remaining four, the R255; R33 and R36 chose to attack their alternative target, Dover, instead of pressing on to London. Only the R12 opted for its primary target, possibly because it had a longer range.

All four approached the British coast on a 6-mile front close to Maplin Sands at around 2140. The R12 was in front, crossing the coast at an altitude of 8,200ft. By the time it reached London it was at a height of only 9,500ft, and faced with a balloon apron that extended up to 10,000ft. Whether or not the crew was aware of this is unknown. What is certain is that at 2215 the starboard wing hit one of the cables over Woolwich. The pilot, Lieutenant Götte, shut off power to his engines and then fired up his two port engines to maintain a level, a manoeuvre that cost 1,000ft in altitude. Whilst a mechanic scrambled along the wing to deal with the problem, the pilot struggled to maintain control. The mechanic burnt his hands on the exhaust and as the aircraft lurched, two large 660lb bombs fell on Woolwich. Undeterred, the R12 bombed Beckenham and managed to make it all the way home to base, arriving there at 0125.

The R39 was by now over London and believing it was dropping the first 1,000kg bomb on the city, hit the Chelsea Royal Hospital. It then headed south and crossed over Folkestone at 2340.

The R33 approached Deal at around 2045, but it was experiencing problems with both of its port engines. The commander decided to drop his bombs on nearby shipping before turning for home. The forward unit of the port engine failed, followed by the rear port engine. The rear starboard engine then lost power. The crew desperately threw as much equipment overboard as they could find, but they were still dropping like a stone and in a short period had dropped to just 650ft. A mechanic discovered that the primary problem was the cold. He quickly punctured one of the oil tanks, cupped oil in his hands and poured it into the rear port engine, managing to get it going again. In this way the R33 managed to limp home.

On the following night, 17/18 February, another RFA 501 attack was reduced to just one serviceable Giant, the R25. Again the target was London and the aircraft crossed the British coastline at All Hallows at around 2145. At around 2245 it began dropping eighteen bombs in the Eltham area. The full stick extended in a north-westerly direction and the last eight hit the railway station and hotel at St Pancras. It was here that the majority of the casualties were inflicted, some twenty-one killed and thirty-two injured. It also inflicted nearly £39,000 worth of damage, which was £20,000 more than had been achieved by four Giants the previous night. The R25, now much lighter, headed off across Kent at a height of 9,800ft, crossing the British coast at Folkestone at 0013. The RFC launched sixty-nine sorties, not one of which came anywhere near the raider.

The next Giant attack, the greatest effort so far by RFA 501, took place on 7/8 March. Six aircraft were launched, targeting London, but once again one of them had to return to base. Nos. 37, 39, 44, 50, 61, 78, 112, 141 and 143 Squadrons launched no less than forty-two defensive sorties that night. The first Giant, in all likelihood the R27, was spotted over Deal at 2256. Three more were seen over Maplin Sands in a twenty-minute period from 2300. The final one was spotted at 2335 over Broadstairs.

Commencing at 0010 R13, R27 and R39 bombed London for twenty-five minutes. The worst damage of the night was the levelling of several houses in Maidevale. One of the three bombers that had crossed at Maplin Sands did not head for London but struck out to the north-west and flew over Bedfordshire. It dropped several bombs close to Ware at around midnight. One dropped its bombs on Southminster and Herne Bay. Having done their work the first Giant disappeared at 0110 over Dymchurch and the others were gone by 0200.

Whilst the British had been unable to engage the Giants, two of them did not return home intact. The R27 crash landed close to the German lines at Courtrai; it may well have run out of fuel. One of the other Giants, unidentified, was badly damaged when it landed at Ghistelles.

There was a double tragedy for the British. Captain Alex B. Kynoch of No. 37 Squadron, Stow Maries, in a BE12, took off at 2329 and Captain H. Clifford Stroud of No. 61 Squadron, Rochford, at 2330 in a BE5A. They collided with one another over Rayleigh, probably in cloud. Kynoch was out of his patrol area and possibly chasing a Giant. Both men were killed in the collision.

The night of 12/13 March saw the return of the German navy Zeppelins, which had not launched an attack since October 1917. The L53, L54, L61, L62 and L63 were involved. The target was the Midlands, but the night was typified by thick cloud, which caused the Zeppelins navigational problems.

The L61, L62 and L63, were spotted crossing between Hornsey and Bridlington at various times between 2030 and 2150. They had targeted Leeds but they actually bombed targets near to Hull. The remaining L53 and L54, believing they were much further west than they were, ended up dropping their bombs into the sea.

Only nine defensive sorties were launched that night, by Nos. 33, 36 and 76 Squadrons because of the same problem that caused difficulties for the Germans: the cloud cover; in some cases the clouds were as low as 150ft, so those flights that were made were relatively short.

This Zeppelin raid had been launched to coincide with three Giants striking London, but the R33 turned back early with engine problems, the R13 developed difficulties and instead targeted Boulogne, and rather than tackle London alone the R39 turned and joined the R13 in its attack.

The Zeppelins killed one person and inflicted just £3,500 worth of damage. This did not deter them from attempting a similar attack the following night, 13/14 March. This time the L42, L52 and L56 were earmarked for the attack, but, just one Zeppelin, the L42 commanded by Captain Martin Dietrich, made the attack. The other two airships were recalled when the German navy received adverse weather forecasts, predicting strong north-easterly winds. By the time the message was transmitted at 1915, Dietrich was close enough to the British coast to continue his flight. He came in over the Norfolk coast and headed towards the dock area in West Hartlepool, flying at a height of 16,400ft. He dropped twenty-one bombs, killing eight people, injuring thirty-nine and doing £14,280 worth of damage.

The British responded with fifteen sorties, but only two of the aircraft launched that night had any chance of seeing the L42. They were from C Flight, No. 36 Squadron, Seaton Carew. Second Lieutenant E. C. Morris and Second Lieutenant R. D. Linford in an FE2D briefly spotted it over Redcar at a height of around 18,000ft. As it turned for home Morris desperately tried to coax his aircraft into range, but turned back having failed 40 miles out to sea.

There was a respite for Britain for the rest of the month and when the next attack did come, on the night of 12/13 April it, too, was launched by German navy Zeppelins. This time the Germans deployed five with more reliable Maybach engines: the L60, L61, L62, L63 and L64. Once again the target was the Midlands.

The force was spotted at various points between Spurnhead and Cromer between 2120 and 2200. The L60 headed for the Humber area and dropped bombs to the south of the river. The L61, believing it was over Sheffield, bombed Runcorn and then Wigan. The L62 had approached the British coast at Cromer and headed for Birmingham, having bombed the Tydd St Mary airfield, home to No. 51 Squadron. It then dropped bombs to the south of Coventry and to the south-west of Birmingham, before exiting over Great Yarmouth at 0335. The L63 and L64 did not penetrate far into Britain and dropped their bombs on Lincolnshire.

The British responded by launching twenty-seven defensive sorties, including aircraft scrambled by the RNAS (on April 1 the RNAS and the RFC had become the RAF, but the aircraft and bases were still listed as being RNAS) out of Great Yarmouth, Bacton, Burgh Castle and Covehithe. The RFC scrambled aircraft from Nos. 33, 38, 51 and 75 Squadrons. They were ordered to get aloft at 2205. Probably the first sighting was by Lieutenant L. Murphy in an FE2B of A Flight, No. 33 Squadron, Scampton. He was patrolling near Grimsby at around 2300 when he spotted the L64, but quickly realized that there was no way that his aircraft could intercept it.

Lieutenant F. Sergeant of B Flight, No. 51 Squadron, was flying at a height of 14,000ft over his own airfield at Tydd St Mary in an FE2B when he spotted the L62 flying at an altitude of around 19,000ft. As it moved south-west he tried to pursue it, but was unable to get within 4,000ft of it and he reluctantly peeled off to return home somewhere over Rugby at 2345.

Lieutenant C. H. Noble-Campbell had left the airfield at Buckminster, the home of B Flight, No. 38 Squadron, at 2325. At 0015 and at an altitude of 16,000ft, he saw the L62 to the north-east of Birmingham. He quickly decided that his aircraft had very little chance of climbing the additional 1,500ft to draw level with the Zeppelin. It was already experiencing problems at this altitude, but nonetheless he climbed to within 500 yards and opened fire. He later crashed near Coventry at 0130 and walked away uninjured.

His colleague, Lieutenant W. A. Brown of C Flight, and based at Stamford, lifted off at 2318. He reported seeing the L62 at around 0100 and he too had tried to chase it and gain height, but he was also forced to come down, also near Coventry, at 2325. Noble-Campbell was temporarily knocked out when part of his propeller hit him on the head, while Brown's aircraft's engine failed. They were both lucky to have escaped uninjured.

The L62 now headed at an altitude of 11,000ft towards Great Yarmouth. There was bad fog along the Norfolk coast, which prevented the RNAS aircraft based there from lifting off. Had they been able to they would have seen that the Zeppelin was in trouble. Noble-Campbell had in fact scored a hit and one of its gas cells was leaking; and it dropped to a height of 5,000ft. As it was, however, there was just one sighting much later on, when Flight Commander G. E. Livock and Flight Commander R. Leckie took off in an F2A at 0430 in pursuit. They in fact sighted the L61, which rapidly rose to 22,000ft and escaped them.

CHAPTER TEN

The Final Raids:
May–August 1918

The first aircraft raid of the next phase of German operations over Britain took place on the night of 19/20 May. For a considerable time only the Zeppelins had carried on the fight. Indeed, *Bogohl* 3 had been licking its wounds and reorganizing for no less than sixteen weeks. The lack of Giant aircraft, innumerable mechanical and engine problems and a shortage of experienced crew had also forced RFA 501 out of the fight for the best part of ten weeks.

When the Germans launched their spring offensive, Gothas and Giants were temporarily required for tactical and strategic bombing missions on the Western Front to support the ground effort, and by the time they restarted their bombing offensive against Britain, the British defences had been radically reorganized. No. 37 Squadron, based at Goldhanger and Stow Maries with a mixture of BE12, BE12A and BE12B aircraft, was responsible for covering the area from Northey Island to Tiptree and from Hatfield Peverel to Stow Maries. No. 39 Squadron, based at North Weald and flying Bristol Fighters, covered the area from Balls Park through North Weald to Crabtree Hill. No. 44 Squadron at Hainault, with Sopwith Camels, covered from Greensted Farm to Suttons Farm. No. 50 Squadron at Bekesbourne, with some SE5As, BE12s and BE12Bs, patrolled the Wingham to Margate area. No. 61 Squadron, based at Rochford and equipped with SE5As, picked up the patrol area to the south of Stow Maries, through Leigh-on-Sea to Yantlet Creek. No. 78 Squadron, based at Suttons Farm and equipped with Sopwith Camels, covered the South Weald to Tilbury area. No. 112 Squadron, at Throwley and also equipped with Sopwith Camels, covered the area from Throwley to Judds Hill and Warden Point. No. 141 Squadron, based at Biggin Hill with Bristol Fighters, covered the Joyce Green, South Ash and Biggin Hill area. Finally, No. 143 Squadron, based at Detling with SE5As, covered the Detling to Marden area.

There were new rules once a patrol order had been issued. Each affected squadron would scramble three or four aircraft and cover their area at a height of between 10,000 and 12,000ft. Each aircraft would operate no closer than 500ft from one of its partners, thereby assuring that any aircraft that was encountered was not a friendly but a raider. The weak point in the line was No. 37 Squadron, which was still equipped with BE12, BE12A and BE12B aircraft, although they were beginning to receive some SE5As.

In addition to the raids from May 1918, there were no less than nine photo-reconnaissance flights launched by the German navy. Since these aircraft came in fast, carried out their reconnaissance quickly and disappeared back to base, it was incredibly difficult for the defence squadrons to launch any effective counter. Indeed only three of the German reconnaissance flights were ever detected in time for defence aircraft to be scrambled.

By early May Brandenburg was champing at the bit to launch his Gothas once more against Britain. Gradually the strength of the force had been built up and all that Brandenburg needed was a favourable weather forecast. Whilst he impatiently waited for the right conditions he was tempted by half chances. His decision not to launch a premature assault in inclement weather was vindicated, when on 9 May three out of four Giants of RFA 501, returning from a bombing raid against the French coast, were wrecked when they tried to land in thick fog.

The weather conditions finally appeared to be favourable for the night of 19/20 May. Brandenburg had amassed no fewer than thirty-eight Gothas, although RFA 501 could only muster three Giants, the R12, R13 and R39. In addition, a pair of Rumpler CVII weather reconnaissance aircraft were to accompany the attack force. This was to be the biggest bomber raid on Britain of the war.

In the event only twenty-eight Gothas were involved in the raid. The first aircraft was seen off the North Foreland at 2217, but it was a Rumpler, as it dropped flares to indicate that the weather conditions ahead were favourable. The aircraft then turned south and bombed London. The Gothas themselves began appearing off Foreness at around 2237 and others were seen near the Isle of Sheppey at 2300. More began appearing between Dover and the Blackwater River before 2400.

Eighteen Gothas and a Giant attacked London, beginning at 2330. In total the Germans dropped between 23,724 and 32,000lb of bombs; London received between 12,128 and 17,850lb. All forty-nine deaths that night were as a result of the London bombings. In addition the Germans injured 177 people and inflicted £177,317 worth of damage.

The British defence squadrons were ordered to begin their patrols at 2253 and within five minutes eight were preparing their aircraft for take-off. Only No. 61 Squadron did not receive the patrol order until later, apparently at 2307. They immediately scrambled four SE5As and by this time the British had twelve Sopwith Camels, eight SE5As, eight Bristol Fighters and three BE12As aloft.

The first contact of the night was over Faversham. Major C. J. Q. Brand, the commanding officer of 112 Squadron, took off at 2315 in his Sopwith Camel heading for Warden Point, his patrol area, at a height of 8,500ft. He clearly saw a Gotha no more than 200ft higher and swung around to attack. The enemy opened fire as he closed in but Brand fired at the bomber's starboard engine with two bursts of twenty rounds. The German's engine stopped and it tried to get away to the north-east. Brand followed up his attack firing three more twenty-five-round bursts. The Gotha immediately burst into flames and began to break up; Brand was so close that the nose of his Camel and his own face and moustache were scorched. He estimated that he had encountered the Gotha at 2323 and that the Gotha hit the ground at 2326. He followed it all the way down to an altitude of 3,000ft.

Lieutenant Anthony J. Arkell and Aircraftman Albert T. C. Stagg, his gunner, took off at 2256 to patrol to the north of Hainault. They were flying at a height of 11,000ft at around 0005 when they spotted the exhaust flames of a Gotha at approximately 10,000ft. They dived down to engage and at 200 yards, behind the Gotha, Stagg opened up and fired half a drum of ammunition. Arkell then fired his Vickers machine-guns and swung around so that Stagg could fire again. The Gotha was desperately trying to evade them but Arkell fired more bursts and then assumed a position underneath the Gotha's tail, allowing Stagg to fire off two more drums. They came around once more, firing 350 rounds with his Vickers at the Gotha. During the engagement the Gotha lost height in an attempt to evade the Bristol Fighter. Arkell now swooped down so that he was no more than 1,500ft from the ground. Stagg fired a burst from his Lewis gun and they saw the Gotha's starboard engine catch fire. The Gotha then spun out of control and hit the ground at 0020 at East Ham. Two of the crew members attempted to jump out and fell to their deaths, whilst a third, who may already have been dead, was found in the wreckage.

There is some dispute as to who destroyed the third German aircraft over Britain that night. Officially, the commanding officer of No. 143 Squadron, Major Frederick Sowrey, who left Detling at 2330, was credited with the kill. He engaged a Gotha at 2345 to the north-east of Maidstone and emptied a drum from his Lewis gun into it, but whilst reloading, he lost sight of it. Later, at 0025 he engaged another Gotha, firing two drums from his Lewis gun. He tried to turn to engage the Gotha with his Vickers guns but his aircraft stalled and he lost sight of it.

In its attempts to evade Sowrey the Gotha had strayed to the west and was seen by Lieutenant Edward E. Turner and Lieutenant Henry B. Barwise, who had left No. 141 Squadron, Biggin Hill, in a Bristol Fighter at 2302. They spotted the Gotha near South Ash at 0030. Turner managed to get behind it and Barwise fired his Lewis gun with RTS ammunition. It hit the Gotha's port engine and the raider began to lose height. Barwise fired two more bursts, hitting both the starboard wings and the fuselage before his gun jammed. Turner tried to follow it but lost sight of it. He became lost whilst trying to relocate it and, low on fuel, landed at Detling.

The aircraft they had attacked was GV/979/16, which crashed near Frinsted at 0045. Only the fuselage gunner survived the crash, and he had a broken arm. The survivor, Hermann Tasche, confirmed that they had been attacked first by Sowrey and possibly the pilot had been wounded during this attack, but the attack by Turner had been the one that had finished them off. In the end the kill was shared between Sowrey and Turner.

As a result of this action, Brand was awarded the DSO, Arkell the MC, Stagg the MM and Turner and Barwise the DFC.

A Fourth Gotha was lost over Britain that night, but not as a result of any action by British pilots or anti-aircraft gunners. GV/925/16 was approaching the British coast and had dropped its altitude to 2,000ft in order to aid navigation. The crew mistook the Blackwater River for the Thames Estuary and they tried to climb to regain height, but at this point the starboard engine cut out. Immediately they jettisoned their bombs but could not gain sufficient height and the aircraft hit the ground at 2350 at St. Osyth. The captain and observer, Lieutenant Rist, was killed.

There were other close encounters that night. Captain C. E. Holman left Bekesbourne in an SE5A at 2300. Twenty minutes later he engaged a German bomber near Canterbury, firing 300 rounds at it. He reported that it turned away from him and began to dive, he believed that it was spinning out of control, but he then lost sight of it.

Meanwhile, over Whitstable, Captain J. T. Collier encountered another Gotha bomber. He made one attack, but then was dazzled by a British searchlight. Undeterred, he continued his patrol and at 2353, near Frinsted and at a height of 10,000ft, he encountered another Gotha. It desperately tried to evade him but he got off 500 rounds before his guns jammed.

Over Romford Captain W. H. Haynes in his Sopwith Camel out of No. 44 Squadron Hainault encountered a German bomber at 8,500ft at

2330. He tracked it over east London and then began to follow it home. He fired at it from the rear at 500ft below. It tried to evade him, but he responded by firing his Lewis guns. He was now receiving return fire and was almost out of ammunition. When he returned home he found several bullet holes near his propeller and some in his lower starboard wing. In all probability he had encountered a Giant rather than a Gotha.

Just three minutes after Haynes first encountered his bomber Lieutenant W. E. Nicholson attacked another bomber over Loughton. He made two passes but then his aircraft developed a pressure valve problem and he was forced to peel away and land at Chingford.

At 2355, Captain S. Cockerell of No. 78 Squadron encountered a Gotha over Orsett, flying at a height of 11,000ft. He made several sweeping attacks against it, receiving return fire. Eventually, after emptying all his drums of ammunition at the target, he realized that he had done very little damage and returned to Suttons Farm at 0030.

The most significant of reconnaissance flights took place on 21 May, just after this raid. It was undertaken by a Rumpler with auxiliary petrol tanks to give it a longer endurance. It took off from Tournai and crossed the British coast at Shoeburyness at a height of 18,700ft. It carried out its mission over London at around 1130 and was back at base by 1400, and it was not even spotted. The aircraft had been airborne for six hours and it had covered 375 miles.

Although Britain was not to know it at the time, the raid on 19/20 May was the last Gotha or Giant attack. The bomber menace had been defeated and German priorities now lay elsewhere. What remained of the fight over Britain would now be conducted by the German navy Zeppelins once more, even though they had suffered huge casualties. They had lost the L62 during a reconnaissance of the North Sea on 10 May and on 19 July Sopwith Camels had attacked the naval base at Tondern and destroyed the L54 and L60.

Nonetheless the Germans were still developing better Zeppelins and launched an attack on 5/6 August – the very last time that the Germans would appear over the British Isles. It was led by the L70, a new Zeppelin which could carry up to 8,000lb of bombs. It was 694ft long and had a maximum speed of 81mph. The other airships were the L53, L56, L63 and L65. Unfortunately for the Germans, the British were waiting.

The first Zeppelins to reach the coast were the L56 and the L63, which were approximately 30 miles to the south of the other three airships and less than 10 miles from the airfields of RAF No. 4 Group, which now included the former RNAS stations at Great Yarmouth, Burgh Castle and Covehithe.

By 1830 the L53, L65 and L70 were 60 miles from the British coastline. This was a serious miscalculation. The Leman Tail Light Vessel, positioned 30 miles north-east of Happisburgh, sighted them at 2010 and continued to report their progress for over an hour. The Germans clearly believed that by flying at an extreme height, even in daylight, they would be impervious to any British defensive moves.

The alert was given at 2050 and two DH4s were launched from Great Yarmouth. The Germans were about to face two highly experienced pilots. Lieutenant R. E. Keyes piloted the first aircraft and his gunner was Aircraftsman A. T. Harman. Shortly behind them was Major Edgar Cadbury, with his gunner, Captain R. Leckie.

Cadbury was the first to spot the Zeppelins. He saw the L70 at a height of around 17,400ft at 2210. He had already jettisoned a pair of 100lb bombs in order to aid the aircraft's climb, and then Leckie discovered to his horror that his Lewis gun did not have a sight. Nonetheless, Cadbury moved in for the attack. Leckie fired at the nose of the airship with Pomeroy explosive bullets, and almost immediately a huge hole developed in the Zeppelin. L70 broke into two pieces and began falling.

Keyes also attacked it from a range of around 100 yards, but his front guns jammed. Harman fired seventy armour piercing and tracer bullets. They then saw it burst into flames and assumed that they had destroyed the raider. There was considerable debate as to who was responsible, but eventually the official nod was given to Cadbury and Leckie, who were both awarded the DFC.

The L70 came down some 8 miles off Wells-next-the-Sea at around 2215. Captain C. B. Sproatt and his gunner, Captain J. Hodson in a DH9, had also attacked it at 2200, firing 100 rounds at a range of 4,000ft, as they were unable to gain altitude beyond 13,000ft. It is not very likely that they caused any significant damage.

Cadbury and Keyes were still aloft and ready to engage a second airship. Cadbury swung in to attack the L65, coming to within 500ft below it. He opened fire with his front guns but they quickly jammed. Then Leckie opened fire. They do not seem to have done any great damage and in trying to clear the jam Cadbury became lost and eventually landed at Sedgeford, at 2305.

Keyes, meanwhile, climbed to attack the L65. Harman managed to fire over a drum of ammunition at it but then the DH4's engine cut out. With the aircraft struggling, Keyes lost altitude and began hunting for somewhere to land. Eventually he saw a flare path and managed to land at Kelstern in Lincolnshire at 0110.

Captain C. S. Iron and Lieutenant H. G. Owen in a DH9 from Great Yarmouth had also tried to engage the German airships. They saw the

L56 and the L63, but after they had climbed to an altitude of 15,500ft the aircraft began to struggle and they eventually decided to land at Sedgeford at 2315, having taken off at 2110.

Captain Kirkpatrick had taken off from Great Yarmouth in a Sopwith Camel at 2110. He spotted the L56 and L63 at around 2120 and climbed to an altitude of 17,000ft but could not coax his aircraft any higher. He decided to abandon the pursuit and landed at Saxthorpe, near Cromer, at 2315.

Also aloft were Captain B. G. Jardine and Lieutenant E. R. Munday. They had taken off in a DH9 from Great Yarmouth at 2055. This was Jardine's first sortie and it is likely that he ditched into the sea. No trace of either man was ever found. Another aircraft was also missing, a Sopwith Camel flown by Lieutenant G. F. Hodson, who had taken off from Burgh Castle at 2105.

After the loss of the L70 the three other Zeppelins in the area, the L53, L63 and L65, climbed higher than 19,400ft. They later reported that they had bombed the Humber area, Boston and King's Lynn, but in fact all their bombs had fallen out to sea. Only the L56 showed any fortitude. The captain, Walter Zaeschmar, later claimed that he had bombed Norwich at 0010 but in fact he had tried to bomb Lowestoft and all his bombs had fallen out to sea.

Of particular significance was the fact that the US navy launched a sortie that night. Their aircraft at Killingholme, an F2A, was scrambled to patrol the Wash and Robin Hood's Bay. The crew got hopelessly lost, however, and eventually landed at Tynemouth, over 100 miles from Killingholme.

Even though the Zeppelins had dropped all their bombs out to sea, the explosions could be heard well inland, which added to the confusion that night. No. 33 Squadron was informed at 2230 that four Zeppelins had been seen off Great Yarmouth and another off Spurnhead. This prompted them to launch an FE2B, and two FE2Ds, in addition to two Bristol Fighters. Lieutenant F. A. Benitz and Lieutenant H. Lloyd-Williams of the squadron's A Flight at Scampton took off at 2237, returning just thirteen minutes later because of petrol pressure problems. They were aloft again at 2310, but probably as a result of the same problem the aircraft crashed at Atwick at 0055. Benitz was killed and Lloyd-Williams was seriously injured.

There was one other crash that night. Lieutenant M. Aymard of No. 50 Squadron, Bekesbourne, was close enough to see the destruction of the L70, but by then he was well off course and his fuel was virtually depleted. He crash landed, escaping with just a broken ankle.

The losses of 19/20 May, followed by the destruction of the L70 on the night of 5/6 August, convinced the Germans that the bombing offensive against Britain had now become too great a risk. The British defences had improved markedly since the first Zeppelin raids. They were now able to deal effectively with the lumbering airships, as well as improving their chances of intercepting bombers. The Germans, of course, had made a huge mistake by exposing their Zeppelins to the British defences on 5/6 August.

Henceforth Germany decided to concentrate its bombers on the Western Front. They had originally determined that as and when it was appropriate they would launch further raids against the British mainland, but in August this plan was abandoned and in order to deploy all its resources against a possible defeat on the continent, the bombing of England was now officially cancelled. They also realized that the British had an effective counter-weapon which could launch devastating reprisal raids, even against Berlin. They had built up their own bomber strength and as the German ground forces were gradually forced back, Berlin was now within range.

CHAPTER ELEVEN

The Legacy of the Raids

A s we have seen, the British first became aware of the potential threat of the German heavy bombers in October 1917, and General Smuts proposed the creation of a separate air force. The Prime Minister, David Lloyd George, however, considered it premature.

The first task would be the creation of an Air Ministry, but the Air Board ruled it out. Various people were keen to ensure that the British air effort became more co-ordinated, amongst them Lord Cowdray. One of his closest friends was Rear Admiral Mark Kerr, who was so convinced that aircraft would be useful in anti-submarine warfare that he had taken pilot training in 1914. Kerr had discovered from Italian sources that the Germans were in the process of building 4,000 large bombers. He wrote a memorandum, which was presented to the Air Board via Cowdray and became known as the 'bombshell'. He claimed that the Germans would soon have the capacity to flatten Britain's factories and that London and the south-east of England would be prime targets. He argued that an Air Ministry should be set up immediately, which would be able to prioritize output to build at least 2,000 British bombers.

This memorandum, which was addressed to the President of the Air Board, prompted Cowdray to see the Prime Minister. It had the desired effect. The War Cabinet ordered the British Secret Service to send agents to discover whether claims in the memorandum had any basis of fact. None was disproved.

On 16 October 1917 the House of Commons was formally told that an Air Ministry would be established. The Air Force Bill was introduced in November. It had many opponents, but it also had a huge number of supporters. Many politicians and senior military figures had advocated the continued bombing of key German industrial targets in order to prevent the Germans from achieving technological superiority. The Bill passed easily through both the House of Commons and the House of Lords and received Royal Assent on 29 November 1917. The speed of the change was unprecedented, but the move occurred only just in time to have a marked effect on the coming Gotha and Giant offensives.

The first Air Council was established on 2 January 1918. As we have seen, Lord Rothermere became head of the Air Ministry, supported by Major General Hugh Trenchard, with Mark Kerr as Deputy Chief of the Air Staff. Lieutenant General Sir David Henderson became the Vice President of the Air Council. The Ministry, for the time being, was based at the Hotel Cecil, in London.

The creation of the Air Ministry brought about an unhappy marriage of the RNAS and the army's RFC. The services overtly despised one another and the final insult as far as the army was concerned was the adoption of a pale blue uniform. In practice, the men wore a variety of khaki, blue, khaki with naval ranks, and every other variation possible. The RAF officially came into existence on 1 April 1918, with a paper strength of 25,000 officers and 140,000 other ranks.

It was believed that the Air Ministry would only survive until the end of the war and that at that point the RAF would be disbanded and its responsibilities returned to the army and the navy. As it was, political manoeuvring brought about Trenchard's resignation and Major General Frederick H. Sykes replaced him. Kerr had already left, having failed to agree with Trenchard on strategic matters. As we have seen, Rothermere also departed, to be replaced by Sir William Weir.

As far as the British knew, these raids of May 1918 heralded the beginning of large-scale bomber offensives. What was needed was a fully integrated system of alarms and controls, coupled with the facility to engage the German aircraft from artillery batteries and from scrambled fighter squadrons. Such a system was up and running by 12 September. Brigadier General Edward B Ashmore was responsible for the warning control system, and three hours after the system became operational, he ordered British aircraft to fly a practice raid. From estimates made from the warnings, the interception rate was four times better than it had been before.

By October, however, the German Western Front had been shattered, and some sixteen squadrons lay in wait in Britain for bombers that never returned. Gradually they were given orders to transfer to France, although only one had established itself there before the armistice. Even though the German bomber offensive had been broken, the British still maintained huge numbers of forces in southern England in case it should resume.

What the British had not known was that the May attacks had shattered the strength of the German bomber fleet. With the continued pressure on the Western front, the bombers were needed for tactical bombing along the front. A planned raid against England was called off on 1 July and although Paris was bombed in September, the Gothas had to be pressed into action against British bombers over Belgium during the night. The German squadrons had taken enormous casualties and possibly the last time they were involved in offensive operations was against Menin, a British supply depot, on 30 October.

After the armistice, the German bombers were specifically named as weapons, and had to be turned over to the victorious Allies. RFA 501 was officially disbanded early in 1919. Its total casualties were 137 dead, eighty-eight missing and over 200 wounded. These figures included actions on the Western Front. It suffered sixty aircraft losses in their attacks against Britain, twenty-four either shot down by British aircraft or otherwise lost and thirty-six were lost in crashes and other accidents.

The British learned many lessons from the German bomber squadrons. The independent Royal Air Force came into existence on 5 June 1918, with an express purpose of striking German industrial targets.

It was able to strike against German towns and cities, which prompted civilians to ask the German High Command to stop bombing Allied civilian targets, as attacks on German towns and cities were being made in reprisal. By April German politicians had joined the call to begin negotiation with the Allies to cease air raids on civilian targets. But the German government would do nothing unless first approached by the Allies.

Shortly after the Air Ministry suggested that the Allied bomber fleet be expanded to sixty squadrons, but it faced strong opposition from Allied ground commanders, such as Field Marshall Douglas Haig and the French Marshal, Ferdinand Foch. Even the chief of the French air service, General Duval, questioned the Independent Air Force's right to be independent. It was felt that the key objective of the Allies had shifted from defeating the enemy in the field to bombing them into submission. It was also felt that the creation of the Independent Air Force was siphoning off men and equipment needed for the ground war.

The Air Ministry found an ally in Colonel, later General, William Mitchell, commanding the air squadrons of the US 1st Army. US aircrews were trained and supplied by the British and it was proposed that they become part of the bomber offensive.

In June around 70 tons of bombs were dropped on Germany. By August this had increased to 100 tons. By September the British front-line bombers numbered around 120. It also became clear that the Air Ministry wanted the Independent Air Force to perform something particularly spectacular. In essence they wanted to drop incendiaries on an old part of a German town or city and level it to the ground. The morale and propaganda value of such an action was believed to be enormous.

Trenchard became Commander-in-Chief of the Allied air force on 26 October. Along with British squadrons, he commanded French, Italian and American units. The decision to unite proved too late for the new Allied Air Force to launch any large-scale air offensive against Germany; had the war continued into 1919, beyond doubt all of these squadrons would have been unleashed against Germany. Three Handley Page V/1500, four-engined bombers, with a bomb capacity of 7,500 lb, were due to launch the first raid against Berlin on the very day that the armistice was declared.

By mid-November the Allied squadrons allocated to Trenchard's new force were back in their home countries' hands and the Independent Air Force was transferred to General Haig's overall command. Although the post-war years were difficult for the RAF, the basic idea of the need for a strategic bomber force had become ingrained and assisted by the fact that Winston Churchill had become Minister for War and Air in 1919, as part of the Lloyd George government. He ignored Lloyd George's policy of bringing the RAF back into the hands of the army and the navy, and when he left the Air Ministry in 1922 following the collapse of Lloyd George's government, Trenchard was still at hand to fight the RAF's corner.

Gotha and Giant raids accounted for around 60 per cent of all casualties inflicted on the British by air attacks. There were fifty-one airship attacks on Britain during the war and fifty-two by aircraft. Slightly over 1,400 people had been killed and just over 3,400 injured. Infrastructure damage had totalled around £3 million.

Comparing this with the huge losses of ground troops on the Western Front, many have dismissed the German air raids against Britain as being insignificant, but both the British and the Germans learned lessons. Both nations now realized that air raids were both practicable and effective. They not only instilled terror in the civilian population, but they also tied up thousands of men and millions of pounds of military equipment in air defences.

The German air raids had a huge psychological impact and many, Winston Churchill included, would not forget their power and terror. In the summer of 1918 Churchill had predicted that 3 or 4 million Londoners would flee the capital and seek shelter and food in the countryside, he was not far wrong.

Nearly twenty years later, Sir Malcolm Campbell, who had been a pilot during the war, warned that, based on the experience of Gotha and Giant raids against Britain, the growing new German air force, the

Luftwaffe, would be able to drop 1,000 tons of bombs a night, four times the combined tonnage dropped during all the Gotha and Giant bomber raids in the First World War. At about the same time, the Air Ministry predicted that Britain would suffer fifty casualties per ton of explosives dropped, based on casualty figures from the Gotha and Giant raids. Indeed, these raids had killed or wounded fifty-two people for every ton. As it transpired, the experience of German bombing raids during 1940 and 1941 showed that this was a gross overestimate.

Again based on the Gotha and Giant raids, the Air Ministry calculated that Britain would suffer 600,000 dead and 1.2 million wounded during the first few months of the Second World War, on the assumption that the Germans would drop 3,500 tons of bombs on the first day and 600 tons every day thereafter. These figures were not inconceivable, as a full third of the British population at that time lived in fifteen cities around the country.

The longer-term psychological implications of the raids clearly weighed heavily with people such as Neville Chamberlain, the future Chief of the Imperial General Staff, Field Marshal Lord Ironside and, of course, the French. Chamberlain had been the Lord Mayor of Birmingham in 1916 and had seen at first hand the terror instilled in the local population and officials of a Zeppelin attack. He was also acutely aware of the effectiveness of German air power nearly twenty years later, when they had devastated targets such as Barcelona during the Spanish Civil War.

In March 1938 Chamberlain, prior to making any decision about the German's effective annexion of Austria and their increasingly bellicose attitude towards Czechoslovakia, asked the British Chiefs of Staff what were the military implications of going to war once more. They were unanimous in their opinion that if Britain went to war in defence of Czechoslovakia then the war would be lost. Paramount was their fear that the Germans could, at will, devastate British cities. Britain would be relatively powerless to stop them and impotent to strike back at strategic targets in Germany.

The bomber offensive had also acutely affected Ironside during the First World War. He was certain the Cabinet believed that the Germans had the ability to wipe out Britain in fairly short order. In his diaries he wrote: 'We cannot expose ourselves now to a German attack. We simply commit suicide if we do. At no time could we stand up against German air bombing. What a mess we are in.'

Despite the lessons of air power in the First World War, Britain failed to follow a considered rearmament policy until 1934. Only then did the Government realize that the main danger lay in bombardment from the air. Rather belatedly, priority was then given to the RAF.

Administrative control of the Fleet Air Arm was given to the Admiralty in 1937, two years later they had to face the Germans in biplanes. In 1939 the British lacked a tactical arm to support their infantry and tank divisions and shortly after May 1940, the country was in imminent danger of a sea-borne invasion.

The fear of aerial destruction continued, and at the outbreak of war on 3 September 1939, two million Londoners fled the capital, although it would not be a target for the *Luftwaffe* for at least another year. The Germans were also certain that air power could bring Britain to its knees. Hermann Göring boasted that the *Luftwaffe* would strike with such ferocity that Britain would sue for peace. However, paradoxically, the Germans had neglected to develop four-engined bombers. Their aircraft were more suited to supporting a ground offensive, and their tactics were to devastate tactical and strategic targets close to the front. The problem arose when the *panzer* divisions needed to cross the English Channel.

The first Chief of the German Air Staff, General Max von Wever, had proposed the construction of heavy bombers with extreme range. He had ordered prototypes to be completed as early as 1936 and had these developments continued, squadrons of them would have been ready for action against Britain by 1940. As it was, von Wever died in an air crash and the Germans seemed from that point to be obsessed with numbers of aircraft rather than their size and capacity.

Even the development of radar and the Spitfire, arguably one of the best defensive fighters ever produced, can be regarded as a legacy of the Gotha and Giant raids of the First World War. It meant that Britain had adequate, although stretched, air defences by the time the Germans unleashed the *Luftwaffe* against them during the Battle of Britain in 1940. Learning from the raids of twenty-two years earlier, Britain also had an effective heavy bomber-striking arm.

Bomber Command itself came into existence in 1936 as the result of the reorganization of the RAF. Sir Cyril Newall became Chief of the Air Staff in 1937. It was a significant appointment, as he had been involved in the reprisal bomber raids against Germany in October 1917. He called for 1,360 front-line bomber aircraft, with 300 per cent reserves. In 1939 he began to think more in terms of 3,500 heavy bombers, but production never reached a point where it could overtake casualties and by 1945 there were only 1,700 heavy bombers.

Another legacy of the raids was in the production of aircraft. Handley Page had only managed to produce four bombers from an order of 255 by the armistice in 1918. Yet during the Second World War they produced 40 per cent of all heavy bombers, notably the Halifax. Indeed the Halifax aircraft had dropped a total of 225,000 tons of bombs by 1945.

Although in both the First and the Second World Wars the Germans patently failed to bomb Britain into submission, by 1941 the British were considering the possibility, that strategic bombing could knock Germany or Italy out of the war, the fact that Churchill, back in October 1917, had been clear that bombing, whilst terrorizing the civilian population, would never force a country to capitulate. Perhaps it was just part of his overall desire to make the Germans suffer for inflicting a Second World War on Britain. Churchill is quoted as saying that strategic bombing was just another way 'to make the enemy burn and bleed in every way'.

Prior to the surrender of the French, the British government still held back from targeting civilians. This was due to a number of factors, not least amongst which was the fact that they believed it was against international law. They were also concerned that it would alienate pro-British feeling in the United States. They would not attack German civilian targets until they had irrefutable evidence that the Germans had done so, overlooking the fact that the Germans had bombed Warsaw and Poland into submission.

Bomber Command launched its first raid against Germany on 10 May 1940, the very day that the Germans launched their attack on the Low Countries and ultimately France. Five days later, on the 15th, whilst the Germans were launching a devastating raid on Rotterdam, 100 British bombers raided Germany.

Although the Germans did not attack London during the summer of 1940, Bomber Command struck at Bremen, Essen, Hamburg and several other German cities. It was not until 24 August that twelve German bombers, whose actual targets were Thameshaven and Rochester, dropped their bombs on central London. This gave the British the excuse that they had been waiting for and the following week they carried out reprisal raids on Berlin.

On 7 September 1940, on the twenty-fifth anniversary of the first major Zeppelin raid against the city, 300 German bombers with fighter escorts attacked London, claiming 1,600 casualties.

The British had also learned from the Gotha and Giant raids of the First World War and, more recently, the *Luftwaffe* attacks of 1940, that precise, surgical attacks on strategic targets were rarely effective. In May 1942 they adopted a rather more indiscriminate use for their bomber fleets, 1,000 British bombers struck Cologne. The effects of this raid, and the later attacks on Hamburg and Dresden, were far more devastating on German morale and their willingness to continue the struggle than anything that the German pilots in 1917 had ever contemplated.

The legacy of the tiny, silver specks in the sky over London in 1917 can be traced to the vast armadas of Allied aircraft over enemy occupied Europe less than twenty-five years later.

APPENDIX I

British Air Defences and Air Raid Casualties Inflicted by Gotha and Giant Raids 1917–18

In January 1918 the air defences in the London Air Defence area amounted to 249 guns, 323 searchlights, four balloon aprons and eight fighter squadrons with an authorized complement of twenty-four aircraft each. By November 1918 they had been improved to 304 guns, 415 searchlights, ten balloon aprons and eleven fighter squadrons.

No. 47 Wing was formed in October 1917 and consisted of No. 51 Squadron, with its headquarters at Thetford, Norfolk, and bases at Harling Road, Hingham, Marham, Mattishall and Tydd St Mary. It was equipped with FE2B and FE2D aircraft.

No. 49 Wing was created at Upminster in September 1917. It consisted of four squadrons. No. 39 Squadron had headquarters at Hounslow and Woodford, and operated out of Biggin Hill, Hainault Farm, North Weald and Suttons Farm. It was primarily equipped with BE2C, BE2E, BE12, BE12A, Armstrong Whitworth FK8s, SE5s, Sopwith Camels and Bristol Fighters. No. 44 Squadron was based at Hainault Farm and equipped with Sopwith 1$^1/_2$ Strutters and Sopwith Camels. No. 78 Squadron had its headquarters at Harrietsham and operated from Telscombe Cliffs, Chiddingstone Causeway, Gosport, Biggin Hill and Suttons Farm. Like No. 39 Squadron, it was equipped with various BE aircraft and also Sopwith 1$^1/_2$ Strutters, FE2Ds and Sopwith Camels. No. 141 Squadron, also part of No. 49 Wing, was based at Rochford and at Biggin Hill. It too had various BE aircraft, as well as Bristol Fighters and Sopwith Dolphins.

No. 50 Wing was formed in August 1917 and consisted of Nos. 37, 61 and 75 Squadrons. No. 37 Squadron had its headquarters at Woodham Mortimer and operated out of Goldhanger, Rochford and Stow Maries. It was equipped with various BE aircraft, RE7s, Sopwith 1$^1/_2$ Strutters, Pups and Camels, and SE5As. No. 61 Squadron, based at Rochford, was equipped with Sopwith Pups and Camels and SE5As. No. 75 Squadron had its headquarters at Goldington and operated out of Therfield, St Neots, Thrapston, Elmswell, Hadleigh and Harling Road. It was equipped with BE2Cs, BE2Es, BE12s, BE12Bs and Avro 504Ks.

The final wing was No. 53, consisting of Nos. 50, 112 and 143 Squadrons. It was formed in March 1918. No. 50 Squadron had its headquarters at Dover and Harrietsham, and operated out of Bekesbourne, Detling and Throwley. It was equipped with various BE aircraft, Armstrong Whitworth FK8s, Sopwith Camels and SE5As. No. 112 Squadron was based at Throwley, Kent, and equipped with Sopwith Pups and Camels. Finally No. 43 Squadron, based at Detling, Kent, was equipped with Armstrong Whitworth FK8s, SE5As and Sopwith Camels.

Total casualties caused by Gotha and Giant raids 1917–18

Area	Number Killed	Number Wounded	Total
London and surrounding area	488	1437	1925 (including those killed by British anti-aircraft fire and air raid shelter stampedes)
Folkestone and Shorncliff Camp	89	184	273
Chatham and naval installations	132	96	228
Harwich, Felixstowe and the naval air station	27	56	83
Southend, Shoeburyness and Rochford airfield	34	47	81
Sheerness	17	51	68
Dover	12	36	48 (including casualties caused by another German aircraft on 2 September 1917)
Margate	15	24	39
Ramsgate	10	23	33
Kent (other)	8	25	33
Essex	1	3	4
Suffolk	3	0	3
Total	**836**	**1982**	**2818**

APPENDIX II

Chronological Breakdown of Gotha and Giant Raids on Britain 1917–18

Date	Target	Number Despatched & Type	Number Attacked & Type	Bombs Dropped (kg)	Ground Casualties k – killed l – injured	Defensive Sorties Flown	Air Casualties
25 May 1917 (Daylight)	Folkestone/ Shorncliffe Camp	23 Gothas	21 Gothas	5,200	95k/195i £19,405 damage	77	1 Gotha lost over English Channel 1 Gotha crashed
5 June 1917 (Daylight)	Sheerness/ Shoeburyness	22 Gothas	22 Gothas	5,000	13k/34i £5,003 damage	62	1 Gotha shot down
13 June 1917 (Daylight)	London/ Margate	20 Gothas	18 Gothas	4,400	162k/432i £129,498 damage	94	1 British aircraft forced down
4 July 1917 (Daylight)	Harwich/ Felixstowe	25 Gothas	18 Gothas	4,400	17k/30i £2,065 damage	103	1 British aircraft forced down
7 July 1917 (Daylight)	London	24 Gothas	22 Gothas	4,475	57k/193i £205,622 damage	108	1 Gotha shot down 4 Gothas crashed on landing 1 British aircraft shot down 1 British aircraft forced down
22 July 1917 (Daylight)	Harwich/ Felixstowe	23 Gothas	21 Gothas	5,225	13k/26i £2,780 damage	122	1 Gotha crashed on landing
12 August 1917 (Daylight)	Southend/ Shoeburyness/ Margate	13 Gothas	11 Gothas	2,125	33k/46i £9,600 damage	139	1 Gotha shot down 4 Gothas crashed on landing

Date	Target	Number Despatched & Type	Number Attacked & Type	Bombs Dropped (kg)	Ground Casualties k – killed l – injured	Defensive Sorties Flown	Air Casualties
22 August 1917 (Daylight)	Margate/ Ramsgate/ Dover	15 Gothas	10 Gothas	1,900	12k/27i £17,145 damage	138	3 Gothas shot down
3/4 September 1917 (Night)	Chatham/ Sheerness/ Margate	5 Gothas	4 Gothas	1,315	132k/96i £3,993 damage	16	None
4/5 September 1917 (Night)	London/ Margate/ Dover	11 Gothas	9 Gothas	3,060	19k/17i £46,047 damage	18	1 Gotha missing
24/25 September 1917 (Night)	London/ Dover	16 Gothas	13 Gothas	4,285	21k/70i £30,818 damage	30	1 Gotha crashed on return trip 1 British aircraft crashed
25/26 September 1917 (Night)	London/ East Kent	15 Gothas	14 Gothas	4,000	9k/23i £16,394 damage	20	1 Gotha missing 2 British aircraft crashed
28/29 September 1917 (Night)	London/ Coast of Suffolk/ Kent/Essex	23 Gothas 2 Giants	3 Gothas 2 Giants	3,100	£129 damage	23	3 Gothas shot down 6 Gothas crashed on landing 1 British aircraft crashed
29/30 September 1917 (night)	London/ Sheerness	7 Gothas 3 Giants	4 Gothas 3 Giants	£3,375	40k/87i £23,154 damage	33	1 Gotha shot down 1 Gotha forced down in Holland
30 September/ 1 October 1917 (Night)	London/ Margate/ Dover	11 Gothas 1 Single-engined aircraft	10 Gothas 1 single-engined aircraft	£3,690	14k/38i £21,482 damage	37	None
1/2 October 1917 (Night)	London/ Kent/ Essex	18 Gothas	12 Gothas	3,705	11k/42i £42,570 damage	19	Unknown
29/30 October 1917 (Night)	Essex coast	3 Gothas	1 Gotha	450	–	7	1 British aircraft crashed
31 October/ 1 November 1917 (Night)	London/ Ramsgate/ Dover	22 Gothas	22 Gothas	5,815	10k/22i £22,822 damage	50	5 Gothas crashed on landing 2 British aircraft crashed
5/6 December 1917 (Night)	London/ Sheerness/ Margate/ Dover	19 Gothas 2 Giants	16 Gothas 2 Giants	7,770	8k/28i £103,408 damage	34	5 Gothas crashed on landing 2 British aircraft crashed

Date	Target	Number Despatched & Type	Number Attacked & Type	Bombs Dropped (kg)	Ground Casualties k – killed l – injured	Defensive Sorties Flown	Air Casualties
18/19 December 1917 (Night)	London/ Margate	15 Gothas 1 Giant	13 Gothas 1 Giant	5,125	14k/83i £238,816 damage	47	2 Gothas shot down by anti-aircraft guns 1 Gotha missing 1 Gotha crashed on landing
22/23 December 1917 (Night)	Kent coast	2 Giants	2 Giants	2,000	None	18	None
28/29 January 1918 (Night)	London/ Sheerness/ Margate/ Dover	13 Gothas 2 Giants	7 Gothas 1 Giant	3,700	67k/166i £187,350 damage	103	1 Gotha shot down 1 Gotha crashed on landing 1 British aircraft forced down
29/30 January 1918 (Night)	London/ Essex coast	4 Giants	3 Giants	3,000	10k/10i £8,968 damage	80	None
16/17 February 1918 (Night)	London/ Dover	5 Giants	5 Giants (German records) 3 Giants (British records)	4,250	12k/6i £19,264	60	None
17/18 February 1918 (Night)	London	1 Giant	1 Giant	1,000	21k/32i £38,992 damage	69	1 British aircraft crashed
7/8 March 1918 (Night)	London/ Herne Bay	6 Giants	5 Giants	5,020	23k/39i £42,655 damage	42	2 Giants crash landed during return flight 2 British aircraft lost in aerial collision
19/20 May 1918 (Night)	London/ Faversham/ Dover	38 Gothas 3 Giants 2 Recon aircraft	28 Gothas 3 Giants 2 Recon aircraft	14,550	49k/177i £177,317 damage	88	1 Gotha forced down over England 5 Gothas shot down 1 Gotha crashed on return journey

APPENDIX III

Summary of Staaken Aircraft that Flew Over Britain

The most numerous Staaken aircraft that flew bombing raids against Britain were the RVI models. They were covered in a printed camouflage fabric, usually of a dark colour, mostly a mixture of Prussian and ultramarine blue. Their serial numbers were painted in large, white figures near the rear fuselage side. Several of them had successful careers as bombers during a short period in 1918.

Aircraft Number	Service History and Known Fate
R12	The R12 was the only Giant to join a Gotha attack on London on the night of 18/19 December 1917. It crossed the British coast north of the Crouch at 2220 and dropped a pair of 660lb bombs and incendiaries on London at around 2110. It then headed back over the coastline at around 2200.

It was back and involved in an attack on the south-eastern coastal towns on the night of 22/23 December. It apparently attacked shipping in the Thames Estuary, along with the R39, but all their bombs missed their targets and landed in the sea between Ramsgate and Sandwich.

On the night of 28/29 January 1918 it was then involved in an attack on London. It crossed Hollesley Bay at 2225 and was over central London at 0015. Its two 660lb bombs hit the Oldhams Press building in Long Acre, killing thirty-eight and injuring eighty-five.

The R12 had escaped a potentially fatal encounter over Harlow during its approach to London. It was attacked by a Bristol of No. 39 Squadron. The aircraft, crewed by John Goodyear and Walter Merchant, encountered it at 10,000ft at around 2300. On its second attack the Bristol came under fire from the R12 and a burst shattered the main petrol tank and wounded Merchant. Goodyear was forced to make an emergency landing.

It had a second close call over Chingford, when it hit the balloon barrage.

The following night it was due to be involved in another attack on London, but this time it suffered engine trouble over the Channel and instead bombed Allied fortifications near Gravelines.

On the night of 16/17 February 1918 it crossed the British coast at Maplin at around 2140 hours. It approached London at around 9,500ft, too low to avoid the balloon apron at Woolwich. The starboard wing hit one of the cables and the aircraft began to spin out of control. The pilot, Lieutenant Götte, shut off the power then opened up his two port engines and managed to restore control. Two 660lb bombs fell out over Woolwich, but the aircraft flew on and bombed Beckenham, returning to base at 0125.

The next verifiable attack it was involved in took place on the night of 19/20 May 1918, the target being London. It probably crossed the British coastline at 2217 and may have been the aircraft that then bombed Dover. Alternatively it may have been part of the main force that went on to London. The attacks began on London at 2330.

R13   The R13 was one of six aircraft that attacked London on the night of 7/8 March 1918. Its front starboard engine failed over London, but it continued on its mission and was involved in the bombing between 0010 and 0035.

The only other verifiable occasion when it was involved was on the night of 19/20 May 1918, when it was one of three Giants that accompanied twenty-eight Gothas on another attack on London.

R25   Built at Staaken in late 1916, the R25 was accepted into service on 6 June 1917 and posted to RFA 500, on the Eastern Front, for trials. With a full combat load it completed a $6^1/_2$-hour test flight on 28 July 1917. It was then flown to Cologne on 5 August, where it became operational as part of RFA 501.

On the night of 29/30 September 1917 it was involved in an air raid on London. It was again positively identified on the night of 29/30 January 1918 in another attack on London. On this occasion it was picked up over North Benfleet at 2315 and attacked by Second Lieutenant R. N. Hall of No. 44 Squadron, flying a Sopwith Camel out of Hainault. His guns jammed after five rounds and the R25 took evasive action. Other members of his squadron joined him. At around 2325 hours, over Brentwood, one of the R25's port engines seized, but it continued on course for

London. It could not maintain height and its speed was down to 58mph. It commenced bombing at midnight from a height of 5,900ft and continued to lose height during its return journey. When it landed it was discovered that it had been hit eighty-eight times.

On the night of 16/17 February 1918 it was part of a group of four Giants that attacked the London and Dover areas. It was primarily responsible for the attack on Dover, where it dropped eighteen bombs at around 2240.

On the following night it made a solo attack on St Pancras Station in London. It was the only serviceable Giant and it was being flown by Lieutenant Max Borchers. It dropped eighteen bombs, with the final eight hitting the station and hotel. It then climbed to 9,800ft and crossed the British coastline at Folkestone at 0013 hours. It had made an average speed of 62mph over its six hours and twenty-three minutes.

Its last known attack over Britain took place on the night of 7/8 March 1918, when it was part of a five-Giant attack on London.

R26   Built at Staaken, the R26 was accepted into service on 24 July 1917 and became operational as part of RFA 501. It was commanded by Fritz Pheiffer and piloted by Lieutenant Wilhelm Pier.

It was involved in the attack on London on 29/30 September 1917, and was also in the attack on London on the night of 29/30 January 1918. Its crew mistook the Blackwater for the Thames, and instead of crossing the British coast at Southend at 2244 hours, it crossed at the Naze. Around forty minutes later, whilst at 10,000ft, two of its engines developed problems and it rapidly began to lose height. Its bomb load was jettisoned over Rayleigh. The crew managed to maintain a height of around 5,000ft on two engines, reaching Ostend at around 0150.

It crash landed and burned on the night of 9/10 May 1918 at Scheldewideke, in heavy fog.

R27   Built by Schütte-Lanz, the R27 successfully negotiated its acceptance flights in October 1917 and joined RFA 501 on 23 January 1918. During its involvement in the raids over Britain Captain Schoeller commanded it.

Its last contribution took place on the night of 7/8 March 1918, when it was one of five Giants involved in a raid on London. It came over the British coastline at Deal at 2256. Explanations vary as to its fate, but it was certainly suffering from navigational problems fairly early on in the raid. It crashed just inside the German lines at Courtrai. This meant that the aircraft was way off course and had, perhaps, run out of fuel. According to German records it crash landed because of frozen fuel lines. The crew managed to escape and the engines and instrumentation were salvaged from the wreck, but the rest was destroyed by Allied artillery fire.

R33   This aircraft was built by Aviatik and accepted into service in October 1917, becoming operational with RFA 501.

It was one of a group of four Giants that attacked London and Dover on the night of 16/17 February 1918. It approached Deal at around 2045, with difficulties with both port engines. The forward one had already stopped. The crew dropped their bombs on shipping and turned for home. Immediately the rear port engine stopped and the rear starboard one dropped to half power. The aircraft was losing height, so the machine-guns and other equipment were jettisoned. It continued to descend from 7,200ft to 650ft. The problem was that the cold weather had affected the oil circulation. One of the mechanics punctured the oil tank with his knife and transferred the oil in his hands to the rear port engine in order to keep it running. The aircraft limped into safety at Scheldewindeke. It was not so fortunate on 15 October 1918 when it crashed.

R35   Built by Aviatik, and accepted into service on 26 February 1918, the R35 flew its first test flights during June and July 1918.

It was due to be part of an operation in late January 1918, but it had developed engine trouble and jettisoned its bombs to the north of Ostend.

No other details of this aircraft are known.

R36   Built by Albatros, the R36 was accepted in October 1917 and became operational with RFA 501. It was involved in the raid on London and Dover on the night of 16/17 February 1918. It had bomb door problems and only dropped two 550lb bombs. Even these completely missed their targets. The aircraft was dismantled and used for spare parts after it made an emergency landing on the night of 7/8 March 1918.

R39   Built by Staaken and completed on 18 July 1917, this aircraft was accepted into service on 9 August 1917 and became operational as part of RFA 501.

Captain von Bentivegni commanded it, with Lieutenant von Lenz and Lieutenant Buth as pilots. It was the most successful of all of the R-planes and was estimated to have dropped 26,000kg of bombs in twenty bombing raids.

Over Britain it was involved in the attack on Sheerness on the night of 29/30 September 1917.

It was again involved against Margate on 6 December 1917 and against London on 29 January, 16 February and 7 March 1918. It returned to attack Dover on 9 May 1918 and Chelmsford on 19 May 1918.

The aircraft also has the distinction of being the only one to have dropped all three 1,000kg bombs on Britain during the war.

APPENDIX IV

RNAS and RFC Squadrons Scrambled During Gotha and Giant Raids, 1917–18

Formation	25/5/17	5/6/17	13/6/17	4/7/17	7/7/17	22/7/17	12/8/17	22/8/17	3–4/9/17	4–5/9/17	24–25/9/17	25–26/9/17	28–29/9/17	29–30/9/17	30/09–01/10/17	1–2/10/17	29–30/10/17	13/10–01/11/17	5–6/12/17	18–19/12/17	22–23/12/17	28–29/1/18	29–30/1/18	16–17/2/18	17–18/2/18	07–08/3/18	19–20/5/18
RNAS Dover	*	*	*	*	*	*	*	*																		*	*
RNAS Eastchurch	*	*	*			*	*	*										*								*	
RNAS Felixstowe	*		*																								
RNAS Grain	*	*	*			*		*																			
RNAS Manston	*		*	*	*	*	*	*					*		*	*		*									
RNAS Westgate	*	*	*			*																					
RNAS Walmer	*	*	*	*	*	*	*	*															*				
RFC 37 Squadron	*	*	*	*	*	*	*	*	*	*	*	*	*	*		*	*	*	*	*	*	*	*	*	*	*	*
RFC 39 Squadron	*	*	*	*	*	*	*	*	*	*	*	*	*	*		*	*	*	*	*	*	*	*	*	*	*	*
RFC 50 Squadron	*	*	*	*	*	*	*	*	*	*	*	*	*			*	*		*	*	*	*	*	*	*	*	*
RFC 44 Squadron								*	*	*	*	*	*	*	*	*	*	*		*	*	*	*	*	*	*	*
RFC 78 Squadron	*	*	*			*	*	*					*	*	*	*	*	*		*	*	*	*	*	*	*	*
No 8 AAP	*			*	*	*	*	*																			
RFC 65 Squadron	*		*	*			*	*																			
RFC 35 (T) Squadron	*		*	*	*			*																			
No 2 AAP	*		*	*	*	*																					
No 198 Depot Squadron				*		*		*									*										
RFC 40 (T) Squadron				*	*	*		*	*																		
RFC 62 (T) Squadron					*		*	*	*																		

Formation	25/5/17	5/6/17	13/6/17	4/7/17	7/7/17	22/7/17	12/8/17	22/8/17	3-4/9/17	4-5/9/17	24-25/9/17	25-26/9/17	28-29/9/17	29-30/9/17	30/09-01/10/17	1-2/10/17	29-30/10/17	13/10-01/11/17	5-6/12/17	18-19/12/17	22-23/12/17	28-29/1/18	29-30/1/18	16-17/2/18	17-18/2/18	07-08/3/18	19-20/5/18
Experimental Station Orford Ness	*	*	*	*	*	*					*			*	*												
RNAS Great Yarmouth				*		*																					
RNAS Burgh Castle				*																							
RNAS Covehithe				*																							
RFC 56 Squadron				*																							
RFC 56 (T) Squadron				*	*				*	*																	
Training Squadron Martlesham Heath				*	*	*	*	*																			
No 66 Squadron Calais				*																							
No 7 AAP					*			*																			
RFC 46 Squadron								*	*	*																	
RFC 63 (T) Squadron			*		*				*	*																	
RFC 61 Squadron								*	*													*	*	*	*	*	*
RFC 112 Squadron								*	*																	*	*
RFC 75 Squadron																						*	*				
RFC 141 Squadron																								*	*	*	*
RFC 143 Squadron																								*	*	*	*

* Denotes that the squadron was scrambled for that raid.

APPENDIX V

RFC Squadrons and Pilots Deployed Against Gotha and Giant Raids 1917–18

In the lists of pilots we have identified them by their rank the first time they were scrambled for that squadron. The lists include not just pilots but gunners and observers. Note also that several of the pilots appear more than once in different squadrons. This illustrates the fact that some of the new squadrons in particular were created with a cadre of experienced pilots from other squadrons. This is particularly the case in No. 143 Squadron, which was created on 1 February 1918. The pilots that were scrambled to deal with the four Giants that attacked the British Isles on the night of 16/17 February 1918 had had experience in other squadrons.

No. 37 Squadron
No. 37 Squadron's origins derived from the Experimental Station at Orford Ness, which was created on 15 April 1916. It officially came into existence on 15 September 1916 and was originally headquartered at Woodham Manor and operated flights from Goldhanger, Rochford and Stow Maries. One of its BE12s was responsible for the destruction of the German navy Zeppelin L48 over Suffolk on the night of 16/17 June 1917.

After the war, in March 1919, the squadron moved to Biggin Hill. It was officially disbanded on 1 July 1919, but in effect it lived on in a new guise, as No. 39 Squadron.

No. 37 Squadron Pilots Scrambled
Lieutenant C. D. Kershaw, Lieutenant W. R. S. Humphreys, Lieutenant L. P. Watkins, Lieutenant L. F. Hutcheon, Captain C. A. Ridley, Captain C. B. Cook, Lieutenant Orr-Ewing, Captain K. N. Pearson, Captain W. Sowrey, Lieutenant R. F. Oakes, Second Lieutenant H. A. Blane, Second Lieutenant J. E. R. Young, Second Lieutenant G. V. A. Gleed, Lieutenant A. A. C. Garnons-Williams, Lieutenant Bennett, Lieutenant G. D. F. Keddie, Corporal W. Rowley, Second

Lieutenant H. A. Edwardes, Captain E. B. Mason, Captain E. S. Cotterill, Lieutenant J. Potter, Captain C. E. Holman, Second Lieutenant G. A. Thompson, Aircraftsman Burtenshaw, Lieutenant Brooks, Sergeant MacDonald, Lieutenant C. V. Clayton, Lieutenant P. R. Cawdell, Second Lieutenant S. Armstrong, Second Lieutenant C. L. Milburn, Second Lieutenant L. T. Onslow, Captain J. L. Horridge, Second Lieutenant J. H. Hayward, Captain A. Dennis, Second Lieutenant O. A. Beckett, Second Lieutenant N. H. Colson, Second Lieutenant E. H. Chater, Second Lieutenant S. Hay, Second Lieutenant A. C. Goldsmith, Second Lieutenant F. R. Kitton, Second Lieutenant A. D. de Fleury, Lieutenant C. L. Blake, Lieutenant H. Lingard, Captain A. B. Kynoch, Captain A. B. Fanstone, Second Lieutenant Foster, Second Lieutenant Murray, Lieutenant Lawrence, Second Lieutenant Spencer, Second Lieutenant Burfoot.

No. 39 Squadron
No. 39 Squadron was created at Hounslow on 15 April 1916. Initially it operated flights out of Hainault Farm and Suttons Farm. In August 1916 a further flight was established at North Weald. Initially it operated with BE2s but in September 1917 it was equipped with Bristol Fighters. The squadron remained operational against Gotha and Giant attacks until November 1918, when it was transferred to France. It was only in Europe for five days prior to the armistice and was eventually disbanded on 16 November 1918.

No. 39 Squadron Pilots Scrambled
Lieutenant E. M. Gilbert, Second Lieutenant A. A. Wilcock, Captain L. F. Hursthouse, Captain S. R. Stammers, Captain R. G. H. Murray, Lieutenant E. S. Moulton-Barrett, Captain J. I. Mackay, Captain W. T. F. Holland, Captain W. H. Haynes, Lieutenant G. T. Wix, Captain T. Gran, Lieutenant Fraser, Second Lieutenant C. L. Brock, Captain O. V. Thomas, Lieutenant C. B. van Leonhof, Lieutenant G. T. Stoneham, Captain J. O. C. Orton, Captain Hope, Aircraftsman Gellan, Lieutenant R. S. Bozman, Lieutenant P. W. L. Jarvis, Captain G. D. F. Keddie, Lieutenant C. J. Chabot, Second Lieutenant W. B. Thomson, Second Lieutenant A. M. Bennett, Captain W. St John Boultbee, Second Lieutenant L. Taylor, Captain J. M. Clarke, Second Lieutenant N. H. Auret, Second Lieutenant A. T. Kemp, Second Lieutenant V. C. Chapman, Second Lieutenant E. J. Stockman, Captain J. A. Dennistoun, Second Lieutenant P. F. O. Frith, Second Lieutenant T. B. Pritchard, Second Lieutenant W. Hunt, Captain L. E. Eeman, Second Lieutenant A. E. Simmons, Lieutenant V. A. Lanos, Second Lieutenant A. J. Winstanley, Lieutenant Robbins, Corporal Gee, Lieutenant C. R. W. Knight, Lieutenant L. Speller, Lieutenant A. L. Harrow-Bunn, Lieutenant P. W. Deane, Lieutenant J. G. Goodyear, Aircraftsman W. T. Merchant, Lieutenant E. S. C. Brooks, Second Lieutenant J. T. Baugh, Aircraftsman Coombes, Second Lieutenant F. J. B. de S la Terriere, Second Lieutenant E. J. Ralli, Sergeant Riches, Aircraftsman W. Eatock, Second Lieutenant H. P. Lale, Lieutenant L. B. Hawkswell, Aircraftsman E. Gudgeon, Aircraftsman A. T. C. Stagg, Aircraftsman L. Card, Lieutenant C. Evans, Aircraftsman Parks, Sergeant Major

Wyatt, Aircraftsman Easton, Lieutenant J. L. N. Bennett-Baggs, Lieutenant A. J. F. Bawden, Lieutenant Forest.

No. 44 Squadron
No. 44 Squadron was created at Hainault Farm on 24 July 1917 and was initially equipped with Sopwith $1^1/_2$ Strutters, but Sopwith Camels later replaced these. One of the early commanding officers was a Major Arthur T. Harris, who would later become known as 'Bomber Harris' during the Second World War.

The Squadron launched innumerable sorties during the night against German raiders. The first Gotha to be shot down at night was attacked in January 1918, and Captain G. H. Hackwill and Second Lieutenant C. C. Banks claimed the first kill. This was unfortunately the squadron's only clear-cut kill of the war. It was finally disbanded on 31 December 1919.

No. 44 Squadron Pilots Scrambled
Captain C. J. Q. Brand, Lieutenant D. V. Armstrong, Lieutenant C. A. Lewis, Lieutenant C. Patteson, Captain J. I. Mackay, Captain T. Gran, Lieutenant E. S. Moulton-Barrett, Captain G. A. H. Pidcock, Lieutenant G. R. Craig, Captain G. W. M. Green, Captain W. H. Haynes, Lieutenant R. G. H. Adams, Lieutenant G. H. Hackwill, Lieutenant L. F. Lomas, Sergeant S. W. Smith, Second Lieutenant Smith, Lieutenant E. M. Gilbert, Lieutenant A. H. Orlebar, Second Lieutenant C. C. Banks, Major T. Hubbard, Second Lieutenant C. H. Clifford, Second Lieutenant R. M. Foster, Second Lieutenant R. N. Hall, Lieutenant E. Gribbon, Lieutenant T. M. O'Neill, Second Lieutenant A. E. Godfrey, Lieutenant J. T. Collier, Lieutenant G. W. Gathergood, Captain C. J. Marchant, Second Lieutenant H. A. Edwardes, Second Lieutenant L. S. V. Gedge, Second Lieutenant W. A. Pritt, Second Lieutenant J. L. Wingate, Second Lieutenant J. H. Summers, Lieutenant W. E. Nicholson, Lieutenant G. O. Shiner.

No. 46 Squadron
No. 46 Squadron was formed out of No. 2 Reserve Squadron and created at Wyton on 19 April 1916. Initially it was deployed for artillery spotting and photographic reconnaissance on the Western Front from October 1916. It was re-equipped with Sopwith Pups in April 1917 and in July of the same year it was briefly stationed to cover the German air raids on London. A lull in the attacks meant that it returned to France in August 1917.

The squadron's Pups were replaced with Sopwith Camels in November 1917 and amongst its new duties were ground-attack missions. It was particularly in evidence during the German spring offensive in March 1918.

When the war ended the squadron was brought back to Rendcombe in February 1919, and it was disbanded on 31 December 1919.

No. 46 Squadron Pilots Scrambled
Lieutenant E. F. Hughes, Second Lieutenant R. S. Asher, Lieutenant C. A. Brewster-Joske, Lieutenant A. W. Wilcox, Lieutenant A. F. Bird, Second Lieutenant F. B. Barager, Second Lieutenant R. L. Ferrie, Second Lieutenant N.

H. Dimmock, Second Lieutenant L. M. Shadwell, Lieutenant A. S. G. Lee, Major P. Babington, Lieutenant C. Courtneidge, Second Lieutenant E. Armitage, Second Lieutenant G. Thompson, Second Lieutenant C. W. Odell, Captain M. D. G. Scott, Captain S. H. Long, Lieutenant MacDonald.

No. 50 Squadron
No. 50 Squadron was created at Dover on 15 May 1916. Over the period of the war it was equipped with a variety of different aircraft, including several variants of the BE2, BE12, RE8, FK8 and Sopwith Pup. It was finally equipped with Sopwith Camels in February 1918. The squadron was based in Kent and used for home defences throughout. The squadron was finally disbanded on 13 June 1919.

No. 50 Squadron Pilots Scrambled
Second Lieutenant C. C. White, Second Lieutenant W. R. Oulton, Second Lieutenant A. J. Arkel, Lieutenant Carmichael, Lieutenant R. W. Le Gallais, Second Lieutenant L. Lucas, Second Lieutenant N. E. Chandler, Lieutenant H, T. O. Windsor, Captain T. R. Irons, Second Lieutenant F. A. D. Grace, Captain A. J. Capel, Captain C. R. Rowden, Second Lieutenant J. G. Goodyear, Second Lieutenant F. V. Bryant, Second Lieutenant N. F. Perris, Second Lieutenant S. Cockerell, Second Lieutenant I. M. Davies, Second Lieutenant G. Murray, Second Lieutenant W. G. Latham, Lieutenant J. Metcalfe, Second Lieutenant T. V. Villiers, Second Lieutenant T. A. Lloyd, Captain C. J. Truran, Lieutenant R. Robertson, Second Lieutenant H. T. W. Oswell, Captain Kirkby, Captain J. S. Shaw, Lieutenant W. L. Phillips, Second Lieutenant Lamb, Lieutenant Stocks, Lieutenant H. Harris, Second Lieutenant J. A. C. Kempe-Roberts, Second Lieutenant A. C. Goldsmith, Major A. A. B. Thomson, Lieutenant T. E. Garside, Lieutenant C. Ossenton, Second Lieutenant V. H. Newton, Second Lieutenant R. C. Cowl, Aircraftsman H. G. Brothers, Lieutenant C. H. Chabot, Lieutenant J. E. King, Second Lieutenant W. J. McSweeney, Second Lieutenant Packham.

No. 56 Squadron
No. 56 Squadron was created out of No. 28 Squadron at Gosport on 9 June 1916. It was transferred to London Colney in July 1916 and to begin with used a number of different aircraft until it was equipped with the SE5 in March 1917. In April 1917 it was sent to France, where it continued its operations for the majority of the war, except for the period June–July 1917, when it was brought back to England to assist in the air defence of the country. It finally returned from Europe in February 1919 and was formally disbanded at Shotwick on 22 January 1920.

B and C Flights out of Bekesbourne flew thirteen sorties between 0731 and 0930 on 4 July 1917.

No. 61 Squadron
No. 61 Squadron was created at Rochford on 24 July 1917. It operated with Sopwith Pups until January 1918, when it was re-equipped with SE5As. It was

engaged in just one anti-Gotha operation on 12 August 1917, when a number of Sopwith Pups from the squadron intercepted the Gothas some 40 miles out to sea. The squadron's SE5As were replaced in October 1918 with Sopwith Camels and the squadron was finally disbanded in June 1919.

No. 61 Squadron Pilots Scrambled
Lieutenant L. F. Hutchin, Lieutenant J. D. Belgrave, Second Lieutenant P. Thompson, Lieutenant J. T. Collier, Captain C. B. Cooke, Captain S. H. Starey, Captain C. E. Holman, Captain E. B. Mason, Second Lieutenant A. H. Bird, Captain C. A. Ridley, Sergeant W. A. E. Taylor, Second Lieutenant H. A. Blain, Second Lieutenant E. E. Turner, Second Lieutenant J. S. Wood, Captain H. C. Stroud, Second Lieutenant G. Howe, Lieutenant L. B. Blaxland.

No. 65 Squadron
No. 65 Squadron was originally created at Wyton on 1 August 1916. It operated with a number of different aircraft until October 1917 when it was issued with Sopwith Camels. Around this time it was moved to France and was involved in anti-aircraft patrols until February 1918. It was then transferred to ground-attack operations before moving to the Belgian coast in August 1918, when it was deployed to escort day bombing missions against Germany. The squadron stayed in Belgium after the war and returned to Britain in February 1919. It was disbanded at Watesbury on 25 October 1919.

No. 65 Squadron Pilots Scrambled
Captain L. E. Whitehead, Second Lieutenant E. Churcher, Captain T. E. Withington, Lieutenant V. Wigg.

No. 75 Squadron
No. 75 Squadron was created at Goldington on 1 October 1916. It was initially given BE2Cs and soon afterwards BE12s. In January 1917 it was re-equipped with BE2Es. In September 1917 it transferred from Goldington to Elmswell and was re-equipped with FE2Bs. The squadron moved once again in May 1918, when it was transferred to North Weald. In July 1918 the squadron traded in its FE2Bs for Avro 504K night-fighters. In October 1918 these, too, were changed for Sopwith Pups. The squadron did not receive Sopwith Camels until after the war, in December 1918. In March of the following year they were equipped with Snipes. The squadron was finally disbanded on 13 June 1919.

No. 75 Squadron Pilots Scrambled
Captain C. W. Mackey, Lieutenant W. A. Forsyth, Second Lieutenant C. F. Cowper, Second Lieutenant J. E. G. Hassall, Lieutenant L. Neville Smith, Captain C. B. Cooke, Lieutenant E. A. Lloyd, Lieutenant C. F. Wolley-Dod, Lieutenant P. Plant.

No. 78 Squadron
No. 78 Squadron was created on 1 November 1916. For some time it operated BE2s and BE12s, but in October 1917 it was issued with Sopwith $1^1/_2$ Strutters. The squadron now moved to Suttons Farm and during the period April–July 1918 the $1^1/_2$ Strutters were gradually replaced with Camels. By November 1918 the squadron now had some Snipes. It was finally disbanded on 31 December 1919.

No. 78 Squadron Pilots Scrambled
Lieutenant J. S. Castle, Captain E. R. Pretyman, Second Lieutenant W. H. Howell, Captain S. P. Gamon, Lieutenant H. Hamer, Second Lieutenant F. L. Luxmoore, Lieutenant C. J. Marchant, Second Lieutenant R. F. W. Moore, Second Lieutenant A. Barker, Second Lieutenant N. H. Auret, Second Lieutenant A. T. Kemp, Second Lieutenant J. F. Ellor, Second Lieutenant N. L. Garstin, Lieutenant H. I. Fordred, Second Lieutenant F. H. Barton, Aircraftsman W. Merchant, Captain D. J. Bell, Second Lieutenant G. G. Williams, Captain F. Billinge, Aircraftsman E. Cooper, Aircraftsman H, L. Daws, Lieutenant G. T. Stoneham, Aircraftsman A. T. C. Stagg, Second Lieutenant W. Hubbard, Aircraftsman W. Eatoc, Lieutenant W. N. Fraser, Captain F. W. Honnett, Lieutenant N. C. Crombie, Captain G. M. Boumphrey, Second Lieutenant J. W. D. Smith, Aircraftsman A. Coombs, Aircraftsman J. Morgan, Aircraftsman L. Card, Lieutenant N. H. Dimmock, Aircraftsman I. Elder, Second Lieutenant J. R. Cote, Captain J. Potter, Major C. R. Rowden, Second Lieutenant W. Hunt, Second Lieutenant A. M. Bennett, Second Lieutenant A. J. Winstanley, Second Lieutenant D. J. Lewis, Second Lieutenant M. H. G. Liddle, Lieutenant I. M. Davies, Second Lieutenant W. Algie, Second Lieutenant F. D. Hudson, Captain S. Cockerell, Second Lieutenant G. Clapham, Lieutenant Colonel M. G. Christie, Captain A. E. Godfrey.

No. 112 Squadron
No. 112 Squadron was formed at Throwley on 30 July 1917. It was initially equipped with Sopwith Pups and did not receive its Sopwith Camels until 1918. It was involved in air defences against German bombers and was disbanded on 13 June 1919. One of its commanding officers, Major Brand, later became one of Fighter Command's group commanders during the Battle of Britain in the Second World War.

No. 112 Squadron Pilots Scrambled
Second Lieutenant A. J. Arkel, Second Lieutenant I. M. Davies, Captain C. Sutton, Lieutenant R. W. Le Gallais, Second Lieutenant Cox, Captain Thomas, Lieutenant C. R. W. Knight, Second Lieutenant J. W. R. Thompson, Second Lieutenant N. E. Chandler, Lieutenant J. S. Poole, Second Lieutenant S. Cockerell, Captain C. J. Q. Brand.

No. 141 Squadron
No. 141 Squadron was not created until 1 January 1918 at Rochford. Initially it had a wide range of different aircraft, until the majority of the unit was issued with Bristol Fighters in March 1918. It operated from Biggin Hill between February 1918 and March 1919 and was then posted to Ireland, where it disbanded on 1 February 1920.

No. 141 Squadron Pilots Scrambled
Lieutenant J. S. Castle, Lieutenant E. J. Stockman, Lieutenant E. E. Turner, Captain E. Pownall, Lieutenant A. F. Barker, Lieutenant A. M. Bennett, Captain M. H. Dimmock, Second Lieutenant J. Hetherington.

No. 143 Squadron
Of the squadrons involved in the first Battle of Britain, No. 143 was the last to be created. It was formed at Throwley on 1 February 1918. In March it was transferred to Detling, operating a mixture of Sopwith Camels and SE5As. After the war it was issued with Snipes. It was finally disbanded on 31 October 1919.

No. 143 Squadron Pilots Scrambled
Captain C. J. Truran, Lieutenant T. E. Garside, Lieutenant F. V. Bryant, Second Lieutenant V. H. Newton, Second Lieutenant W. R. Oulton, Lieutenant J. Tennant, Second Lieutenant N. F. Perris, Second Lieutenant R. C. Cowl, Lieutenant C. Ossenton.

Bibliography

Ashmore, E.B., *Air Defence*, Longman, 1929

Boyne, Walter J., Colonel, *The Influence of Air Power upon History*, Pelican Publishing Company, 2003

Bushby, John R. *Air Defence of Britain*, Ian Allan, 1973

Cole, Christopher & Cheeseman, E.F., *The Air Defence of Britain 1914–1918*, Putnam 1984

Dallas, Brett, *The History of British Aviation, 1908–1914*, Hamilton, 1933

Fredette, Raymond H. *The Sky on Fire*, Smithsonian Institute Press, 1999

Grosz P, *Gotha G.I.* Windsock Datafile 83, Albatros Productions Ltd, 2000

Hallion, Richard P., *Rise of the Fighter Aircraft 1914–1918*, Ian Allan, 1971

Hook, Alex, *World War I Day by Day*, Grange Books, 2004

Imrie, Alex, *Pictorial History Of The German Army Air Service 1914–1918*, Ian Allan, 1971

Jones, H.A., *War in the Air: Being the Story of the part played in the Great War by the Royal air force*, Naval & Military Press, 2002 (Reprint of 1935 original)

Mason, Francis. K., *Battle over Britain. A history of the German Air assaults on Grwat Britain, 1917–18 and July–December 1940 and of the development of Britains air defences between the world Wars*, McWhirter, 1969

Morris, J, *The German Air Raids on Great Britain 1914–1918*, Sampson, Low and Marston, 1925

Neumann, G.P., *The German Air Force in The Great War*, Cedric Chivers Ltd, 1969 (reprint of 1921 original)

Philpott, Bryan, *History of the German Airforce*, Gallery, 1986

Rimell, Raymond L., *Airway over Great Britain, 1914–1918*, Arms and Armour Press, 1987

Index